SOVEREIGN DEBT AND SOCIO-ECONOMIC RIGHTS BEYOND CRISIS

This book offers a distinctive critical discussion of the relationship between sovereign debt and socio-economic human rights in the context of the contemporary global neoliberal economic order, going beyond strictly 'post-crisis' approaches and emphasising the structural character and consistent growth of public and private indebtedness. It reflects on the implications of mounting debt for the actual ability of States to realise human rights in a world of escalating indebtedness, inequality and insecurity. It expands existing definitions of neoliberalism by reflecting in particular on neoliberalism's epistemological underpinnings, and provides a comprehensive and systematic analysis of the 2009 Greek debt crisis and the main elements of post-crisis developments in international and EU law, arguing that the 'neoliberalisation of law' has essentially been advanced in the wake of the Eurozone debt crisis.

Emma Luce Scali is Lecturer in Law at Birmingham City University and Roma Tre University, where she teaches, among others, a course on the 'crisis' of human rights. Her current research interests and publications centre around human rights, sovereign financing and the global economic order.

Sovereign Debt and Socio-Economic Rights Beyond Crisis

THE NEOLIBERALISATION OF INTERNATIONAL LAW

EMMA LUCE SCALI
Birmingham City University

CAMBRIDGE
UNIVERSITY PRESS

CAMBRIDGE
UNIVERSITY PRESS

University Printing House, Cambridge CB2 8BS, United Kingdom

One Liberty Plaza, 20th Floor, New York, NY 10006, USA

477 Williamstown Road, Port Melbourne, VIC 3207, Australia

314–321, 3rd Floor, Plot 3, Splendor Forum, Jasola District Centre, New Delhi – 110025, India

103 Penang Road, #05–06/07, Visioncrest Commercial, Singapore 238467

Cambridge University Press is part of the University of Cambridge.

It furthers the University's mission by disseminating knowledge in the pursuit of education, learning, and research at the highest international levels of excellence.

www.cambridge.org
Information on this title: www.cambridge.org/9781108494007
DOI: 10.1017/9781108625029

First published 2022

A catalogue record for this publication is available from the British Library.

ISBN 978-1-108-49400-7 Hardback

To Professor Carlo Focarelli

Contents

Figures

Tables

Foreword

With this book Dr Emma Luce Scali has demonstrated conceptual clarity and ability as an original thinker in confronting some of the most significant topics in human rights scholarship today and in the lived reality of people in Europe. These are exacting times to be writing about socio-economic rights; at the forefront of many a mind is how they might be made to do the heavy lifting required of them in these dark times and that was already the case before the pandemic. The influence of socio-economic rights seems dwarfed by the scale of the predicament and the obduracy of dominant solutions. The place to start an exercise of this importance is with diagnosing the problem. On that central task this work provides a compelling account.

Dr Scali's main argument, and one she sets out with exhaustive research and lucid prose, is that there is a key link between the ascent of neoliberalism and international legal developments or the lack thereof. The regimes she maps in detail for their recent neoliberal turns are the legal framework for economic and fiscal law of the EU's Economic and Monetary Union, in particular in the wake of the 2009 financial crisis, the European Court of Human Rights' recent austerity judgments, and quasi-judicial pronouncements of the UN Committee on Economic, Social and Cultural Rights (CESCR) from the same period. Characterising neoliberalism as 'anti-humanist and totalistic', she draws explanatory power from Hayek to foreground and condemn how its epistemology leads to bypassing human agency in the construction of the social order. Call it what you will, real flesh-and-blood people have been imperceptible in the evolution of legal projects that restructure their lives while promising deliverance in some post-crisis (contested and unproven) future. Responses to the debt crisis in Europe saw this unrelenting process brought to bear on its expunged people. I am prompted to recall Martti Koskenniemi's searing observation, all the more so for being axiomatic. In a recent set of reflections on the International Monetary Fund

(IMF) and human rights, Koskenniemi remarked: 'If the question is never raised about the effect of those politics on the rights of the affected groups, it is hard to see how they could be justified beyond the small group of experts having produced them.'[1]

It is one matter that some institutions disown human rights on the basis that they are neither relevant nor required for the execution of their mandates, as the IMF has long done. Other institutions incorporate human rights but subordinate social rights in defence of other interests, as per a critique of the EU. It is a separate but related query that seeks to explore how human rights may be inadvertently subverted by the legal bodies charged with their protection. What this work helps to expose is quite how states have failed to transpose human rights to the world of economic decision-making and finance and how, and perhaps why, human rights bodies have fallen prey to prevailing assumptions.

On this last point, among Dr Scali's hypotheses is the belief that 'there is no alternative' has been 'reflexively' internalised by human rights bodies. This is a stark warning that has elsewhere been underscored with regards to CESCR's commitment to redistribution from the gains of predatory capitalism[2] and how the rejection by the Right of socio-economic rights (for fear of requiring radical domestic and international redistribution of wealth), has been countered by CESCR – misguidedly – with guarantees as to their neutrality and compatibility with free market economies.[3]

In addressing the concern among some states, from the drafting of the International Covenant on Economic, Social and Cultural Rights to date, that obligations in the area of socio-economic rights would not subvert their chosen economic policy agendas (and to complicate matters, I note that respect for national policy space is a legitimate demand against conditionality by international financial institutions and foreign economic intervention), the

1 Martti Koskenniemi, 'Prólogo', Edición Especial 'Fondo Monetario Internationacional y Derechos Humanos, Juan Pablo Bohoslavsky and Francisco Cantamutto (Editores Invitados) 6 *Revista Derechos en Acción* 18 (Verano 2020–2021), 25. For the English version, Juan Pablo Bohoslavsky and Francisco Cantamutto (Guest eds.), 'The International Monetary Fund and Human Rights: Interviews' SPEAK OUT at Laboratory for Advanced Research on the Global Economy, LSE Human Rights, LSE, Spring 2021, www.lse.ac.uk/sociology/assets/documents/human-rights/IMF-HRs-LSE-final.pdf.

2 John Linarelli, Margot E. Salomon and Muthucumaraswamy Sornarajah, *The Misery of International Law: Confrontations with Injustice in the Global Economy* (Oxford University Press, 2018), chapter 7 and Margot E. Salomon, 'Sustaining Neoliberal Capital through Socio-Economic Rights', Critical Legal Thinking, October 2017, http://criticallegalthinking.com/2017/10/18/sustaining-neoliberal-capital-socio-economic-rights/.

3 Zachary Manfredi, 'Against "Ideological Neutrality": On the Limits of Liberal and Neoliberal Economic and Social Human Rights' (2020) 8 *London Review of International Law* 2, 287.

Committee has taken pains to defend the neutrality of the Covenant. But the salient idea introduced in this book, and addressed head-on in recent scholarship, is that given the irreconcilability of socio-economic rights with market dependence, they cannot be neutral. Instead, the argument goes, it is time to shun the defence of neutrality altogether and replace it with an explicit, radically rethought, socialist agenda.[4]

Dr Scali's work reflects normative impartiality and is stronger for that careful balance. In her own words, she attempts at 'reconstructing a faithful narrative of the facts, taking stock of the existing law, and identifying the underlying problem(s)'. Still, to her merit, the author wears her heart on her sleeve, her loyalties to the victims of contested economic policies clear. Another strength of this work is Dr Scali's literacy across legal regimes and social scientific disciplines. As much as anything else, that points to the abilities of a new generation of scholars who are especially well equipped to make sense of the parlous state of the world and hence to do something about it.

Margot E. Salomon, LSE

[4] *Ibid* (a socialist political economy); Ugo Mattei and Margot E. Salomon, 'From Poverty and Development to People's International Law' in Ruth M. Buchanan, Luis Eslava and Sundhya Pahuja (eds.), *Oxford Handbook of International Law and Development* (forthcoming, Oxford University Press, 2022) (beyond the public and private to a socialist political ecology based on a commons vision).

Acknowledgements

This book is a revised version of the doctoral thesis that I defended at the University of Nottingham in 2018. I am most grateful to my supervisors Mary E. Footer and Christopher Bevan for their invaluable support and guidance. They had the foresight and courage to do what eventually turned out to be for the best. I also wish to express my thanks to my two examiners, Margot E. Salomon and James Harrison, who made my viva the stimulating and rewarding intellectual experience that convinced me to attempt to write this book. My gratitude also extends to my family, whose encouragement has always been unflinching, my absence notwithstanding, and to Raffaella Nigro, Amina Maneggia, Elisa Longoni and Elena Cavagni for their far-travelling wisdom and affection. Finally, I am most indebted to Carlo Focarelli, to whom this book is dedicated, for having been, throughout the years, an irreplaceable mentor and inspiration: a debt forever to remain unpaid.

Table of Cases

INTERNATIONAL COURT OF JUSTICE (ICJ)

Interpretation of the Agreement of 25 March 1951 between the WHO and Egypt, Advisory Opinion of 20 December 1980 [1980] ICJ Rep 73

EUROPEAN COURT OF HUMAN RIGHTS (ECTHR)

Mamatas and others v. *Greece*, Judgment of 21 July 2016, Apps 63066/14, 64297/14 and 66106/14

Koufaki and ADEDY v. *Greece*, Judgment of 7 May 2013, Apps 57665/12 and 57657/12

UN COMMITTEE ON ECONOMIC SOCIAL AND CULTURAL RIGHTS (CESCR)

Views

Views adopted by the Committee on the case *Rosario Gómez-Limón Pardo* (Spain), 5 March 2020, communication No. 052/2018, UN Doc. E/C.12/67/D/52/2018

Views adopted by the Committee on the case *López Albán and others* (Spain), 11 October 2019, communication No. 037/201, UN Doc. E/C.12/66/D/37/2018

Views adopted by the Committee on the case *S.C. and G.P.* (Italy), 7 March 2019, communication No. 022/2017, UN Doc. E/C.12/65/D/22/2017

Views adopted by the Committee on the case *Trujillo Calero* (Ecuador), 26 March 2018, communication No. 010/2015, UN Doc. E/C.12/63/D/10/2015

Views adopted by the Committee on the case *Ben Djazia and others* (Spain), 21 July 2017, communication No. 005/2015, UN Doc. E/C.12/61/D/5/2015

Views adopted by the Committee on the case *López Rodríguez* (Spain), 20 April 2016, communication No. 001/2013, UN Doc. E/C.12/57/D/1/2013

Views adopted by the Committee on the case *I.D.G.* (Spain), 13 October 2015, communication No. 002/2014, UN Doc. E/C.12/55/D/2/2014

Concluding Observations

Concluding observations on the sixth periodic report of Cyprus (28 October 2016) E/C.12/CYP/CO/6

Concluding observations on the sixth periodic report of the United Kingdom of Great Britain and Northern Ireland (14 July 2016) E/C.12/GBR/CO/6

Concluding observations on the fifth periodic report of Italy (28 October 2015) E/C.12/ITA/CO/5

Concluding observations on the second periodic report of Greece (27 October 2015) E/C.12/GRC/CO/2

Concluding observations on the initial report of Zambia (23 June 2005) E/C.12/1/Add.106

Concluding observations on the initial report of Benin (5 June 2002) E/C.12/1/Add.78

Concluding observations on the second periodic report of Morocco (1 December 2001) E/C.12/1/Add.55

Concluding observations on the second periodic report of Algeria (30 November 2001) E/C.12/1/Add.71

Concluding observations on the initial report of Nepal (24 September 2001) E/C.12/1/Add.66

Concluding observations on the third periodic report of the Syrian Arab Republic (24 September 2001) E/C.12/1/Add.63

Concluding observations on the second periodic report of Senegal (24 September 2001) E/C.12/1/Add.62

Concluding observations on the initial report of Bolivia (21 May 2001) E/C.12/1/Add.60

Concluding observations on the initial report of Honduras (21 May 2001) E/C.12/1/Add.57

Concluding observations on the initial report of Kyrgyzstan (1 September 2000) E/C.12/1/Add.49

Concluding observations on the initial report of Sudan (1 September 2000) E/C.12/1/Add.48

Concluding observations on the third periodic report of Mexico, in CESCR, 'Report on the Twentieth and Twenty-First Sessions (26 April–14 May 1999, 15 November–3 December 1999)' (2000) E/2000/22

Concluding observations on the third periodic report of Canada, in CESCR, 'Report on the Eighteenth and Nineteenth Sessions (27 April–15 May 1998, 16 November–4 December 1998)' (1999) E/1999/22
Concluding observations on the second periodic report of Uruguay, in CESCR, 'Report on the Sixteenth and Seventeenth Sessions (28 April–16 May 1997, 17 November–5 December 1997)' (1998) E/1998/22
Concluding observations on the initial report of Azerbaijan, in CESCR, 'Report on the Sixteenth and Seventeenth Sessions (28 April–16 May 1997, 17 November–5 December 1997)' (1998) E/1998/22
Concluding observations on the initial report of the Philippines, in CESCR, 'Report on the Twelfth and Thirteenth Sessions (1–19 May 1995, 20 November–8 December 1995)' (1996) E/1996/22
Concluding observations on the second periodic report of the Dominican Republic, in CESCR, 'Report on the Twelfth and Thirteenth Sessions (1–19 May 1995, 20 November–8 December 1995)' (1996) E/1996/22
Concluding observations on the initial report of the Republic of Korea, in CESCR, 'Report on the Twelfth and Thirteenth Sessions (1–19 May 1995, 20 November–8 December 1995)' (1996) E/1996/22
Concluding observations on the second periodic report of Portugal, in CESCR, 'Report on the Twelfth and Thirteenth Sessions (1–19 May 1995, 20 November–8 December 1995)' (1996) E/1996/22
Concluding observations on the third periodic report of Colombia, in CESCR, 'Report on the Twelfth and Thirteenth Sessions (1–19 May 1995, 20 November–8 December 1995)' (1996) E/1996/22

EUROPEAN COMMITTEE OF SOCIAL RIGHTS (ECSR)

Conclusions XX-3 of 15 December 2014, *Greece – Article 4-1*, XX-3/def/GRC/4/1/EN
Decision on the merits of 7 December 2012, *Federation of Employed Pensioners of Greece (IKA-ETAM)* v. *Greece*, Complaint No. 76/2012
Decision on the merits of 7 December 2012, *Panhellenic Federation of Public Service Pensioners (POPS)* v. *Greece*, Complaint No. 77/2012
Decision on the merits of 7 December 2012, *Pensioners' Union of the Athens-Piraeus Electric Railways (I.S.A.P.)* v. *Greece*, Complaint No. 78/2012
Decision on the merits of 7 December 2012, *Panhellenic Federation of Pensioners of the Public Electricity Corporation (POSDEI)* v. *Greece*, Complaint No. 79/2012
Decision on the merits of 7 December 2012, *Pensioners' Union of the Agricultural Bank of Greece (ATE)* v. *Greece*, Complaint No. 80/2012

Decision on the merits of 23 May 2012, *General Federation of Employees of the National Electric Power Corporation (GENOP-DEI)/Confederation of Greek Civil Servants' Trade Unions (ADEDY)* v. *Greece*, Complaint No. 65/2011

Decision on the merits of 23 May 2012, *General Federation of Employees of the National Electric Power Corporation (GENOP-DEI)/Confederation of Greek Civil Servants' Trade Unions (ADEDY)* v. *Greece*, Complaint No. 66/2011

COURT OF JUSTICE OF THE EUROPEAN UNION (CJEU)

General Court, Judgment of 7 October 2015, *Alessandro Accorinti and others* v. *ECB*, Case T-39/13

Court of Justice, Judgment of 27 November 2012, *Thomas Pringle* v. *Government of Ireland*, Case C-370/12

DOMESTIC COURTS

Argentina

Supreme Court, Judgment of 1 February 2002, *Smith* v. *Poder Ejecutivo Nacional*

Greece

Council of State, Judgment No. 1116/2014 of 21 March 2014

Council of State, Judgment No. 668/2012 of 20 February 2012

Portugal

Constitutional Court, Decision No. 187/2013 of 5 April 2013, www.tribunalconstitucional.pt/tc/acordaos/20130187.html

United States

Court of Appeals for the Second Circuit, Judgement of 26 October 2012, *NML Capital, Ltd.* v. *Republic of Argentina*, 699 F.3d 246, 250 (2d Cir. 2012)

Table of International Treaties and Other Instruments

Constitution of the International Labour Organization (ILO Constitution) (1919)

ILO Convention (No. 29) concerning Forced or Compulsory Labour (adopted 28 June 1930, entered into force 1 May 1932) 39 UNTS 55

ILO, Declaration concerning the aims and purposes of the International Labour Organization (Declaration of Philadelphia) (10 May 1944)

Charter of the United Nations (26 June 1945)

ILO Convention (No. 87) concerning Freedom of Association and Protection of the Right to Organize (adopted 9 July 1948, entered into force 4 July 1950) 68 UNTS 17

ILO Convention (No. 98) concerning the Application of the Principles of the Right to Organize and to Bargain Collectively (adopted 1 July 1949, entered into force 18 July 1951) 96 UNTS 258

ILO Convention (No. 100) concerning Equal Remuneration for Men and Women Workers for Work of Equal Value (adopted 29 June 1951, entered into force 23 May 1953) 165 UNTS 303

Convention for the Protection of Human Rights and Fundamental Freedoms ('European Convention on Human Rights') (signed 4 November 1950, entered into force 3 September 1953)

ILO Convention (No. 105) concerning the Abolition of Forced Labour (adopted 25 June 1957, entered into force 17 January 1959) 320 UNTS 291

ILO Convention (No. 111) concerning Discrimination in Respect of Employment and Occupation Discrimination (adopted 25 June 1958, entered into force 15 June 1960) 362 UNTS 31

International Convention on the Elimination of All Forms of Racial Discrimination (7 March 1966)

International Covenant on Civil and Political Rights (adopted 16 December 1966, entered into force 3 January 1976) 999 UNTS 3

International Covenant on Economic, Social and Cultural Rights (adopted 16 December 1966, entered into force 3 January 1976) 993 UNTS 3
Optional Protocol to the International Covenant on Civil and Political Rights (adopted 16 December 1966, entered into force 23 March 1976) 999 UNTS 171
ILO Convention (No. 138) concerning Minimum Age for Admission to Employment (adopted 26 June 1973, entered into force 19 June 1976) 1015 UNTS 297
Convention on the Elimination of All Forms of Discrimination against Women (18 December 1979)
Vienna Convention on Succession of States in respect of State Property, Archives and Debts (8 April 1983)
Convention on the Rights of the Child (20 November 1989)
European Social Charter (Revised) (3 May 1996) ETS 163
ILO Convention (No. 182) concerning the Prohibition and Immediate Action for the Elimination of the Worst Forms of Child Labour (adopted 17 June 1999, entered into force 19 November 2000) 2133 UNTS 161
Convention on the Rights of Persons with Disabilities (13 December 2006)
Optional Protocol to the International Covenant on Economic, Social and Cultural Rights (adopted 10 December 2008, entered into force 5 May 2013) A/RES/63/117
ILO Convention (No. 189) concerning Decent Work for Domestic Workers (adopted 16 June 2011, entered into force 5 September 2013)

OTHER INTERNATIONAL INSTRUMENTS

Atlantic Charter (14 August 1941)
Proclamation of Teheran, Final Act of the International Conference on Human Rights (Teheran, 22 April–13 May 1968) A/CONF. 32/41 at 3 (1968)
The Limburg Principles on the Implementation of the International Covenant on Economic, Social and Cultural Rights (1987) 9 *Human Rights Quarterly* 122
Vienna Declaration and Programme of Action (25 June 1993)
Bangalore Declaration and Plan of Action (1995) *ICJ Review* 55, 219–227
The Maastricht Guidelines on Violations of Economic, Social and Cultural Rights (1998) 20 *Human Rights Quarterly* 691
Quito Declaration on the Enforcement and Realization of Economic, Social and Cultural Rights in Latin America and the Caribbean (1999) 2 *Yale Human Rights and Development Law Journal* 6
UNCTAD, Principles on Promoting Responsible Sovereign Lending and Borrowing (10 January 2012)

UNITED NATIONS

General Assembly (UNGA) Resolutions

Res 217 A (III) of 10 December 1948, 'Universal Declaration of Human Rights'
Res 124 (II) of 15 November 1947, 'Agreements with Specialized Agencies'
Res 543 (VI), 'Preparation of Two Drafts International Covenants on Human Rights' (5 February 1952)
Res 60/1 of 16 September 2005, '2005 World Summit Outcome', A/RES/60/1 (24 October 2005)
Res 60/251 of 15 March 2006, 'Human Rights Council', A/RES/60/251 (3 April 2006)
Report of the International Law Commission, 'Articles on the Responsibility of International Organizations' A/66/10 (2011)
Res 69/247 of 29 December 2014, 'Modalities for the Implementation of Resolution 68/304, Entitled "Towards the Establishment of a Multilateral Legal Framework for Sovereign Debt Restructuring Processes"', A/RES/69/247 (13 January 2015)
Res 69/313 of 27 July 2015, 'Addis Ababa Action Agenda on Financing for Development (Addis Ababa Action Agenda)', A/RES/69/313 (17 August 2015)
Res 69/319 of 10 September 2015, 'Basic Principles on Sovereign Debt Restructuring Processes', A/RES/69/319 (29 September 2015)

Human Rights Council (HRC) Resolutions

Res 25/16 of 15 April 2014, Mandate of the Independent Expert on the effects of foreign debt and other related international financial obligations of states on the full enjoyment of all human rights, particularly economic, social and cultural rights, A/HRC/RES/25/16
Res 21/11 of 18 October 2012, Guiding Principles on Extreme Poverty and Human Rights, A/HRC/RES/21/11
Res 20/10 of 18 July 2012, The effects of foreign debt and other related international financial obligations of states on the full enjoyment of all human rights, particularly economic, social and cultural rights, A/HRC/RES/20/10
Res 7/4 of 27 March 2008, Mandate of the Independent Expert on the effects of foreign debt and other related international financial obligations of states on the full enjoyment of all human rights, particularly economic, social and cultural rights, A/HRC/RES/7/4

Committee on Economic Social and Cultural Rights (CESCR)

General Comments

General Comment No. 22, 'The right to sexual and reproductive health (art. 12)' (2 May 2016) E/C.12/GC/22
General Comment No. 19, 'The right to social security (art. 9)' (4 February 2008) E/C.12/GC/19
General Comment No. 18, 'The right to work (art. 6)' (6 February 2006) E/C.12/GC/18
General Comment No. 17, 'The right of everyone to benefit from the protection of the moral and material interests resulting from any scientific, literary or artistic production of which he or she is the author (article 15, paragraph 1 (c), of the Covenant)' (12 January 2006) E/C.12/GC/17
General Comment No. 15, 'The right to water (arts. 11 and 12)' (20 January 2003) E/C.12/2002/11
General Comment No. 14, 'The right to the highest attainable standard of health (art. 12)' (11 August 2000) E/C.12/2000/4
General Comment No. 13, 'The right to education (art. 13)' (8 December 1999) E/C.12/1999/10
General Comment No. 12, 'The right to adequate food (art. 11)' (12 May 1999) E/C.12/1999/5
General Comment No. 6, 'The economic, social and cultural rights of older persons' (7 October 1996)
General Comment No. 5, 'Persons with disabilities' (1 January 1995)
General Comment No. 4, 'The right to adequate housing (art. 11, para. 1)' (13 December 1991) E/1992/23
General Comment No. 3, 'The nature of states parties' obligations (art. 2, para. 1)' (1 January 1991) E/1991/23
General Comment No. 1, 'Reporting by states parties' (27 July 1981) E/1989/22

Letters and Statements

'Public debt, austerity measures and the International Covenant on Economic, Social and Cultural Rights' (22 July 2016) E/C.12/2016/1
'Letter dated 16 May 2012 addressed by the Chairperson of the Committee on Economic, Social and Cultural Rights to States Parties to the International Covenant on Economic, Social and Cultural Rights'

'An evaluation of the obligation to take steps to the "maximum of available resources" under an optional protocol to the Covenant' (21 September 2007) E/C.12/2007/1

Economic and Social Council (ECOSOC) Resolutions

Res 1985/17 (28 May 1985), 'Review of the composition, organization and administrative arrangements of the Sessional Working Group of Governmental Experts on the Implementation of the International Covenant on Economic, Social and Cultural Rights', E/C.12/1989/4 (27 October 1988)

Res 1982/33 (6 May 1982), 'Review of the composition, organization and administrative arrangements of the Sessional Working Group (of Governmental Experts) on the Implementation of the International Covenant on Economic, Social and Cultural Rights', E/C.12/1989/4 (27 October 1988)

Decision 1978/10 (3 May 1978), 'Composition of the Sessional Working Group on the Implementation of the International Covenant on Economic, Social and Cultural Rights', E/C.12/1989/4 (27 October 1988)

Res 1988 (LX) (11 May 1976), 'Procedures for the implementation of the International Covenant on Economic, Social and Cultural Rights', E/C.12/1989/4 (27 October 1988)

INTERNATIONAL MONETARY FUND (IMF)

Decision No. 14064-(08/18) of 22 February 2008, as amended by Decision Nos. 14184-(08/93) of 29 October 2008, 14284-(09/29) of 24 March 2009, BUFF/10/56 of 9 May 2010 and 14716-(10/83) of 30 August 2010, 'Access Policy and Limits in the Credit Tranches and under the Extended Fund Facility and on Overall Access to the Fund's General Resources, and Exceptional Access Policy – Review and Modification' in IMF, *Selected Decisions and Selected Documents of the International Monetary Fund*, 35th Issue (31 December 2010) 426–427

EU LAW

Treaty on European Union (signed 7 February 1992, entered into force 1 November 1993) [2012] OJ C326

Resolution of the European Council on the Stability and Growth Pact of 17 June 1997 [1997] OJ C236/1

Council Regulation (EC) No. 1466/97 of 7 July 1997 on strengthening of the surveillance of budgetary positions and the surveillance and coordination of economic policies [1997] OJ L209/1

Council Regulation (EC) No. 1467/97 of 7 July 1997 speeding up and clarifying the implementation of excessive deficit procedure [1997] OJ L209/6

Council Regulation (EC) No. 332/2002 of 18 February 2002 establishing a facility providing medium-term financial assistance for Member States' balances of payments [2002] OJ L053

Draft Treaty establishing a Constitution for Europe [2003] OJ C169

Council Regulation (EC) No. 1055/2005 amending Regulation (EC) No. 1466/1997 on the strengthening of the surveillance of the budgetary positions and the surveillance and coordination of economic policies [2005] OJ L174

Council Regulation (EC) No. 1056/2005 amending Regulation (EC) No. 1467/1997 on speeding up and clarifying the implementation of excessive deficit procedure [2005] OJ L174

Treaty of Lisbon amending the Treaty on European Union and the Treaty establishing the European Community (signed 13 December 2007, entered into force 1 December 2009) [2007] OJ C306/01

Charter of Fundamental Rights of the European Union (adopted 12 December 2007, entered into force 1 December 2009) [2012] OJ C326/391

Council Regulation (EC) No. 479/2009 of 25 May 2009 on the application of the Protocol on the excessive deficit procedure annexed to the Treaty establishing the European Community [2009] OJ L145/1

Intercreditor Agreement between Kingdom of Belgium, Federal Republic of Germany, Ireland, Kingdom of Spain, French Republic, Italian Republic, Republic of Cyprus, Grand Duchy of Luxembourg, Republic of Malta, Kingdom of the Netherlands, Republic of Austria, Portuguese Republic, Republic of Slovenia, Slovak Republic and Republic of Finland, 8 May 2010, *Euro Area Loan Facility Act 2010* [Ireland], Schedule 1

Loan Facility Agreement between the following Member States whose currency is the Euro: Kingdom of Belgium, Ireland, Kingdom of Spain, French Republic, Italian Republic, Republic of Cyprus, Grand Duchy of Luxembourg, Republic of Malta, Kingdom of the Netherlands, Republic of Austria, Portuguese Republic, Republic of Slovenia, Slovak Republic and Republic of Finland and KfW, acting in the public interest, subject to the instructions of and with the benefit of the guarantee of the Federal Republic of Germany, as Lenders and The Hellenic Republic as Borrower, the Bank of Greece as Agent to the Borrower, 8 May 2010, *Euro Area Loan Facility Act 2010* [Ireland], Schedule 2

EFSF Framework Agreement (7 June 2010)
Council Regulation (EU) 407/2010 of 11 May 2010 establishing a European Financial Stabilisation Mechanism [2010] OJ L118
Council Decision 2011/199/EU of 25 March 2011 amending Article 136 of the Treaty on the Functioning of the European Union with regard to a stability mechanism for Member States whose currency is the euro [2011] OJ L91
Regulation (EU) No. 1173/2011 of the European Parliament and of the Council of 16 November 2011 on the effective enforcement of budgetary surveillance in the Euro Area [2011] OJ L306
Regulation (EU) No. 1174/2011 of the European Parliament and of the Council of 16 November 2011 on enforcement measures to correct excessive macroeconomic imbalances in the Euro Area [2011] OJ L306
Regulation (EU) No. 1175/2011 of the European Parliament and of the Council of 16 November 2011 amending Council Regulation (EC) No. 1466/97 on the strengthening of the surveillance of budgetary positions and the surveillance and coordination of economic policies [2011] OJ L306
Regulation (EU) No. 1176/2011 of the European Parliament and of the Council of 16 November 2011 on the prevention and correction of macroeconomic imbalances [2011] OJ L306
Council Regulation (EU) No. 1177/2011 of 8 November 2011 amending Regulation (EC) No. 1467/97 on speeding up and clarifying the implementation of the excessive deficit procedure [2011] OJ L306
Council Directive 2011/85/EU on requirements for budgetary frameworks of the Member States [2011] OJ L306
Treaty establishing the European Stability Mechanism (signed 1 February 2012, entered into force 27 September 2012) D/12/3
Treaty on the Functioning of the European Union (Consolidated version) [2012] OJ C326/49
Protocol (No. 12) on the Excessive Deficit Procedure in Consolidated version of the Treaty on the Functioning of the European Union [2012] OJ C326/47
Communication from the Commission: Common principles on national fiscal correction mechanisms (20 June 2012) COM (2012) 342 final
Regulation (EU) 472/2013 of the European Parliament and of the Council of 21 May 2013 on the strengthening of economic and budgetary surveillance of Member States in the Euro Area experiencing or threatened with serious difficulties with respect to their financial stability [2013] OJ L140
Regulation (EU) No. 473/2013 on the European Parliament and of the Council of 21 May 2013 on common provisions for monitoring and assessing draft budgetary plans and ensuring the correction of excessive deficit of the Member States in the Euro Area [2013] OJ L140

Commission Regulation (EU) No. 220/2014 of 7 March 2014 amending Council Regulation (EC) No. 479/2009 as regards references to the European system of national and regional accounts in the European Union [2014] OJ L69/101

Council Recommendation (EU) 2015/1184 of 14 July 2015 on broad guidelines for the economic policies of the Member States and of the European Union [2015] OJ L192

Council Regulation (EU) 2015/1360 of 4 August 2015 amending Regulation (EU) No. 407/2010 establishing a European financial stabilisation mechanism [2015] OJ L210

DOMESTIC LEGISLATION

Germany

Kaiser Wilhelm I's Royal Proclamation on Social Policy, in *Stenographische Berichte über die Verhandlungen des Reichstags* [Stenographic Reports on the Proceedings of the Reichstag] 5th Legislative Period, First Session 1881/82: Opening Session, 17 November 1881, Berlin (Printing Office of the Norddeutsche Allgemeine Zeitung, 1882) 1–3, http://germanhistorydocs.ghi-dc.org/sub_document.cfm?document_id=1808

Anti-Socialist Law (21 October 1878), in German History in Documents and Images (GHDI), *Documents – Politics II: Parties and Political Mobilization*, 'Law Against the Publicly Dangerous Endeavours of Social Democracy', 21 October 1878 [German text in SB, IV, i (1878), vol. 1, No. 47, pp. 132–135], http://germanhistorydocs.ghi-dc.org/sub_document.cfm?document_id=1843

France

French Declaration of the Rights of Man and of the Citizen, adopted by France's National Constituent Assembly on 26 August 1789

Comité de la mendicité de la Constituante, 1st Report, 1790

Greece

The Constitution of Greece (1975), www.hellenicparliament.gr/UserFiles/f3c70a23-7696-49db-9148-f24dce6a27c8/001-156%20aggliko.pdf

Law No. 4270 of 28 June 2014 on Fiscal Management and Supervision Principles, as amended by Law No. 4336 of 14 August 2015

Invitation of the Hellenic Republic (to the bondholders of Greek debt) of 24 February 2012, http://ftalphaville.ft.com/files/2012/02/Reg_S_Invitation_Memorandum.pdf

Law 4050/2012 of 23 February 2012 on Rules relating to the adjustment of securities, their issue or guarantee by the Greek state with the agreement of the bond holders

Italy

Law 243/2012 of 24 December 2012 on Provisions for implementation of the balanced budget principle pursuant to Article 81 paragraph 6 of the Constitution, as amended by Law No. 164 of 12 August 2016

Constitutional Law No. 1 of 20 April 2012, 'Introduzione del principio del pareggio di bilancio nella Carta Costituzionale', GU No. 95 of 23 April 2012

Law No. 99 of 22 June 2010, 'Conversione in legge del decreto-legge 10 maggio 2010, n. 67, recante disposizioni urgenti per la salvaguardia della stabilità finanziaria dell'area euro. Ordine di esecuzione dell'accordo denominato "Intercreditor Agreement" e dell'accordo denominato "Loan Facility Agreement" stipulati in data 8 maggio 2010', GU No. 150 of 30 June 2010

United States

Declaration of Independence of the Thirteen United States of America, adopted by the US Congress on 4 July 1776

Virginia Declaration of Rights, adopted by the Virginia Constitutional Convention on 12 June 1776

Abbreviations

AMR	alert mechanism report
BEPGs	Broad Economic Policy Guidelines
BIS	Bank for International Settlements
CESCR	UN Committee on Economic, Social and Cultural Rights
CJEU	Court of Justice of the European Union
CRAs	credit rating agencies
ECB	European Central Bank
ECOSOC	UN Economic and Social Council
ECtHR	European Court of Human Rights
EDP	excessive deficit procedure
EFSF	European Financial Stability Facility
EFSM	European Financial Stabilisation Mechanism
EIP	excessive imbalance procedure
EMU	Economic and Monetary Union (European Union)
ESM	European Stability Mechanism
ESR	Economic and Social Rights
EU	European Union
FAO	Food and Agriculture Organization
GC	General Comment (CESCR)
GDP	gross domestic product
GNP	gross national product
IBRD	International Bank for Reconstruction and Development
ICCPR	International Covenant on Civil and Political Rights
ICESCR	International Covenant on Economic, Social and Cultural Rights
ICJ	International Court of Justice
IDR	in-depth review
IE	Independent Expert (UN)

IFIs	international financial institutions
IHRL	international human rights law
IKA	Social Insurance Institute (Greece)
ILO	International Labour Organization
IMF	International Monetary Fund
MIP	Macroeconomic Imbalance Procedure
MoU	memorandum of understanding
MTOs	medium-term budgetary objectives
OECD	Organisation for Economic Co-operation and Development
OMTs	outright monetary transactions
OP-ICESCR	Optional Protocol to the International Covenant on Economic, Social and Cultural Rights
SGP	Stability and Growth Pact
TEU	Treaty on European Union
TFEU	Treaty on the Functioning of the European Union
TSCG	Treaty on Stability, Coordination and Governance in the Economic and Monetary Union
UDHR	Universal Declaration on Human Rights
UNCTAD	United Nations Conference on Trade and Development
UNESCO	United Nations Educational, Scientific and Cultural Organization
WHO	World Health Organization

1

Introduction

1.1 BEYOND CRISIS: RECASTING THE APPROACH TO THE SOVEREIGN DEBT–HUMAN RIGHTS RELATIONSHIP AND OUTLINE OF THE BOOK

Today, when the relationship between sovereign debt and economic and social rights (ESR)[1] is mentioned, austerity[2] inevitably comes to mind. At least in Europe, austerity materialised, in the aftermath of the 2008 Global Financial Crisis, as a consequence of the Eurozone debt crisis, negatively affecting the realisation of many of the rights enshrined in core international human rights instruments, such as the International Covenant on Economic, Social and Cultural Rights (ICESCR) and the European Social Charter, and producing what, in hindsight, clearly appears as a *permanent* restructuring of the welfare systems of several European countries.

The attention of human rights scholars, monitoring bodies and civil society has, therefore, largely refocused on the human rights impacts of austerity and economic reform policies[3] (and, more recently, on the strains put by the coronavirus disease COVID-19 pandemic on state resources, and the impact of pre-existing debt on the emergency response efforts of several countries),[4]

[1] For a preliminary definition of the term, see Section 1.2 later.

[2] The term broadly identifies a rather typical set of economic policies (including public spending cuts, reforms of the public sector and privatisations) supposedly aimed at 'consolidating' the public budget and which are generally demanded by lenders/investors as a prerequisite to grant a loan, financial assistance or debt relief. On austerity and conditionality more generally, see Chapter 4.

[3] See Chapters 3 and 4.

[4] See e.g. UN General Assembly, 'Addressing, from a human rights perspective, the debt-related problems of developing countries caused by the coronavirus disease (COVID-19) pandemic', Report of the Independent Expert on the effects of foreign debt and other related international financial obligations of states on the full enjoyment of all human rights, particularly economic, social and cultural rights, Yuefen Li, UN Doc. A/75/164 (31 July 2020).

after that, in recent decades, it had been mainly directed to issues of debt restructuring,[5] debt relief[6] and odious debt.[7]

However, austerity and, more generally, the typology of economic reforms implemented, since the Global Financial Crisis increasingly also in Europe, are not a novel phenomenon, nor are their social consequences. In terms of economic rationale, objectives, instruments and impacts, they have echoed earlier International Monetary Fund structural adjustment programmes, and it seems very unlikely that the main European and international institutions involved were genuinely unaware of their social implications. Already in 1978, for instance, the Special Rapporteur on the Situation of Human Rights in Chile had published a 'Study of the impact of foreign economic aid and assistance on respect for human rights in Chile',[8] and in 1990 the IMF had acknowledged that policies which 'include fiscal retrenchment and public sector reform' – such as those more recently enforced in Greece and other European countries – 'particularly when accompanied by a freezing of public sector employment or wages [... are] likely to affect the poor'.[9] The IMF has reaffirmed the negative distributional effects of austerity, inter alia, in a Working Paper of 2013.[10]

More importantly, since the Global Financial Crisis, austerity has become a global phenomenon not necessarily linked to excessive debt levels. In 2013, the Office of the High Commissioner for Human Rights (OHCHR) reported how developing countries – which weathered the initial consequences of the crisis better than their more economically developed counterparts – nonetheless

[5] See i.a. Michael Waibel, *Sovereign Defaults before International Courts and Tribunals* (Cambridge University Press, 2011); Rodrigo Olivares-Caminal, *Legal Aspects of Sovereign Debt Restructuring* (London: Sweet and Maxwell, 2009); August Reinisch, *State Responsibility for Debts: International Law Aspects of External Debt and Debt Restructuring* (Vienna: Böhlau, 1995).

[6] See i.a. Celine Tan, 'Life, Debt and Human Rights: Contextualising the International Regime for Sovereign Debt Relief' in Krista Nadakavukaren Schefer (ed.), *Poverty and the International Economic Law System: Duties to the Poor* (Cambridge University Press, 2013) 307–324; Robert K Rasmussen, 'Sovereign Debt Restructuring, Odious Debt and the Politics of Debt Relief' (2007) 70 *Law and Contemporary Problems* 4, 249–261.

[7] See i.a. Jeff King, *The Doctrine of Odious Debt in International Law*: A Restatement (Cambridge University Press, 2016); Sabine Michalowski, *Unconstitutional Regimes and the Validity of Sovereign Debt: A Legal Perspective* (Farnham: Ashgate, 2007).

[8] Special Rapporteur on the Situation of Human Rights in Chile, 'Study of the impact of foreign economic aid and assistance on respect for human rights in Chile', Report prepared by Antonio Cassese (1978) E/CN.4/Sub.2/412 (Vol. IV).

[9] IMF, 'Annual Report of the Executive Board for the Financial Year Ended April 30, 1990', 1990, 41–42.

[10] Laurence Ball, Davide Furceri, Daniel Leigh and Prakash Loungani, 'The Distributional Effects of Fiscal Consolidation' (June 2013) *IMF Working Paper*, WP/13/151.

adopted austerity measures 'for "pre-emptive reasons," i.e. [. . .] to avert negative reactions from financial markets'.[11] The Council of Europe Commissioner for Human Rights noted how 'contractions in public spending as an ongoing consequence of the global economic downturn affect[ed] [. . .] 80% of the global population in 2013, increasing to [. . .] 90% of persons worldwide by 2015'.[12] Therefore, while austerity has certainly been linked in Europe to the sovereign debt crisis, it appears to be the 'tip of the iceberg', the symptom of a more generalised, constrained fiscal climate associated with increased supranational control over national economic and fiscal policies.[13] Likewise, the resulting regression in the enjoyment of ESR (not significantly hindered, as the Greek case addressed in this book will illustrate, by existing international human rights law)[14] seems the most recent and visible manifestation of a halt, to say the least, in their realisation, which seems to have been accelerated, rather than entirely caused by the crisis.

This book is premised on three different assumptions. First, the increasing and increasingly widespread indebtedness, described in Chapter 2, and the more general proliferation of debt relationships at all levels of economic interaction (see, for instance, the rise in private household debt noted later,[15] or the typology of measures and instruments put in place by the European Union to assist the Member States in their efforts to counter the economic consequences of the COVID-19 pandemic)[16] are a symptom of the structural shortcomings of global financialised capitalism and its neoliberal configuration. Therefore, to be truly meaningful, any discussion of the sovereign debt–human

11 Office of the High Commissioner for Human Rights (OHCHR), 'Report on austerity measures and economic and social rights', 2013, 8.

12 Council of Europe (CoE) Commissioner for Human Rights, 'Safeguarding human rights in times of economic crisis', November 2013, 15.

13 See Chapter 2.

14 In this book, the disputed expression 'international human rights law' (IHRL) is used to refer to all international norms (not necessarily contained in a legal instrument explicitly identified as a human rights instrument) that have the object of safeguarding those rights which are considered to represent (see below) human rights (although, of course, also according to this definition, the clear identification of such norms is not necessarily straightforward). In particular, these include the 'core' international human rights treaties, as identified i.a. by the OHCHR at www.ohchr.org/en/professionalinterest/pages/coreinstruments.aspx.

15 See Chapter 2, footnote 29.

16 See i.a. Emma Luce Scali, 'Sovereign Financing during the COVID-19 Pandemic: The Debt Implications of Italy's Socio-Economic Measures for 2020 and the Response of the European Union' in Pia Acconci and Elisa Baroncini (eds.), *Gli effetti della pandemia Covid-19 su commercio, investimenti e strumenti finanziari* (Napoli: Editoriale Scientifica, 2020) 369–387; Poonam Shokar, 'Will COVID-19 Usher on Another Decade of Austerity within the United Kingdom? What Does this Mean for the Protection of Economic, Social and Cultural Rights (ESCR)?', EJIL: Talk!, 13 May 2020.

rights relationship needs to be recast beyond the contingencies of the latest (actually, of any recent) crisis to consider the nature, meaning and implications of indebtedness in the current global economic order,[17] and the actual significance of debt financing for the ability of states to realise human rights, including ESR.

Secondly, this book is premised on the idea that to understand the lamented inefficacy of international human rights law in confronting pressures to reverse prior legal and practical achievements in the protection of human rights, a more explicit and purposeful analysis of the political economy implications of human rights (especially ESR), on one side, and the (material and ideational) implications for human rights conceptions of the current global economic system, on the other, is necessary.

Thirdly, this book is premised on the idea that the affirmation and totalistic and hegemonic expansion of neoliberalism – not much (or not merely) as a theory of political economy, but more generally as a belief system grounded on a distinctive epistemology (see Section 1.3) and whose core tenets greatly diverge from the fundamental beliefs that inspired the affirmation and development of international human rights in the twentieth century[18] – has (largely 'invisible') implications[19] not only for the nature of the global economic system (including the above-mentioned ascent, within it, of debt relationships) but also for conceptions of the human person (and qualities generally attached to it, such as agency, autonomy, freedom, responsibility and human

[17] With the term 'global economic order', I intend to refer in this book to the ordering of global economic relations resulting inter alia from specific international norms, not necessarily to the fact that such ordering has a coherent structure or specific nature (although it is deemed to be an increasingly neoliberal economic order).

[18] See also Margot E Salomon, 'Poverty, Privilege and International Law: The Millennium Development Goals and the Guise of Humanitarianism' (2008–2009) 51 *German Yearbook of International Law* 39–73, 46 (noting how '[f]rom the perspective of human rights theory, we can see quite fundamental ontological and legal incompatibilities between this model of Darwinian economics and a favouring of private (corporate) property on the one hand, and the notions of dignity, universal minimum entitlements and the state as active duty bearer on the other').

[19] Neoliberalised conceptions appear so ingrained in our present-day experience and understanding of the world (down to the intimacy of the individual, see i.a. the chapter on 'Everyday Neoliberalism' in Philip Mirowski, *Never Let a Serious Crisis Go to Waste: How Neoliberalism Survived the Financial Meltdown* (London: Verso, 2014) and Byung-Chul Han, *The Agony of Eros*, trans. by Erik Butler (Cambridge, MA: MIT Press, 2017), to have become largely 'invisible to the mind' or, according to some, 'the common sense of the age', Corinne Blalock, 'Neoliberalism and the Crisis of Legal Theory' (2014) 77 *Law and Contemporary Problems* 4, 71–103, p. 83; see also Philip Mirowski and Dieter Plehwe (eds.), *The Road from Mont Pèlerin: The Making of the Neoliberal Thought Collective* (Cambridge, MA: Harvard University Press, 2009), p. 427.

rights) and of social phenomena and institutions, such as poverty, inequality, the state and the law. Consequently, it has implications for our understanding and (re)interpretation of existing international law.

This book essentially argues that – at least as far as the debt–ESR relationship is concerned – responses to the crisis, relevant post-crisis legal developments and even, in some instances, the assessment of both from a human rights perspective seem to have reflected neoliberalised conceptions, and thus to fall into a larger (and pre-existing) trend of *neoliberalisation* of international law.

Therefore, after a preliminary introduction, in the remainder of this chapter, of this book's understanding of ESR (Section 1.2) and neoliberalism (Section 1.3), the next chapters will revisit some of the post-crisis debt-and-ESR-related developments in light of the above-mentioned assumptions.

Chapter 2 will provide a general definition of sovereign debt and illustrate the trend, dating back to the 1970s, of rising global public indebtedness, including in advanced economies, to reflect on the actual role of debt in the current global economic system. Afterwards, it will analyse the main elements of the post-crisis reform of the legal framework for economic and fiscal policymaking in the European Economic and Monetary Union (a reform linked, inter alia, to the intensified need to subject the fiscal conduct of increasingly indebted states to stricter controls) and discuss how these seem to evidence its increased neoliberalisation.

Chapter 3 will critically review the existing international law on ESR, namely the ICESCR, and briefly outline existing standards on sovereign debt and human rights. Considering the surviving peculiarities of the ICESCR (due, inter alia, to the historical contingencies that influenced its elaboration in the 1950s–60s) and the nature of the economic and fiscal policy measures that have been generally recommended over the years by its monitoring body (i.e. the CESCR), this chapter will, first, challenge the purported economic neutrality of the Covenant (and, more generally, of the international ESR regime) as currently interpreted. Secondly, it will highlight the increased influence of neoliberalism on this legal framework's post-crisis developments, especially the more recent (re)interpretation by the CESCR of the prohibition of retrogressive measures.

Finally, Chapter 4 will provide an illustration of the trends and dynamics discussed in the previous chapters through a comprehensive and contextualised examination of the specific, but paradigmatic, Greek debt crisis, arguing that, in this case as well, both the responses devised by national and supranational institutions, and their scrutiny by some human rights monitoring bodies in particular, seem to reflect an increasingly neoliberalised conception of human rights and of the debt–ESR relationship.

1.2 PRELIMINARY DEFINITIONS: (A) ECONOMIC AND SOCIAL RIGHTS AS INTERNATIONAL HUMAN RIGHTS

Human rights are generally described as rights that all persons have simply by virtue of their humanity, that is, inherent and inalienable rights (see e.g. the Preamble and Article 1 of the Universal Declaration on Human Rights or the founding document of international human rights law). Their protection – including by means of international law – is meant to preserve something deemed to be *quintessential* to the human person[20] and, for that reason, to be safeguarded at all costs. No definitive agreement exists, however, as to the exact meaning of this *being human* that human rights are meant to protect, so that 'no single, homogeneous, coherent set of human rights' exists in international law, reflecting some univocal conception (and any use of the expression 'human rights', unspecified, risks being misleading and 'scientifically unsound').[21] Actually, if any agreement is reached on one (or more) definite notion(s) of (what are) the human rights that international law is meant to protect, it is on the notion(s) that have temporarily prevailed over alternative conceptions. Any conception, thus, is bound to remain always contestable and dependent on the possible redefinition of (and on the ultimate belief in the need to protect) this quintessence of the human person.

For the purposes of a discussion of existing international human rights law – like the one in the present book – we may take (as we indeed do, see later) *legal* human rights to correspond to the rights that are affirmed and protected as such in international legal sources, as interpreted by relevant monitoring bodies.[22] Before providing a general definition of international ESR in this sense, however, I would like to clarify succinctly some fundamental characteristics of *legal* rights that appear necessary to understand what it means for human rights, and notably ESR, to be considered (or not) as such, and accordingly to assess the nature and possible limitations of the existing international legal framework for their protection.

According to the famous and influential classification proposed, at the beginning of the twentieth century, by the American jurist Wesley Newcomb

[20] For a discussion (also of a specific conception) of the 'human person' as the key foundation of human rights, see Carlo Focarelli, 'International Human Rights "in Crisis" and the Neoliberalization of the Human Person' (2020) 19 *Chinese Journal of International Law* 1, 53–100.

[21] *Ibid.*, 80. See also Ilias Bantekas and Lutz Oette, *International Human Rights Law and Practice*, 3rd ed. (Cambridge University Press, 2020).

[22] For a critical overview of the sources of international human rights law, see Cristine Chinkin, 'Sources' in Daniel Moeckli, Sangeeta Shah and Sandesh Sivakumaran (eds.), *International Human Rights Law*, 3rd ed. (Oxford University Press, 2017) 75–95.

Hohfeld,[23] a legal right, as a specific type of 'jural' or legal relation, is essentially defined by its correlative duty: it is 'an entitlement to the state of affairs [. . .] that is specified in the imposition of a duty on someone else'.[24] In other words, someone (A) has a legal right against someone else (B) in relation to something (X), *if and only if* (B) has a duty towards (A) in relation to the same 'thing'.[25]

This seems to be the notion of rights incorporated by international human rights law, where states (as both the core political institutions of contemporary societies[26] and the core subjects of international law) are the primary duty-bearers and under a general obligation to regulate the conduct of all persons within their jurisdiction so that they respect, protect and fulfil internationally recognised human rights.

Since often, especially in common parlance, rights are also (misleadingly) portrayed as 'liberties', 'freedoms', 'privileges' or 'powers', it seems important to stress the distinction, under the Hohfeldian classification of legal relations, in particular between a legal right and a *liberty* (or privilege). Differently from a legal right, a liberty as a legal relationship corresponds to the negation of a duty upon the 'liberty-holder' with a content or tenor opposite to that of the liberty in question.[27] To put it more simply, (A) has a liberty in relation to (X), for instance to do (X), if s/he has no duty in relation to the opposite of (X), that is, not to do (X).

[23] Wesley N. Hohfeld, 'Fundamental Legal Conceptions as Applied in Judicial Reasoning' (originally published as two articles in the *Yale Law Journal* for 1913 and 1917) in Walter Wheeler Cook (ed.), *Fundamental Legal Conceptions as Applied in Judicial Reasoning: And Other Legal Essays* (New Haven: Yale University Press, 1920). See also Albert Kocourek, 'Various Definitions of Jural Relation' (1920) 20 *Columbia Law Review* 4, 394–412; Arthur Corbin, 'Jural Relations and Their Classification' (1921) *Yale Law School Faculty Scholarship Series*, Paper 2873; Mark Andrews, 'Hohfeld's Cube' (1983) 16 *Akron Law Review* 3, 471–485.

[24] Matthew H. Kramer, 'Rights without Trimmings' in Matthew M. Kramer, N. E. Simmonds and Hillel Steiner (eds.), *A Debate Over Rights* (Oxford University Press, 1999), p. 32; Hohfeld, 'Fundamental Legal Conceptions', p. 38.

[25] Hohfeld identified four core legal concepts (right, privilege, power and immunity) each one entailing a jural correlative and a jural opposite (duty, no-right, liability and disability), and thus resulting in eight different possible jural relations which, according to Hohfeld, represent the 'lowest generic conceptions to which any and all "legal quantities" may be reduced', Hohfeld, 'Fundamental Legal Conceptions', pp. 58–59. As Hohfeld himself admitted, someone's 'legal interest' relating to (X) may consist, in practice, of 'a complex aggregate of rights (or claims), privileges, powers and immunities', *ibid.*, 96. In practice, what we generically call a 'right' may entail several distinct jural relations, but the defining core of a legal right remains its correlative duty. See also Carl Wellman, *The Moral Dimensions of Human Rights* (Oxford University Press, 2011), pp. 18–19.

[26] See e.g. Martha Nussbaum, 'Human Dignity and Political Entitlements' in *Human Dignity and Bioethics: Essays Commissioned by the President's Council on Bioethics* (President's Commission on Bioethics, 2008) 351–380, pp. 359–360 (arguing that the duties correlated to the entitlements that all people have just by virtue of their humanity belong, first and foremost, to the basic political structure of society, i.e. the state); see also her *Creating Capabilities: The Human Development Approach* (Cambridge, MA: The Belknap Press of Harvard University Press, 2011).

[27] Hohfeld, 'Fundamental Legal Conceptions', p. 39.

In this case, (B)'s position towards (A) is defined only by his/her correlate 'no-right' that (A) does the opposite of (X). Therefore, while (A)'s right is consubstantial with (B)'s duty, *(A)'s liberty does not create any duty on (B)*. (A) may or may not do (X), and if s/he does, s/he has violated no right of (B). Furthermore, (B) is under no duty not to interfere with (A)'s attempt at doing (X), since (A) has a liberty but not a right to do (X). The two notions of legal right and liberty, thus, order interpersonal relationships very differently, and there is a great difference in asserting something as a matter of one or the other.[28] In this sense, when we find references to the fact that a legal human right entails both entitlements and freedoms,[29] a distinction is being actually made between correlative duties (i.e. positive ones in relation to the entitlement aspects of a right, and negative ones in relation to its freedom aspects).[30] There are no legal rights that do not create duties.

Furthermore, while contemporary lawyers and legal scholars often seem to refer to rights as 'two-term relations between persons and one subject-matter or (in a broad sense) thing',[31] it is important to emphasise that legal rights are always intrinsically three-term, *inter-personal* relations. They define the relative positions of the *persons* (A) and (B) in a legal relationship whose object is (X). In the strictly legal sense, therefore, (X) itself is not 'a right', but the object of a right, while, as mentioned earlier, (A)'s right to (X) corresponds to a particular type of normative relationship between (A) and (B) vis-à-vis (X): what (A) is actually entitled to is to a certain conduct by (B) in relation to (X), rather than (X) itself.

The occultation of the third term-person in a right relationship make rights appear as abstract assertions made against an indefinite (and sometimes supposedly indefinable) duty-bearer. It is, thus, instrumental both to undermine the actual realisation of human rights and to exploit the notion and language of human rights for political/ideological ends, as 'in political terms it is clearly much more rewarding to promise rights rather than duties'.[32] Thus, any *struggle for rights* should be better fought in terms of *duties*.[33]

[28] There are different theories as to the reasons why some relations are legally ordered specifically as right-relations, see e.g. Horacio Spector, 'Value Pluralism and the Two Concepts of Rights' in Brian H. Bix and Horacio Spector (eds.), *Rights: Concepts and Contexts* (Abingdon: Routledge, 2012) 115–134; John Finnis, *Natural Law and Natural Rights*, 2nd ed. (Oxford University Press, 2011), p. 204.

[29] See e.g. CESCR, General Comment No. 22, 'The right to sexual and reproductive health (art. 12)', UN Doc. E/C.12/GC/22 (2 May 2016), paras. 5–6.

[30] See also Henry Shue, *Basic Rights: Subsistence, Affluence and US Foreign Policy*, 2nd ed. (Princeton University Press, 1996).

[31] Finnis, *Natural Law*, p. 199 ff.

[32] Focarelli, 'International Human Rights "in Crisis"', 79. See also Carlo Focarelli, 'Il Pianeta dei Balocchi. A Proposito della Definizione dei Diritti Umani' (2016) 10 *Diritti Umani e Diritto Internazionale* 3, 659–676, 667.

[33] *Ibid.*

1.2.1 *The Affirmation of Economic and Social Rights as International Human Rights*

The first conceptualisation of economic and social rights as *human* rights (the latter with an acceptation closer to a contemporary understanding of human rights) occurred during the 1791 and 1793 revolutionary constitutional processes in France.[34] It can be traced in the writings of radical actors of the Revolution, such as François-Noël Babeuf and Maximilien Robespierre, as well as in the work of the *Comité de la mendicité de la Constituante*.[35] In 1970, the latter asserted:

> We have always thought to give charity to the poor but never to establish the rights of the poor vis-à-vis the society. [...] This is the great challenge for the French Constitution, since nobody else had till now recognised these *Human Rights*.[36]

In 1793, Robespierre proposed a new Declaration of Rights, where the 'right to exist' of the members of society, through their rights to work and to social assistance, was to be proclaimed as a legally enforceable obligation and a 'debt' of society and the rich towards the poor.[37] Despite these proposals, however, in

34 Indeed, the first declarations of the rights of 'men' in the eighteenth-century constitutions of the American colonies (in particular the 1776 Virginia Declaration of Rights, adopted by the Virginia Constitutional Convention on 12 June 1776, Section 1 and 3), the 1776 Declaration of Independence of the Thirteen United States of America (adopted by the US Congress on 4 July 1776) and the 1789 French Declaration of the Rights of Man and of the Citizen (adopted by France's National Constituent Assembly on 26 August 1789) did not contain any reference to economic and social rights, except for their mention of property (an implicit one, in the case of the American Declaration, see Linda M. Keller, 'The American Rejection of Economic Rights as Human Rights and the Declaration of Independence: Does the Pursuit of Happiness Require Basic Economic Rights?' (2003) 19 *New York Law School Journal of Human Rights* 557).

35 George Katrougalos, 'A Short Genealogy of Social Rights' in Nikitas Aliprantis and Ioannis Papageorgiou (eds.), *Social Rights at European, Regional and International Level: Challenges for the 21st Century* (Brussels: Bruylant, 2010), p. 26.

36 *Comité de la mendicité de la Constituante*, 1st Report, 1790, quoted in *Ibid.*, pp. 26–27 (emphasis added).

37 The 1793 Declaration, indeed, affirmed: 'Art. 11. The society is obliged to ensure the existence of all its members, either by giving work to them, or by providing to those who cannot work the means to survive. Art. 12. The assistance to the miserable is the debt of the rich toward the poor. The law will determine how this duty is going to be paid.' See also Katrougalos, 'A Short Genealogy', p. 27. A year before, in his address to the Convention, Robespierre had already clearly expressed what he considered as 'the first social rule': 'Which is the principal of these [Man's] rights? The right to exist. The first social rule, therefore, is the rule which guarantees to all members of the society their right to exist. All other laws must be subordinate to this first one,' Nikitas Aliprantis, 'Social Rights Beyond the National Level – Findings and Challenges' in Aliprantis and Papageorgiou, *Social Rights at European, Regional and International Level*, p. 4.

the Declaration of Rights adopted by the Constitution of the Convention of 24 June 1793, social rights (to work, to public assistance and to education) received recognition only as 'a sacred debt of society',[38] mere moral rather than legally enforceable rights ('little more than ideological declarations, denuded of legal context or other practical implications').[39]

It is not possible to retrace here the constitutional history of all the countries whose legal traditions influenced the development of international human rights law.[40] However, in the realm of international law, it was only at the end of the Second World War that the ideas originally expressed within the American and French declarations and then progressively embraced by several constitutions across the world translated into international norms.[41]

[38] *Ibid.*

[39] *Ibid.*

[40] In fact, the starting point for the drafting of the 1948 Universal Declaration of Human Rights (on which, see further below) was an Outline Draft prepared by the UN Secretariat's Division for Human Rights on the basis of the different human rights affirmed within the constitutions of UN Member States that were in force at the time, see in particular Commission on Human Rights, Drafting Committee, 'International Bill of Rights: Documented Outline Part I – Texts', UN Doc. E/CN.4/AC.1/3/Add.1 (11 June 1947), www.un.org/en/ga/search/view_doc.asp?symbol=E/CN.4/AC.1/3/Add.1. See also below (n 49).

[41] Although some doctrines and principles existing in pre-1945 international law – and relating, in particular, to the law of armed conflict, state responsibility, the protection of minorities and international criminal law – served as a background to and influenced the development of international human rights law, its origins are commonly traced back to the framing of the UN Charter and the UDHR, see i.a. Philip Alston and Ryan Goodman, *International Human Rights: Text and Materials* (Oxford University Press, 2013), p. 58 ff.; Ed Bates, 'History' in Moeckli, Shah and Sivakumaran, *International Human Rights Law*, p. 23 ff. Despite proposals to the contrary, the UN Charter eventually did not incorporate a bill of rights. The second paragraph of the Charter's preamble proclaims that the members of the United Nations are determined 'to reaffirm faith in fundamental human rights, in the dignity and worth of the human person, in the equal right of men and women and of nations large and small'. Article 1(3) of the UN Charter lists, among the purposes of the UN, the promotion and encouragement of respect for human rights and fundamental freedoms for all without distinction as to race, sex, language, or religion; Article 13(1)(b) urges the General Assembly to initiate studies and make recommendations for the purpose of 'assisting in the realization of human rights and fundamental freedoms for all without distinction as to race, sex, language, or religion'; and Articles 55 and 56 make human rights an integral part of the UN international economic and social cooperation obligations. Human rights are also part of the mandate of the Economic and Social Council (ECOSOC) (Articles 62, 68) and of the international trusteeship system (Article 76(c)). The Charter's drafters perceived, in fact, the protection of human rights as imperative to a new international order conducive to peace, thus emphasising its instrumental value in international relations, Bantekas and Oette, *International Human Rights Law and Practice*, p. 19. Notwithstanding, the generic term 'human rights' appears in the Charter only in provisions referring to the purposes of the UN or the competences of different UN organs, thus having, mainly, a promotional or programmatic character. Only one substantive human right, i.e. that to equality, receives specific mention in the Charter (Articles 1(3), 13(1)(b) and 55), Alston and Goodman, *International Human Rights*, pp. 140–141.

With specific regard to socio-economic rights, the most appropriate starting point for their international legal history is the creation of the International Labour Organization (ILO) in 1919, as part of the Treaty of Versailles that ended the First World War.[42] The impetus for the establishment of an international organisation to regulate labour conditions came from the persuasion that 'peace and justice go hand in hand[, n]ot in the sense that war is always the result of injustice, but rather that social justice is an essential foundation of peace'.[43] The Preamble of the ILO Constitution affirmed, in fact, that 'universal and lasting peace can be established only if it is based upon social justice', and acknowledged that 'conditions of labour exist involving such injustice hardship and privation to large numbers of people as to produce unrest so great that the peace and harmony of the world are imperilled'.[44]

During the interwar period, the ILO adopted several international standards in relation to a broad range of matters, now generally falling under the rubric of ESR, such as social security, freedom of association, the right to organise trade unions and equality of treatment/non-discrimination in the enjoyment of ESR. After a period of reduced activity in the late 1930s, due to the war and the decline of the League of Nations (with which the ILO was associated), in 1944 the twenty-sixth ILO General Conference adopted the historic Declaration of Philadelphia, annexed to the ILO Constitution and representing the Charter of the aims and objectives of the organisation. Article 1 of the Declaration reaffirmed that 'the war against want requires to be carried on with unrelenting vigour within each nation, and by continuous and concerted international effort',[45] while Article 2 solemnly proclaimed that

> (a) all human beings, irrespective of race, creed or sex, have the right to pursue both their material well-being and their spiritual development in conditions of freedom and dignity, of economic security and equal opportunity; (b) the attainment of the conditions in which this shall be possible must constitute the central aim of national and international policy; (c) all national and international policies and measures, in particular those of an economic and financial character, should be judged in this light and accepted only in so far as they may be held to promote and not to hinder the achievement of this fundamental objective [...].[46]

42 Alston and Goodman, *International Human Rights*, p. 279.

43 Gerry Rodgers, Eddy Lee, Lee Swepston and Jasmien van Daele, *The International Labour Organization and the Quest for Social Justice* (ILO, 2009), p. 3.

44 Constitution of the International Labour Organization (ILO Constitution), 1919, Preamble.

45 ILO, Declaration concerning the aims and purposes of the International Labour Organization (Declaration of Philadelphia), 10 May 1944.

46 *Ibid.*

The expression 'war on want' of Article 1 clearly evoked the 1941 'Four Freedoms' speech of US President Franklin Delano Roosevelt (and the famous 1942 Beveridge report).[47] In that speech, Roosevelt had enlisted 'freedom from want' among the 'essential human freedoms' upon which to ground a vision of the future world, a vision that Roosevelt further clarified in his famous 1944 State of the Union speech on a 'Second (Economic) Bill of Rights':

> We cannot be content, no matter how high that [American] general standard of living may be, if some fraction of our people – whether it be one-third or one-fifth or one-tenth – is ill-fed, ill-clothed, ill housed, and insecure. This Republic had its beginning, and grew to its present strength, under the protection of certain inalienable political rights – among them the right of free speech, free press, free worship, trial by jury, freedom from unreasonable searches and seizures. They were our rights to life and liberty. As our Nation has grown in size and stature, however – as our industrial economy expanded – these political rights proved inadequate to assure us equality in the pursuit of happiness. We have come to a clear realization of the fact that true individual freedom cannot exist without economic security and independence. 'Necessitous men are not free men'. People who are hungry and out of a job are the stuff of which dictatorships are made.
>
> In our day these economic truths have become accepted as self-evident. We have accepted, so to speak, a second Bill of Rights under which a new basis of security and prosperity can be established for all regardless of station, race, or creed.[48]

This vision was undoubtedly among the sources of inspiration for the drafting of the UDHR, which the newly established UN Commission on Human Rights entrusted, in 1947, to a Working Group chaired by the US president's wife, Eleanor Roosevelt.

The UDHR was adopted by the United Nations General Assembly on 10 December 1948, and it includes a number of economic, social and cultural rights, namely to social security (art. 22), to work (art. 23), to rest and leisure (art. 24), to an adequate standard of living (art. 25), to education (art. 26) and to

47 William Beveridge, 'Social Insurance and Allied Services' (American edition reproduced photographically from the English edition and published by arrangement with His Majesty's Stationery Office, The Macmillan Company 1942).

48 Franklin D. Roosevelt, *Annual Message to Congress on the State of the Union*, 11 January 1944, fdrlibrary.marist.edu/archives/address_text.html. Roosevelt's mention of the 'rights to life and liberty' and to 'the pursuit of happiness' is a clear reference to the language of the United States' Declaration of Independence of 1776.

participation in cultural and artistic life and in the benefits of scientific advancement (art. 27).[49] Article 22, furthermore, contains language that applies more generally to all the economic, social and cultural rights enshrined in the UDHR:

> Everyone, as a member of society, has the right to social security and is entitled to realization, through national effort and international co-operation and in accordance with the organization and resources of each state, of the economic, social and cultural rights indispensable for his dignity and the free development of his personality.

After long discussion, however, the UDHR was deliberately given the form of a 'recommendation'. Today, many of its provisions are considered as having gained formal legal force by becoming part of customary international law (whether its provisions on economic and social rights have gained such status, however, is still controversial).[50]

A proper binding international human rights regime eventually emerged in the 1960s, with the adoption, in 1966, of the International Covenant on Civil and Political Rights (ICCPR) and the above-mentioned ICESCR. The drafting of two separate Covenants by the UN Commission of Human Rights commenced in 1953, once it became evident that growing ideological tensions between states belonging to the two 'blocs' in the wake of the Cold War were producing an irreconcilable disagreement over the

49 UN General Assembly, Res 217 A (III) of 10 December 1948, 'Universal Declaration of Human Rights'. As mentioned above (n 40), the document that served as the Working Group's first draft had been redacted by the United Nations Secretariat's Division on Human Rights. It listed forty-eight different articles outlining the individual human rights that had been identified as those most frequently appearing in the human rights catalogues in force at the time across the world. They included, under the 'Social Rights' chapter, the rights to 'medical care' (Art. 35), to 'education' (Art. 36), to 'perform socially valuable work' (Art. 37), to 'good working conditions' (Art. 38), to 'such equitable share of the national income as the need for [man's] work and the increment it makes to the common welfare may justify' (Art. 39), to 'public help' for family responsibilities (Art. 40), to 'social security' (Art. 41), to 'good food' and housing (Art. 42), to 'a fair share of rest and leisure' (Art. 43), and to participate in cultural and artistic life and to share in the benefits of science (Art. 44), see 'Draft Outline of International Bill of Rights (prepared by the Division of Human Rights)', UN Doc. E/CN.4/AC.1/3 (4 June 1947), www.un.org/en/ga/search/view_doc.asp?symbol=E/CN.4/AC.1/3. See also Olivier De Schutter (ed.), *Economic, Social and Cultural Rights as Human Rights* (Cheltenham: Edward Elgar, 2013), p. xiv.

50 See i.a. Alston and Goodman, *International Human Rights*, p. 144; Bruno Simma and Philip Alston, 'The Sources of International Human Rights Law: Custom, *Jus Cogens*, and General Principles' (1992) 12 *Australian Yearbook of International Law* 1, 82–108; Eibe Riedel, Gilles Giacca and Christophe Golay, *Economic, Social and Cultural Rights in International Law: Contemporary Issues and Challenges* (Oxford University Press, 2014), p. 21.

appropriate means of implementation of, on one side, civil and political and, on the other, economic, social and cultural rights:

> Western states led by the United States of America – in contradiction with the Four Freedoms Speech of Franklin D. Roosevelt of 1941 and with his Economic Bill of Rights Speech of 1944 – favoured the concept of two separate treaties maintaining that [civil and political] rights and [economic, social and cultural] rights were and are inherently of a different legal nature, insofar as the latter would lack judicial enforceability. Contrary to this position, the so-called Eastern bloc as well as many non-aligned states supported and demanded equal treatment for [economic, social and cultural] rights. At the final count, the supporters of one comprehensive treaty had to compromise and accept two separate treaties [. . .].[51]

The ICCPR and ICESCR were finally adopted in 1966 and entered into force, respectively, on 23 March and 3 January 1976.[52] As of 2020, 176 states have ratified the ICCPR and 171 states the ICESCR.[53] Together with the UDHR, the two Covenants represent today the so-called International Bill of Rights.

1.2.2 *A Definition of International ESR for This Book's Purposes*

The terms 'economic and social rights', 'socio-economic rights' and the abbreviation 'ESR' are used throughout this book to cover the full range of economic and social rights as expressed in international human rights instruments and particularly the ICESCR.[54]

According to a concise description offered by the OHCHR, economic, social and cultural rights are human rights relating to the workplace, social security, family life, participation in cultural life, and access to housing, food, water,

[51] Riedel, Giacca and Golay, *Economic, Social and Cultural Rights in International Law*, 6–7. See UN General Assembly Resolution, Preparation of Two Drafts International Covenants on Human Rights, 5 February 1952, A/RES/543 (VI) (the so-called 'Separation Resolution').

[52] International Covenant on Civil and Political Rights (adopted 16 December 1966, entered into force 3 January 1976) 999 UNTS 3; International Covenant on Economic, Social and Cultural Rights (adopted 16 December 1966, entered into force 3 January 1976) 993 UNTS 3.

[53] Comoros, Cuba, Palau and the United States have signed but not yet ratified the ICESCR, while 22 other countries, including the Holy See, Malaysia, Singapore, South Sudan and the UAE, have taken no action in its regard.

[54] Although of course relevant for ESR in the European context, this book will not address the European Social Charter, this representing a distinct legal regime. Nonetheless, Chapter 4 will include a brief discussion of some of the most recent decisions of the European Committee of Social Rights (i.e. the body entrusted with monitoring the Charter's implementation) that involved Greece, to emphasise the difference with the suggested convergence of the jurisprudence of the other human rights monitoring bodies considered in this book (i.e. the UN Committee on Economic, Social and Cultural Rights and, limitedly, the European Court of Human Rights) towards neoliberalised conceptions of some elements of their respective human rights regimes.

health care and education.[55] A basic list includes *workers' rights* (including freedom from forced labour, the rights to decide freely to accept or choose work, to fair wages and equal pay for equal work, to leisure and reasonable limitation of working hours, to safe and healthy working conditions, to join and form trade unions and to strike); *the right to social security and social protection* (including the right not to be denied social security coverage arbitrarily or unreasonably, and the right to equal enjoyment of adequate protection in the event of unemployment, sickness, old age or other lack of livelihood in circumstances beyond one's control); *protection of and assistance to the family* (including the rights to maternity and paternity protection, and to protection of children from economic and social exploitation); *the right to an adequate standard of living* (including the rights to food and to be free from hunger, to adequate housing, to water and to clothing); *the right to health* (including the rights to access to health facilities, goods and services, to healthy occupational and environmental conditions, to protection against epidemic diseases and to sexual and reproductive health); *the right to education* (including the right to free and compulsory primary education and to available and accessible secondary and higher education, progressively to be made free of charge; and the liberty of parents to choose schools for their children); and *cultural rights* (including the right to participate in cultural life and to share in and benefit from scientific advancement, and the protection of authors' moral and material interests from scientific, literary or artistic production).[56]

International human rights law does not make any explicit distinction between economic, social or cultural rights. The rationale embraced by international instruments was an essentially bureaucratic one, the adjectives 'economic', 'social' and 'cultural' being originally used to identify the rights that fell within the sphere of interest of, respectively, the ILO ('economic' rights), UN agencies such as the Food and Agriculture Organization (FAO) and the World Health Organization (WHO) ('social' rights), and the United Nations Educational, Scientific and Cultural Organization (UNESCO) ('cultural' rights).

Cultural rights, in particular, although conceptually clustered with economic and social rights, in practice have been dealt with more in connection with civil and political rights (inter alia, under the ICCPR's non-discrimination clause, minorities provisions or in connection with specific civil and political rights).[57] For this reason, this work will devote its attention principally to economic and

55 OHCHR, 'Fact Sheet No. 33: Frequently Asked Questions on Economic, Social and Rights' (2008), www.ohchr.org/Documents/Issues/ESCR/FAQ%20on%20ESCR-en.pdf.

56 Alston and Goodman, *International Human Rights*, pp. 285–286.

57 *Ibid.*

social rights (hereinafter, ESR), although many of the considerations herein put forward may well apply to all human rights without distinctions.

1.3 PRELIMINARY DEFINITIONS: (B) NEOLIBERALISM

Neoliberalism is a contested and multifarious concept, eluding any conclusive and fully coherent definition.[58] Over the years, it has come to identify many different phenomena:[59] inter alia, a theory of political economy, or a set of economic policies;[60] a mode of governmentality, or a political rationality;[61] a class-based political project to revive the domination of capitalism and the capitalist classes;[62] an intellectual movement, thought collective, or epistemic community;[63] or a hegemonic discourse.[64] In common parlance, neoliberalism

[58] For some recent attempts at defining the concept and analysing its multiple dimensions, see i.a. Dieter Plehwe, Quinn Slobodian and Philip Mirowski (eds.), *Nine Lives of Neoliberalism* (London: Verso 2020); Simon Dawes and Marc Lenormand (eds.), *Neoliberalism in Context* (London: Palgrave Macmillan, 2020); Damien Cahill, Melinda Cooper, Martijn Konings and David Primrose (eds.), *The SAGE Handbook of Neoliberalism* (London: SAGE, 2018); Simon Springer, Kean Birch and Julie MacLeavy (eds.), *The Handbook of Neoliberalism* (Abingdon: Routledge, 2016); Matthew Eagleton-Pierce, *Neoliberalism: Key Concepts* (Abingdon: Routledge, 2016).

[59] Kean Birch, for instance, has identified seven distinct scholarly approaches to understanding neoliberalism, see his *A Research Agenda for Neoliberalism* (Cheltenham: Edward Elgar, 2017).

[60] E.g. David Harvey, *A Brief History of Neoliberalism* (Oxford University Press, 2005); Mark Blyth, *Austerity: The History of a Dangerous Idea* (Oxford University Press, 2011).

[61] Michel Foucault, *The Birth of Biopolitics: Lectures at the Collège de France, 1978–1979*, ed. by Michel Senellart, General Eds. : François Ewald and Alessandro Fontana, trans. by Graham Burchell (London: Palgrave Macmillan, 2010). Also Pierre Dardot and Christian Laval, *The New Way of the World: On Neoliberal Society* (London: Verso, 2013), and Stephanie Lee Mudge, 'What Is Neo-Liberalism?' (2008) 4 *Socio-Economic Review* 6, 703–731 follow this 'Foucauldian' approach.

[62] For a 'Marxian' approach to neoliberalism, see i.a. Harvey, *A Brief History of Neoliberalism*; Gérard Duménil and Dominique Lévy, *The Crisis of Neoliberalism*(Cambridge, MA: Harvard University Press, 2011); Naomi Klein, *The Shock Doctrine: The Rise of Disaster Capitalism* (New York: Picador, 2008).

[63] A remarkable work on the intellectual genesis of neoliberalism is certainly Martin Beddeleem, 'Fighting for the Mantle of Science: The Epistemological Foundations of Neoliberalism, 1931–1951', unpublished PhD thesis, Université de Montréal (2017). See also, importantly, the works of Philip Mirowski and Dieter Plehwe: besides Mirowski, *Never Let a Serious Crisis Go to Waste* and Mirowski and Plehwe, *The Road from Mont Pèlerin*, see also Dieter Plehwe, Bernhard Walpen and Gisela Neunhöffer, *Neoliberal Hegemony: A Global Critique* (London: Routledge, 2006). On the notion of 'epistemic community', see Peter M. Haas, 'Introduction: Epistemic Communities and International Policy Coordination' (1992) 46 *International Organization* 1, 1–35.

[64] See e.g. Vivien A. Schmidt, 'Ideas and the Rise of Neoliberalism in Europe' in Cahill et al., *The SAGE Handbook of Neoliberalism*, p. 72.

has been alternately associated with neoclassical economics, monetarism, Tatcherism, Reaganism, Howardism, 'pensée unique' or 'strong discourse', economism, market fundamentalism or even 'fetishism' or 'anti-statism'.

To some observers, the elusiveness of the concept is 'deeply embedded within the constitutive features of neoliberalism itself',[65] which 'is not a coherently bounded "ism," a functional system, a stable regime, or an historical "end-state" [… nor] a fixed set of policy preferences and technologies', so that attempts at specifying the concept more stringently are essentially 'mistaken'.[66] Rather, it is 'quite appropriate that the tangle of meanings attached to "neoliberalism" remain both somewhat ambiguous and situationally specific [… as this fact] arguably says something about how neoliberalism exists in the world – as a presence seemingly oppressive, real, and immediate in some respects, but at the same time one that can also be considered to be diffuse, abstract, and liminal'.[67] To a certain extent it is also true that 'neoliberalism seems often to be used as a sort of stand-in term for the political-economic zeitgeist', or that the concept 'has progressively been imbued of its own causal properties – "that is, it [has] become the 'it' that does the explaining, rather than the political phenomenon that needs to be explained"'.[68] Nonetheless, I agree with those who trust the persistent validity of the concept as a 'useful descriptor of real-world phenomena',[69] as long as one does not purport to provide a definitive, all-encompassing definition of neoliberalism to be applicable to all circumstances. This book does not.

For this book's purposes of exploring the purported advancement of international law's neoliberalisation since the Global Financial Crisis, neoliberalism can be best identified with a currently hegemonic, totalistic[70] and at its

65 Damien Cahill, Melinda Cooper, Martijn Konings and David Primrose, 'Introduction: Approaches to Neoliberalism' in Cahill et al. *The SAGE Handbook of Neoliberalism*, p. xxviii.

66 Jamie Peck, Neil Brenner and Nik Theodore, 'Actually Existing Neoliberalism' in Cahill et al., *The SAGE Handbook of Neoliberalism*, pp. 4 and 7. Peck adds, importantly for our discussion of 'neoliberalisation', that this is also why the latter 'must be interpreted as an historically specific, fungible, volatile, and unstable process of market-driven sociospatial restructuring (for all its imperative manifestations and alignments with contemporary power-geometries), rather than as a fully actualized policy regime, complete institutional apparatus or stabilized regulatory framework', *ibid.*

67 *Ibid.*

68 Cahill et al., 'Introduction: Approaches to Neoliberalism', pp. xxvii–xxviii.

69 *Ibid.*, xxix.

70 With the adjective 'hegemonic' I intend to refer here to the dominance of neoliberalism as a belief system (not necessarily, but potentially also, pursued by a social class, as in the Marxist concept of hegemony developed in particular by A. Gramsci) supported by some form of (not necessarily cognisant) consent on the part of those it dominates. Christian Arnsperger has described neoliberalism as 'a theory to end all theories', *Critical Political Economy:*

core anti-humanist[71] and anti-human rights[72] belief system (forming inter alia the basis of a specific theory of political economy), which is grounded in particular on a specific (and, originally, historically contingent) vision of the nature and possibilities of human knowledge (from which also derives a specific conception of the limits and role of social institutions). Such epistemological vision, as will be said shortly, essentially grounds the neoliberal justification and totalistic effort to establish the pre-eminence of the market as a(n epistemic) method to understand the reality of social phenomena and to accordingly (re)order all social relations. Neoliberalisation corresponds, thus, to the reconstruction of various aspects and elements of international law (inter alia, through a preliminary restructuring of the state) according to these normative assumptions and its underlying epistemological stance.

With this definition, I am not suggesting that neoliberalisation necessarily entails a deliberate adherence by its agents to neoliberal epistemology (these are, in fact, often unaware of it, since, as mentioned earlier, neoliberal assumptions have become largely invisible to the mind and operate at what has been defined as the 'psychic' level),[73] but that neoliberal epistemology

Complexity, Rationality and the Logic of Post-Orthodox Pluralism (London: Routledge, 2006), quoted in Mirowski and Plehwe, *The Road from Mont Pèlerin*, p. 445. For a discussion of neoliberalism as a (specific) 'totalizing project', see also Focarelli, 'International Human Rights "in Crisis"'.

71 With the term 'humanism' I intend to refer generally to philosophical/moral stances that (although with remarkable differences) all place central emphasis on the human realm, and on the 'value' and agency of human beings and their implications for the construction of the social order.

72 See further Section 1.3.1, for an explanation of this idea.

73 Focarelli clarifies that the term 'psychic' is meant 'to identify something more radical than what the other similar terms used in the (anti-neoliberal) literature [such as "way of being," "consciousness," "cultural unconscious," "mentality," "logic," "mind-set," "epistemology," or Foucault's "site of truth" or "regime of truth"] refer to [...]'. It denotes a 'broader' concept 'than those denoted by any of the above-mentioned alternative terms', as 'it includes all of them at the deepest and most influential level, thus involving the "psyche" very much in Jung's understanding of it as "the totality of all psychic processes, conscious as well as unconscious"'. It also 'concerns a largely (yet not totally) unaware subject, not differently from an "objective" biological fact, or instinct, or mental health condition; it operates at the level of relatively scarcely-differentiated mental activity'. What seems to be suggested here is that neoliberalism has essentially restructured, and it has become embedded in the human 'cognitive system' itself. For this reason, Focarelli also argues that 'it is insusceptible to being remedied by the subject through his/her sole own (especially rational) forces', and it 'is deeply embedded even in its self-professed critics who, despite their apparent convictions, may be intimately more "neoliberal" than (those considered) neoliberals themselves'. In this sense, according to Focarelli, neoliberalism is today a 'totalizing project', inasmuch as 'any outside or way out [of it] cannot be realised but by applying the [same] criticized methods, thus reinforcing them', see Focarelli, 'International Human Rights "in Crisis"', 73.

unavoidably always underlies neoliberalisation, and thus effects its (dehumanising) consequences (in the terms described later in the text) regardless of its unintentional implementation.

According to this definition of neoliberalism, phenomena that are usually taken to represent it (e.g. specific economic policies such as deregulation, privatisation and liberalisation of trade, or specific conceptions of freedom or welfare) appear as surface and partial manifestations of a deeper and more comprehensive belief system and of its embedded epistemological vision.

Not being reducible to such manifestations, hence, neoliberal 'transformations wrought over the last four decades [cannot] be reversed or transcended through implementation of alternative policy initiatives and programmes alone'.[74] The implications and effects of neoliberalism, including on the law, are to be traced back to, and if necessary contested, at this deeper epistemological (and, if one admits the above-mentioned interpretation, deeper psychic) level.[75]

For this reason, while for the purposes of this book, we can be satisfied with considering some of neoliberalism's more external manifestations – in Section 1.3.2 – the next subsection will nonetheless succinctly outline the core elements of what is deemed here to represent a general neoliberal epistemology. My attempt in this sense must be considered only as a stepping stone to a much larger research endeavour to reveal the possible neoliberal roots of currently prevailing social and possibly legal epistemologies, and their significance for the understanding of our current reality, including the reality of international law.

1.3.1 *Neoliberal Epistemology*

As is well known, neoliberalism emerged in the 1930s as the attempt on the part of what was then a 'fringe' of intellectuals (inter alia, scientists, economists, philosophers and politicians, for the most part European and American) to oppose the rise of socialism and its economic planning ambitions by elaborating a 'new' version of liberalism (the prefix 'neo' was indeed meant to signal a departure from rather than a return to classical nineteenth-century

74 Cahill et al., 'Introduction: Approaches to Neoliberalism', p. xxxi; see also Focarelli, 'International Human Rights "in Crisis"', 78.

75 I see this effort as dual: a first (critical and self-critical) step requires that we bring back to the surface of conscious thought the currently embedded features of neoliberalism, and (try to) become aware of our own modes of (neoliberal) thinking; a second, concurrent (practical) step requires, instead, that we devise/construct and *experience*, in the very practical sense of personal actions and lived life, an alternative 'reality' to the neoliberal one, from which only, I believe, a different way of thinking can emerge.

laissez-faire liberalism).[76] The Great Depression, the rise of totalitarianism and authoritarianism in Europe and the two World Wars had fostered a broad debate over the causes of Europe's 'civilisational breakdown', and an argument increasingly adhered to at the time was that unrestrained capitalism was at the roots of Europe's collapse. The inter- and post-war years, thus, saw the increasing affirmation of alternative welfarist (socialist), statist (Marxist/communist) and Keynesian approaches to political economy, all advocating (although from different perspectives and with different political objectives) for a more active role of the state in economic decision-making. The attack on socialism and the reform of liberalism pursued by early neoliberals (as well as some of neoliberalism's current manifestations, see Section 1.3.2) centred, indeed, around (the contested – from neoliberals' point of view – ability to and, consequently) the role of centralised social institutions, in primis the state, in shaping the social (including economic) order in the best possible way.[77]

A relatively understated aspect of this ideological fight, which has only more recently been brought to the surface by a growing literature on the intellectual history of neoliberalism, is that it was especially couched in methodological, namely epistemological terms. For early neoliberals, in fact, both socialists' and (late-nineteenth and early-twentieth century) liberals' aspiration towards the application (in different directions) of the 'scientific method' to politics (originating, inter alia, in then recent scientific developments) represented 'a methodological delusion built on a misunderstanding of the nature of knowledge and of scientific work, as well as on a hubristic conception of their potential'.[78] Writing in the early 1940s, Fredrick von Hayek (notoriously considered one of the key intellectual figures of neoliberalism) vehemently condemned what he called 'scientism', or the 'slavish imitation' by the social sciences 'of the method and language of Science' (the latter capitalised by Hayek to signal a narrower conception of science, inter alia 'confined to the physical and biological disciplines which [during the first half of the nineteenth century, according to Hayek] began to claim for themselves a special rigorousness and certainty which distinguished them from all others').[79]

[76] The term 'neoliberalism' was first coined by Alexander Rüstow in 1938 during the famous Walter Lippman Colloquium, see i.a. Mirowksi and Plehwe, *The Road from Mont Pèlerin*, p. 12.

[77] *Ibid.*, 10.

[78] Beddeleem, 'Fighting for the Mantle of Science', iii.

[79] Friedrich A. Hayek, 'Scientism and the Study of Society' in Bruce Caldwell (ed.), *The Collected Works of F.A. Hayek: Studies on the Abuse and Decline of Reason: Text and Documents*, vol. 13 (University of Chicago Press, 2010), p. 80.

Scientism was, in Hayek's (and other early neoliberals') opinion,[80] 'hubristic', for it overplayed the potential reach of human rationality, an arrogance to which Hayek meant to oppose, inter alia, the 'humility' of his 'methodological individualism' (see later). As it has been noted, 'the quarrel which neoliberals engaged with their progressive counterparts was [...] centred around methodology'.[81] It essentially was a quarrel over 'who, exactly, was in the best position to gain valid understanding of the "social-totality"', whether 'science, intellectuals, faith, or the proletariat',[82] and thus was in the best position, as well, to act politically upon this knowledge. As eloquently put by Martin Beddeleem, neoliberalism 'made the pursuit of knowledge and truth a political question, and gave the question of social order an epistemological answer: *what we could do depended on what we could know*'.[83] In this sense, Friedrich von Hayek's 'problem of knowledge', or Michael Polany's concept of 'tacit knowledge', among others, emerged between the 1920s and 1940s as 'politically-motivated intellectual devices',[84] to fit, according to some authors, neoliberals' 'overall heuristic of hostility to socialism'.[85]

Of course, it is not possible to retrace and discuss here the substantial epistemological debate that took part among neoliberal intellectuals in the first half of the twentieth century (this has been much more authoritatively done in the literature referred to earlier). Hence, the remainder of this section will outline what I take to be its core elements and their main implications for conceptions of the social and legal orders:

(1) At the beginning of the twentieth century knowledge emerges as unit of analysis (and parameter of legitimacy) of political action.[86] Neoliberalism in particular is concerned with objective knowledge about how to best order in primis (but not exclusively) economic relations, through the political authority of the state.

80 See, generally, Beddeleem, 'Fighting for the Mantle of Science'.

81 *Ibid.*, 8.

82 Richard Hull, 'The Great Lie: Markets, Freedom and Knowledge' in Plehwe, Walpen and Neunhöffer, *Neoliberal Hegemony*, p. 146.

83 Beddeleem, 'Fighting for the Mantle of Science', 5 (emphasis in the original).

84 Hull, 'The Great Lie', p. 141; Philip Mirowski, 'Naturalizing the Market on the Road to Revisionism: Bruce Caldwell's *Hayek's Challenge* and the Challenge of Hayek interpretation' (2007) 3 *Journal of Institutional Economics* 3, 351–317 at 359 noted how 'already in the 1920s, Hayek was pursuing a research program which bore as its major implication the essential inability of governments to successfully plan and control economies; in other words, the overarching heuristic of Hayek's quest was already situated firmly in place'.

85 Mirowski, 'Naturalizing the Market', p. 360.

86 Richard Hull, 'ICTs, the Knowledge Economy, and Neo-liberalism' (2001) 8 *BRIDGES: An Interdisciplinary Journal of Theology, Philosophy, History & Science* 3/4, 1 and 3.

(2) Neoliberal epistemology starts from the assumption that individual subjective knowledge is limited and idiosyncratic, not capable of understanding social processes as a whole. Hayek, for instance, famously observed that

> the concrete knowledge which guides the action of any group of people never exists in a consistent and coherent body. It only exists in the dispersed, incomplete, and inconsistent form in which it appears in many individual minds, and the dispersion and imperfection of all knowledge are two of the basic facts from which the social sciences have to start.[87]

Because no individual can know (and thus act upon) what would be best for the ordering of economic, and more generally social relations, no individual or 'centralised' entity, no matter how benevolent, should take decisions on such ordering (this epistemological vision has, in other words, a normative dimension with political and social consequences).[88] From this idea derives not only the inevitable erroneousness but actually the impossibility of social (for early neoliberals, socialist/communist) planning.

(3) According to this premise, the only possible objective knowledge of the social order that humans can attain derives from the *aggregation* of the subjective knowledge displayed by individual attitudes. In Hayek's vision, the social scientist must follow a 'compositive' (or 'synthetic') method to 'build up' or 'reconstruct' social 'wholes', by 'systematically fitting together' such attitudes (significantly for the implications for human agency that will be mentioned below, not people's theorising about them).[89] Such procedure, according to Hayek, 'often leads to the discovery of principles of structural coherence of the complex phenomena which had not been (and perhaps could not be) established by direct observation'.[90]

(4) It is in this sense that the market is reframed by neoliberalism into an 'epistemic method' and, arguably, the only valid one: it becomes a 'machine-like information processor', where truth emerges through something resembling evolution.[91]

The social order that is allegedly revealed by this method is a spontaneous one – the 'result of individual action but without being designed by any

87 Hayek, 'Scientism and the Study of Society', p. 93. This vision derives from Hayek's philosophy of mind; see in particular his *The Sensory Order: An Inquiry into the Foundations of Theoretical Psychology* (London: Routledge, 1952).

88 See also Mirowksi and Plehwe, *The Road from Mont Pèlerin*, p. 423.

89 Hayek, 'Scientism and the Study of Society', pp. 100 and 102–103.

90 *Ibid.*, 101.

91 Mirowksi and Plehwe, *The Road from Mont Pèlerin*, p. 423.

individual'[92] – and one to which the individual (given the epistemic impossibility of any alternatives) must 'necessarily submit'.[93]

It must be noted that, nowadays, the Internet, social media and artificial intelligence seem to provide the ultimate technology to implement this cumulative epistemic method and to automate the discovery of 'social wholes'.[94] Not only do they embed (and thus actualize, whenever applied, the effects of such) neoliberal epistemological approach, but in a sense the (hegemony of the) latter is also a precondition for the faith (and possible hype around) their possibilities, especially in the realm of the social sciences and the law.

Finally, being treated as external, in a sense 'extraneous', to its partakers, this social order is portrayed as 'a-moral', that is, morally undetermined, and thus supposedly free of any connotations of justice.[95]

However, while this vision apparently removes the possibility of knowledge from the rational planner, placing it outside the human individual and into the market as information processor, it actually consigns knowledge to the market's *interpreter* (in Hayek's case, the social scientist), who is the one that must arrange the data, according to Hayek, 'in such an orderly fashion' to 'build up the structure of possible relationships between individuals'.[96] Such interpreter, however, is no less human, nor less individual than any other person, so that ultimately the social order that s/he purports to discover is no less socially constructed.[97] Moreover, this order inevitably has moral connotations, not only because it reflects the morality that is inevitably embedded in the process of data selection and aggregation operated by the interpreter but also because it ultimately is – if not in its design, certainly in its implementation – an order of *human* social relations: from the standpoint of its subjects, who are intrinsically moral beings, it inevitably always retains moral significance.

92 Hayek used the famous metaphor of 'the way in which footpaths are formed in a wild broken country': '[a]t first everyone will seek for himself what seems to him the best path. But the fact that such a path has been used once is likely to make it easier to traverse and therefore more likely to be used again; and thus gradually more and more clearly defined tracks arise and come to be used to the exclusion of other possible ways. Human movements through the region come to conform to a definite pattern which, although the result of deliberate decisions of many people, has yet not been consciously designed by anyone,' Hayek, 'Scientism and the Study of Society', p. 104.

93 See i.a. Friedrich A. Hayek, *Individualism and Economic Order* (University of Chicago Press, 1948), p. 24.

94 See also Philip Mirowski, *Machine Dreams: Economics Becomes a Cyborg Science* (Cambridge University Press, 2002).

95 See also Foucault, *The Birth of Biopolitics*.

96 Hayek, 'Scientism and the Study of Society', p. 103.

97 See also Mirowksi and Plehwe, *The Road from Mont Pèlerin*, p. 434.

When applied as part of a normative political philosophy to the ordering of social relations, this epistemological orientation implies a form of *governmental* and *legal naturalism* (with possible deterministic consequences): politics and the law must conform to the spontaneous order revealed by the cumulative method of the market, rather than be guided by consciously (and democratically) agreed-upon principles such as equality, justice or the protection of the human person. This neoliberal approach has been epitomised, for instance, by the 'There Is No Alternative' slogan of Margaret Thatcher, but it keeps running underneath many current political debates and, as will be argued in the next chapters, it has been possibly reflexively incorporated – or at least not duly challenged – in the assessment of responses to the Global Financial and Eurozone debt crises, including by some human rights monitoring bodies.

Most importantly, as is being increasingly noted, such 'neoliberal treatment of market as a super information processor, renders human cognition and preferences' – and, as a consequence, human responsibility – 'irrelevant'.[98] While not being necessarily grounded on a denial or limited conception of human agency per se (but rather on the limitations of the human 'mind'),[99] neoliberal epistemology eventually effects, at least to a certain extent, the bypassing of such agency in the construction of the social order, with inevitable dehumanising and undemocratic implications. This approach is clearly antithetical to philosophical outlooks, such as those that have historically grounded human rights and their legal regimes, rather centred on (and aimed at protecting) the dignity, moral equality and agency of all human beings. It is in this sense and because of this underlying epistemological approach that, in my opinion, neoliberalism is ultimately to be considered as an anti-humanist and anti-human rights philosophy.

1.3.2 *Law's Neoliberalisation*

As understood in this book, therefore, neoliberalism does not identify exclusively with specific economic policies but, as mentioned, with a broader belief system – actualised also by means of the law and the political authority of the state – that promotes the aligning of social order to the 'order of the market' (to be understood, first and foremost, as the epistemic method described above), while opposing other, non-market-like (essentially political) modes of social organisation.

[98] Philip Mirowski, 'Markets as Computer Programs in a Theory of Markets', Lecture, 12 December 2017, www.hkw.de/en/app/mediathek/video/62324.

[99] See e.g. Hayek, *The Sensory Order*.

The state and the law are essential to the realisation of this 'market social order', and therefore their role needs to be briefly elucidated.

Contrary to the neoliberal rhetoric on state retrenchment, neoliberalism requires, as is now well acknowledged, a strong state 'as both producer and guarantor of a stable market society'.[100] What neoliberalism actually advances, thus, is a claim for a particular kind of state,[101] leading to a redefinition of the latter (see later), not to its restraint nor, even less, annihilation.[102]

The law, on its part, is not just an institutional vehicle to implement neoliberalism but, as has been observed, the legal form itself, namely the liberal-capitalist legal form – where the law embodies 'a system of generalised rules that are interpreted through reason and applied equally to all, following rational procedural formalities in a manner [supposedly] void of political concerns and outcomes'[103] – is considered to be constitutive of neoliberalism, and particularly suitable to the neoliberal search for a 'technology of government'.[104] Elements of this 'liberal legality' – precisely, its alleged neutrality, equality and rationality – are considered to play an essential role in the construction of the neoliberal order:

> Laws appear to be universal and fixed, independent of historical conjuncture and political will, and legal decisions appear to be technical matters of the interpretation of universal and fixed legal texts in a very formalist sense. In this view, law is a principal means of mediating social relations and shaping subjectivity under capitalism, and, through this process, law configures social relations in its image: the abstraction of laws from the specific social contexts in which they arise obscures their indeterminacy, their historical contingency, and the power relations underpinning them.[105]

In other words, the asserted neutrality, formal equality and rationality of liberal legality are deemed to be particularly well suited to support the

100 Mirowksi and Plehwe, *The Road from Mont Pèlerin*, p. 435.

101 *Ibid.*

102 See i.a. Quinn Slobodian, *Globalists: The End of Empire and the Birth of Neoliberalism* (Cambridge, MA: Harvard University Press, 2018); Raymond Plant, *The Neo-Liberal State* (Oxford University Press, 2010).

103 Honor Brabazon (ed.), *Neoliberal Legality: Understanding the Role of Law in the Neoliberal Project* (London: Routledge, 2017).

104 Foucault, *The Birth of Biopolitics*, p. 321: '[r]egulation has not been sought [by (neo)liberalism] in the "law" because of the supposedly natural legalism of [neo]liberalism, but because the law defines forms of general intervention excluding particular, individual, and exceptional measures [...]'; see also David Trubek and A. Santos, 'Introduction: The Third Moment in Law and Development Theory and the Emergence of a New Critical Practice' in David Trubek and Alvaro Santos (eds.), *The New Law and Economic Development: A Critical Appraisal* (Cambridge University Press, 2006) 1–18.

105 *Ibid.*

realisation of neoliberalism's envisioned *nomocracy*, that is, a rule-governed order not devoted, in principle, to the attainment of any particular collective end[106] – an aspiration linked to neoliberalism's above-mentioned fundamental distrust in the possibility of enacting a collective vision of the 'good society', and thus in democratic governance (a characteristic with inevitable authoritarian implications).[107]

In a nomocracy, the state maintains the sovereign authority to make and promulgate the law, but 'not as it pleases'.[108] If society is a 'factory', to use another metaphor by Hayek, the state is not the factory's managers, who produce goods or services, but rather its maintenance workers, merely entrusted with overseeing and, where necessary, improving the mechanisms (i.e. the market) regulating the factory's production.[109] Neoliberalism seizes on the political authority of the state, but the 'neoliberal state' is reduced to a technocratic administrative entity,[110] as new formats of techno-managerial governance are favoured[111] (whence the preference for supranational institutions and bodies such as the IMF, the World Bank or the Eurogroup, or for technical governments, such as those in charge in some European countries in the aftermath of the Global Financial Crisis, e.g. the 2011–2013 Monti government in Italy) and the state is increasingly controlled through 'numerous audit devices (under the sign of "accountability")'.[112] More generally, neoliberalism seeks to put regulatory institutions beyond the reach of politics, 'developing a politics of anti-politics'.[113]

Therefore, nomocracy entails the transformation of law from a means to achieve a substantive purpose, to a means to enforce a method, notably, in this case, the market. The rule of law is, also, frequently conflated with or

106 Plant, *The Neo-Liberal State*, p. 6.

107 Mirowksi and Plehwe, *The Road from Mont Pèlerin*, pp. 440–446, emphasising how the political solution proposed by some of the founding figures of the neoliberal thought collective, including Hayek himself, de facto resembled Carl Schmitt's 'total state' and his arguments in support of the necessity to repress democracy; Harvey, *A Brief History of Neoliberalism*, pp. 66 and 69–70; Blalock, 'Neoliberalism and the Crisis of Legal Theory'.

108 Blalock, 'Neoliberalism and the Crisis of Legal Theory', p. 86.

109 *Ibid.*, pp. 86–87; Friedrich A. Hayek, *Law, Legislation and Liberty*, vol. 1 (University of Chicago Press, 1973), pp. 47–48.

110 Harvey, *A Brief History of Neoliberalism*, pp. 64–86; Plant, *The Neo-Liberal State*.

111 *Ibid.*

112 Mirowksi and Plehwe, *The Road from Mont Pèlerin*, p. 436. In this sense, see also the discussion, in the next chapter, of the post-crisis reform of the legal framework for economic policy in the EMU.

113 Kanishka Jayasuriya, 'Globalization, Sovereignty, and the Rule of Law: From Political to Economic Constitutionalism?' (2001) 8 *Constellations* 4, 442–460, quoted in Blalock, 'Neoliberalism and the Crisis of Legal Theory', p. 87.

subordinated to conformity with 'market-making'.[114] Neoliberal legality is, thus, characterised, among other things, by its (purported) neutrality in respect of social aims, the prominence devoted to formal equality over substantive inequalities, and a more generally active role of the law, or the increased juridification of social relations, together with a preferential channelling of social and political conflicts towards judicial solutions.[115]

Hence, the neoliberalisation of law, including international law, is manifested not only in (1) the neoliberal content of specific legal rules or decisions (e.g. prescribing neoliberal economic policies or prioritising imperatives that are functional to the proper working of capitalist markets, e.g. financial stability or solvency, over other social claims); (2) the importation and prominence given in legal reasoning to criteria or arguments borrowed from economic theory (such as efficiency or cost–benefit analyses); or (3) the neoliberal reinterpretation of concepts such as personal liberty,[116] dignity, equality, public interest, the rule of law[117] or even human rights. It is also, more generally, manifested in (4) the use of law as a device to implement the 'market as a method' to organise society (also by restructuring and controlling the reach of the state) and to shield such method from other non-market modes of governance, as some of the legal developments discussed in the next chapters may reveal.

[114] Mirowksi and Plehwe, *The Road from Mont Pèlerin*, p. 437; David Singh Grewal and Jedediah Purdy, 'Introduction: Law and Neoliberalism' (2014) 77 *Law and Contemporary Problems* 4, 1–23 at 17–18; Claire Kilpatrick, 'On the Rule of Law and Economic Emergency: The Degradation of Basic Legal Values in Europe's Bailouts' (2015) 35 *Oxford Journal of Legal Studies* 2, 325–353.

[115] Brabazon, *Neoliberal Legality*; Harvey, A *Brief History of Neoliberalism*, p. 66.

[116] With regard to the market-modelled (re)interpretation of legally- relevant concepts, Grewal and Purdy, for instance, have noted how neoliberalism has reshaped the idea of 'personal liberty' under US constitutional law, as a notion centred 'on individual choice in spending, consumption, and self-expression', so that 'the pursuit of individual preferences through spending decisions (including the economic "preferences" of corporate "persons") is *sufficient* as an account of personal liberty *and of the structural relation of that liberty to a scheme of good-enough government*', Grewal and Purdy, 'Introduction: Law and Neoliberalism', 15 and 17 (emphasis in the original). They have further noted the habit cultivated in legal reasoning by decisions based on neoliberal pledges of '*ignoring structure* [. . .] in favour of exclusive concern with the liberty of the choosing individual or corporation', *ibid.*, 15 (emphasis added).

[117] Another example of the evolution of legal concepts associated with neoliberalism is provided by Margot Salomon in relation to the concept of 'expropriation' under international economic law: 'while in the 1970s and 1980s disputes on direct expropriation mainly related to the nationalisation of foreign property, today the central concern is that concepts such as indirect expropriation may be applied to bona fide regulatory measures taken by the host government aimed at protecting the environment, health and other welfare interests in society, giving rise to claims for compensation', M. Salomon, 'Winners and Others: Accounting for International Law's Favourites' in Conor Gearty and Costas Douzinas (eds.), *The Cambridge Companion to Human Rights Law* (Cambridge University Press, 2012), pp. 275–276.

2

Sovereign Debt and Neoliberalism

2.1 INTRODUCTION

In the last couple of decades, several human rights organisations, scholars and monitoring bodies have increasingly come to recognise the relevance of sovereign financing for the realisation of all human rights, and directed their efforts to instruct and assess the process, contents and outcomes of public budgets (including debt-related aspects) and, more generally, of economic policymaking, in terms of states' substantive human rights obligations (see Chapter 3). This (often pragmatical) approach has not only significantly shifted the focus on states' need to raise and allocate (public) resources to *fulfil* rights – when, contrary to this now-conventional assumption, what at times is actually needed (and morally warranted, considering the 'accumulation by dispossession' tendency of the current global economic system)[1] is *protection* of people's economic means and capacity to be self-supporting from the conduct of the individuals and institutions able to undermine them,[2] inter alia *through a different legal ordering of economic*

[1] John Linarelli, Margot E. Salomon and Muthucumaraswamy Sornarajah, *The Misery of International Law: Confrontations with Injustice in the Global Economy* (Oxford University Press, 2018); Harvey, *A Brief History of Neoliberalism*, p. 159. On recent inequality trends, see also Thomas Piketty, *Capital in the Twenty-First Century* (Cambridge, MA: The Belknap Press of Harvard University Press, 2014).

[2] This idea is Henry Shue's. In his seminal 1996 work, Shue provides two examples of what he defines as, respectively, accidental or essential deprivation (i.e. deprivation that respectively is not, or instead is inherent to a particular economic decision or strategy): (1) a business contract between the villagers of a hypothetical peasant village in a developing country and a businessman from the capital, causing widespread malnutrition in the village because of the required shift in land use from the growing of black beans – the major source of protein in the region – to flowers for export; (2) the adoption, i.a., by several Latin American countries, of the political-economic model of so-called illiberal state capitalism (Shue quotes Richard R. Fagen, 'The Carter Administration and Latin America: Business as Usual?' (1978) 57 *Foreign Affairs* 3), causing growing inequality, poverty and political repression. In both cases,

relations.[3] It also tends to overlook fundamental questions about the nature and transformation of contemporary sovereign financing. These questions, which on the contrary this chapter attempts to bring to the fore, raise significant doubts as to whether, in its currently prevailing forms, sovereign financing (and the type of state reflected and affected by it) can be realistically expected to serve the realisation of (what kind of) human rights. What are the prospects and, at this point, the actual connotation and emancipatory potential of, as will be said, increasingly debt-financed human, especially socio-economic rights, in a world of escalating indebtedness, inequality and insecurity? Can we be content with efforts at directing the use of increasingly impoverished public resources towards the full realisation of state human rights obligations, or shall we rather turn our attention to more forcefully addressing the shortcomings of the current economic order and the resulting economic and social injustice?[4]

After briefly outlining a general definition of sovereign debt (Section 2.2), this chapter will present recent global debt trends and their characteristics, and reflect on the possible causes (Section 2.3) and social implications (Section 2.3.1.) of increased debt financing. The chapter will, thus, introduce and reflect upon the post-crisis developments in the legal regime for economic and fiscal policymaking of the European Economic and Monetary Union and its suggested further neoliberalisation (Section 2.4).

as stressed by Shue, 'the honouring of subsistence rights [on which his analysis is focused] may [...] in no way involve transferring commodities to people, but may instead involve preventing people's being deprived of the commodities or the means to grow, make, or buy the commodities', Shue, *Basic Rights*, p. 51. A similar argument could be made, among other issues, with regard to the increasingly widespread, state-enacted, lowering of labour protection standards (see e.g. HRC, Report of the Independent Expert on the effects of foreign debt and other related international financial obligations of states on the full enjoyment of all human rights, particularly economic, social and cultural rights (27 December 2016) A/HRC/34/57) and the expansion of the so-called gig economy, in a capitalist context, characterised for most people (at least in advanced economies) by labour- and wage-dependency.

3 Such different legal ordering, of course, would nonetheless require, first of all, a collective convergence towards a different (normative) understanding of economic relations.

4 On this point, see also 'End-of-mission statement by Mr. Juan Pablo Bohoslavsky, United Nations Independent Expert on the effects of foreign debt and other related international financial obligations of states on the full enjoyment of all human rights, particularly economic, social and cultural rights. Mission to Iceland, 8–15 December 2014' (15 December 2014), where the Independent Expert noted that although '[l]egitimate financial systems require appropriate regulations and institutions aimed at ensuring that they serve the real economy [...] it is also necessary to reflect on the moral driving forces of the colossal over-borrowing that led an entire country [in this case, Iceland] into the crash. *To what extent, and under what circumstances, debt-based-growth strategies are necessary and consistent with the full realization of human rights and happiness?*' (emphasis added).

2.2 SOVEREIGN DEBT: A GENERAL DEFINITION

In a colloquial, non-legal connotation of the term (at least in the modern Western understanding of the concept) a debt is 'any form of obligation, particularly a moral obligation by a person to reciprocate a benefit received from another person in the past'[5] (on this element of reciprocity, see Section 2.3.1). In the broadest legal sense of the term, *debt* is a 'liability on a claim'.[6] Although the notion is more commonly associated with a financial liability or obligation (debt being generally intended as a 'duty [...] to pay money'),[7] as a legal relationship debt may involve different objects, and hence possibly consist also of 'a non-monetary thing that one person owes to another'.[8] *Sovereign debt*, in particular, in its contemporary acceptation, is debt owed by the state (and its sub-entities), that is, today, a transpersonal,[9] sovereign, territorial and exclusive system of rule.[10]

Being shaped around specific normative aspirations and aimed at delimiting the object and circumstances of the *vinculum juris*, existing legal definitions of sovereign debt (also described, depending on the context, as state, public, national or government debt) do not describe the concept in its abstract totality, but only as it is made legally relevant for regulation. Therefore, they only record partial (and, in some cases, surpassed) conceptions of the phenomenon, notably

5 'Debt' in Stephen Michael Sheppard (ed.), *The Wolters Kluwer Bouvier Law Dictionary*, vol. 1 (Alphen aan den Rijn: Wolters Kluwer, 2012), p. 758.

6 'Debt' in *Black's Law Dictionary*, 10th ed. (Toronto: Thomson Reuters, 2014), p. 488. At this abstract level of description, debt represents 'a fundamental element of [any] legal interrelationship', as the term pins down 'the (legal) burden or duty to do or to omit something' that lies on the 'debtor', that is, 'the obligated side of the legal relationship which, on the opposite side, has a party with the entitlement to claim something', Christoph G. Paulus, 'Debts', in Rüdiger Wolfrum (ed.), *The Max Planck Encyclopedia of Public International Law*, vol. 2 (Oxford University Press, 2012), p. 1082.

7 'Debt' in *The Wolters Kluwer Bouvier Law Dictionary*, p. 758.

8 'Debt' in *Black's Law Dictionary*, p. 488.

9 The transpersonal character of the sovereign is considered to be one of the characteristics (and prerequisite for the emergence) of modern public debt and sovereign debt markets since the fourteenth century, see i.a. Mauricio Drelichman and Hans-Joachim Voth, *Lending to the Borrower from Hell: Debt, Taxes, and Default in the Age of Philip II* (Princeton University Press, 2014), p. 25 ff.; Jean-Claude Hocquet, 'City-State and Market Economy' in Richard Bonney (ed.), *Economic Systems and State Finance* (Oxford University Press, 1995), pp. 81–100; Luciano Pezzolo, 'Bonds and Government Debt in Italian City-States, 1250–1650' in William N. Goetzmann and K. Geert Rouwenhorst (eds.), *The Origins of Value: The Financial Innovations that Created Modern Capital Markets* (Oxford University Press, 2005) 145–164.

10 See e.g. Carlo Focarelli, *International Law as Social Construct* (Oxford University Press, 2012), p. 154 ff. For a discussion of the 'sovereign' element of the concept, see Odette Lienau, 'Who Is the "Sovereign" in Sovereign Debt?: Reinterpreting a Rule-of-Law Framework from the Early Twentieth Century' (2008) 33 *The Yale Journal of International Law* 63–111.

those which have attracted regulatory concerns at specific times, prompting the lawmaking process.

EU law contains a broad definition of *government debt*, shaped around the primary preoccupation with operationalising the constraints on budget deficit and public debt provided by the Stability and Growth Pact (SGP) and the Excessive Deficit Procedure (EDP) for the Economic and Monetary Union (EMU).[11] Under Protocol No. 12 on the EDP annexed to the Treaty on the Functioning of the European Union (TFEU), government debt (also called 'EDP' or 'Maastricht debt') corresponds to the sum of the existing general government liabilities under the categories of currency and deposits, debt securities and loans.[12]

In international law, the only instruments that include a definition of sovereign debt are the 1983 Vienna Convention on Succession of States in respect of State Property, Archives and Debts[13] (not yet in force), and the above-mentioned 2012 Guiding Principles on Foreign Debt and Human Rights (as discussed later in the text, a soft law instrument).[14]

11 On which see further Section 2.4.

12 Article 2, Protocol (No. 12) on the Excessive Deficit Procedure in Consolidated version of the Treaty on the Functioning of the European Union [2012] OJ C 326/47, as supplemented by Council Regulation (EC) No. 479/2009 of 25 May 2009 on the application of the Protocol on the excessive deficit procedure annexed to the Treaty establishing the European Community [2009] OJ L 145/1 and by Commission Regulation (EU) No. 220/2014 of 7 March 2014 amending Council Regulation (EC) No. 479/2009 as regards references to the European system of national and regional accounts in the European Union [2014] OJ L 69/101. According to the revised European system of national and regional accounts in the European Union (referred to as ESA 2010, enforceable since 1 September 2014 by Regulation (EU) No. 549/2013), the 'general government' sector consists of all 'institutional units which are non-market producers whose output is intended for individual and collective consumption, and are financed by compulsory payments made by units belonging to other sectors, and institutional units principally engaged in the redistribution of national income and wealth' (ESA 2010, 2.111). It includes, thus, central, state and local governments, and social security funds. The qualification of institutional units as 'non-market producers', that is, 'providing all or most of their output (goods and services) free of charge or at prices that are not "economically significant"' (ESA 2010, 20.19) excludes from the definition all government-controlled units that are considered market produces, that is, 'public corporations' (but includes public corporations and quasi-corporations controlled by government, if their output is mainly non-market). See also Eurostat, *Manual on Government Deficit and Debt: Implementation of ESA 2010* (Luxembourg: European Union, 2016), p. 11 ff.

13 Vienna Convention on Succession of States in respect of State Property, Archives and Debts (8 April 1983).

14 Human Rights Council, Report of the Independent Expert on the effects of foreign debt and other related international financial obligations of states on the full enjoyment of all human rights, particularly economic, social and cultural rights, Cephas Lumina: Guiding Principles on foreign debt and human rights (10 April 2011) A/HRC/20/23 (hereinafter, UN Guiding Principles on foreign debt and human rights), on which, see further Chapter 4.

The 1983 Vienna Convention defines *state debt* as 'any financial obligation of a predecessor State arising in conformity with international law towards another State, an international organization or any other subject of international law'.[15] However, as has been noted, this characterisation of sovereign debt, purposely developed in the context of the law of state succession, is inadequate for two reasons:

> [f]irst, being based on the restriction to 'another State, an international organization or any other subject of international law', it appears to exclude all debt owed to private creditors – [currently, as will be expounded in Section 2.3] the most important type of debt in volume terms. [. . .] Second, even if private creditors were 'other subjects of international law' the qualification 'in conformity with international law' is of doubtful practical value [. . .] [because] [w]ith few exceptions, today's sovereign debt instruments are governed by municipal law.[16]

On the contrary, the relevance of private creditors and the more likely domestic legal dimension of contemporary sovereign debt have been captured by the definition of *foreign debt* provided by the 2012 Guiding Principles on foreign debt and human rights:

> external (or foreign debt) refers to an obligation (including monetary obligation) created under a contractual agreement and owed by a State to a non-resident lender which may either be an international financial institution, a bilateral or multilateral lender, a private financial institution or a bondholder, or is subject to foreign law. It includes: (i) loans, that is, advances of funds to the debtor by the lender on the basis of an undertaking that the borrower will repay the funds at some future point (including deposits, bonds, debentures, commercial loans and buyer's credits); and (ii) suppliers' credits, that is, contracts whereby the supplier allows the customer to defer payment until sometime after the date on which the goods are delivered or the services are provided. The aggregate of a State's outstanding external debts is referred to as its external debt stock.[17]

This definition echoes the distinction between domestic (or internal) and foreign (or external) debt that was originally deemed relevant to circumscribe the mandate on the topic of the UN Human Rights Council (and the Commission on Human Rights before it) and the Independent Expert on Foreign Debt and Human Rights,[18] only to public debt having a foreign, that

[15] Vienna Convention on Succession of States, Article 33.
[16] Waibel, *Sovereign Defaults before International Courts and Tribunals*, p. 12.
[17] UN Guiding Principles on foreign debt and human rights, 11, para. 4.
[18] See Chapter 3.

is, 'international', rather than purely domestic dimension. Debt can be domestic or foreign according to different criteria, for example, the law governing the debt contract, the currency in which the debt is issued or the nationality of creditors,[19] and foreign debt is usually described as debt 'expressed in some foreign currency, typically payable abroad, governed by some external law and subject to the jurisdiction of external courts'.[20] The relevance of each criterion actually depends on the context: for legal purposes, the law governing the contractual relationship is certainly paramount. Nonetheless, in practice, the boundaries between domestic and foreign debt have progressively eroded,[21] so that today the distinction has lost much of its *raison d'être* and certainly is not relevant for a discussion of the relationship and implications of sovereign debt for human rights.

More generally, and for the purposes of this book, sovereign debt can be defined as *the sum of the existing (contractual and non-contractual) obligations (including, but not limited to, financial obligations) owed by a state (and by all entities for whose debts the state is ultimately responsible) to one or more creditor(s)*. The latter can include other states and public institutions (e.g. central banks), international financial institutions (e.g. the International Monetary Fund (IMF), the World Bank or the European Stability Mechanism), as well as private financial institutions and bondholders (e.g. commercial or investment banks, insurance companies, pension or hedge funds and retail investors). Sovereign debt includes, inter alia, trade debt (i.e. obligations arising from the purchase of supplies and services by the state or owed to banks through arrangements such as documentary letters of credit) and other (non-contractual) liabilities (e.g. deriving from arbitral awards).[22]

2.3 RECENT GLOBAL DEBT TRENDS AND THE NATURE OF CONTEMPORARY DEBT FINANCING

The historical (not necessarily linear) development of different modes of sovereign financing, including states' fiscal regimes, has progressed parallel

[19] Hans-Ernst Folz, 'State Debts' in Rudolf Bernhardt and Peter Macalister-Smith (eds.), *Encyclopaedia of Public International Law*, vol. 4 (Amsterdam: North-Holland, 2000), p. 608.

[20] Waibel, *Sovereign Defaults before International Courts and Tribunals*, p. 13.

[21] *Ibid.*

[22] International Law Association, The Hague Conference (2010), Sovereign Insolvency Study Group, 'State Insolvency: Options for the Way Forward' (August 2010), ila.vettoreweb.com/Storage/Download.aspx?DbStorageId=1451&StorageFileGuid=58bc4db7-4213-440c-93fe-978a0a2896cb, 9.

to transformations of the sovereign as a political organisation, its aims and consequent financial necessities and the nature and (later, also legal) ordering of international (economic and political) relations.[23] It would be beyond the scope of this book to retrace the entire modern history of sovereign financing,[24] but a consideration of global trends in sovereign borrowing, especially since the Second World War, is essential to locate relevant international law developments within the broader historical and sociopolitical context.

Since the 1970s, sovereign borrowing has become a routine/non-extraordinary, prevalently market-based state-financing practice (on currently prevailing types of debt instruments and their potential implications for sovereign financing, see further in the text), with a pronounced transnational dimension. In other words, states increasingly rely on debt, global financial markets and international institutions to fund their ordinary sovereign functions.[25]

While historically and up to the first half of the twentieth century, debt financing and episodes of large and rapid public debt accumulation were typically associated with extraordinary events and crises (especially wars and related military expenditure),[26] global public indebtedness, after declining during the decades following the Second World War, has more or less steadily

[23] See e.g. John Ruggie, 'International Regimes, Transactions and Change: Embedded Liberalism in the Postwar Economic Order' (1982) 36 *International Organization* 2, 379–399.

[24] Important works on this history include Richard Bonney (ed.), *Economic Systems and State Finance* (Oxford University Press, 1995) and *The Rise of the Fiscal State in Europe, c. 1200–1815* (Oxford University Press, 1999); Charles Tilly, *Coercion, Capital, and European States: AD 990–1992* (Oxford: Blackwell, 1990); Max Winkler, *Foreign Bonds: An Autopsy. A Study of Default and Repudiations of Government Obligations* (Philadelphia: Roland Swain Company, 1933); Mauricio Drelichman and Hans-Joachim Voth, *Lending to the Borrower from Hell: Debt, Taxes, and Default in the Age of Philip II* (Princeton University Press, 2014); William N. Goetzmann and K. Geert Rouwenhorst (eds.), *The Origins of Value: The Financial Innovations that Created Modern Capital Markets* (Oxford University Press, 2005); and Niall Ferguson, *The Cash Nexus: Money and Power in the Modern World, 1700–2000* (New York: Basic Books, 2001).

[25] See i.a. Andreas F. Lowenfeld, *International Economic Law*, 2nd ed. (Oxford University Press, 2008), p. 670, noting a shift in the 1970s – with syndicated lending especially to developing countries – 'to what in many instances became loans for balance of payment purposes'.

[26] Visibly large spikes in the average debt-to-GDP ratio of several advanced economies, for instance, occurred during the First World War (1914–1918), the Great Depression (1929–1934) and the Second World War (1939–1945), see S. M. Ali Abbas, Laura Blattner, Mark De Broeck, Asmaa El-Ganainy and Malin Hu, 'Sovereign Debt Composition in Advanced Economies: A Historical Perspective' (2014) *IMF Working Paper No. WP/14/162*. For other analyses of sovereign debt trends, see i.a. S. M. Ali Abbas, Nazim Belhocine, Asmaa El-Ganainy and Anke Weber, 'Current Debt Crisis in Historical Perspective' in Carlo Cottarelli, Philip Gerson and Abdelhak Senhadji (eds.), *Post-Crisis Fiscal Policy* (Cambridge, MA: MIT Press, 2014) 161–191; Carmen M. Reinhart, Vincent R. Reinhart and Kenneth Rogoff, 'Public Debt Overhangs: Advanced-Economy Episodes since 1800' (2012) 26 *Journal of Economic Perspectives* 69; Carmen M. Reinhart and Kenneth Rogoff, 'From Financial

increased between the early 1970s and the mid-2000s – a period referred to as the 'Great Accumulation' – despite the absence of a global crisis.[27] In those four decades, the public debt of advanced economies[28] more than doubled, from about 40 per cent of GDP to or above (depending on data sets and specific countries) 80 per cent of GDP.[29] Also, the general government debt of emerging market economies had a parallel trend until the late 1980s (when several debt crises restricted many developing countries' access to international financial markets) and, since the beginning of the 2000s, has returned to its long-term upwards trajectory.

These trends have been exacerbated by the Great Recession following the 2008 Global Financial Crisis – when public debt in advanced economies surpassed 100 per cent of GDP[30] – and, more dramatically, by the coronavirus

Crash to Debt Crisis American Economic Review' (2011) 101 *American Economic Review* 5, 1676–1706; International Monetary Fund, 'World Economic Outlook: Coping with High Debt and Sluggish Growth' (October 2012), Chapter 3: 'The Good, the Bad, and the Ugly: 100 Years of Dealing with Public Debt Overhangs'; and S. M. Ali Abbas, Nazim Belhocine, Asmaa El-Ganainy and Mark Horton, 'Historical Patterns and Dynamics of Public Debt – Evidence from a New Database' (2011) 59 *IMF Economic Review* 4, 717–742.

27 Abbas et al., 'Sovereign Debt Composition in Advanced Economies', 14.

28 Since the relatively few existing historical accounts of trends in sovereign debt levels and composition tend to focus on advanced economies (given the more limited availability of historical data for developing countries), figures in this section tend to refer mostly to the former. Nonetheless, the trend of steadily increasing sovereign indebtedness as well as the prevailing changes in debt composition described later are a global phenomenon. This section's general interpretation of the significance of such trends for sovereign financing and human rights, thus, applies globally. For an economic classification of countries, see further (n 34).

29 Abbas et al., 'Sovereign Debt Composition in Advanced Economies', 14; IMF, 'World Economic Outlook: Coping with High Debt', 101; and i.a. the OECD data reported in Wolfgang Streeck, 'The Politics of Public Debt: Neoliberalism, Capitalist Development and the Restructuring of the State' (2013) 15 *German Economic Review* 1, 145. As correctly pointed out by Streeck, the rise of public indebtedness in OECD countries halted in the mid-1990s for about a decade (in effect, a first period of fiscal consolidation) largely due to deep welfare reforms in many countries (in the case of some European countries, linked as well to the need to reach the fiscal targets required to join the Euro Area). These represented, according to Streeck, 'a time-lagged response to the rise in social spending', particularly on unemployment benefits and active labour market policies, that had characterised the 1980s as a result of the 1970s OECD-wide recession and particularly the Second Oil Crisis of 1979, *ibid.*, 149.

30 As noted by the IMF, global public and private debt stocks had reached '225 percent of GDP in 2019, 30 percentage points above the level prevailing before the global financial crisis', IMF, 'Fiscal Monitor: Policies for the Recovery' (October 2020), ix. On the exceptional rise in private debt in recent decades, its possible causes and human rights implications, see also UN Human Rights Council, 'Private debt and human rights' Report of the Independent Expert on the effects of foreign debt and other related international financial obligations of states on the full enjoyment of human rights, particularly economic, social and cultural rights, UN Doc. A/HRC/43/45 (3 January 2020).

disease (COVID-19) pandemic (at the time of writing, still ongoing), as in 2020 global debt reached wartime levels, for the first time again ever since.[31]

In fact, the social distancing measures imposed in 2020 by most governments across the world to contain and manage the pandemic have caused 'the worst recession since the Great Depression, [. . .] far worse than the Global Financial Crisis'[32] (when the world economy recorded what, in retrospect, seems a mere −0.1 per cent GDP growth). According to the latest IMF data, in 2020, global growth is projected at −4.4 per cent of GDP (−5.8 per cent in advanced economies (AEs), −3.3 per cent in emerging market and middle-income economies (EMMIEs) and −1.2 per cent in low-income developing countries (LIDCs))[33] and, despite an expected rebound in 2021, is forecast to remain, in AEs, 2 percentage points below the pre-virus baseline.[34] The massive fiscal support so far undertaken by states to mitigate the socio-economic consequences of the pandemic – as of September 2020, totalling almost 12 per cent of global GDP, a much larger amount than the one devoted to the global financial crisis[35] – has consisted of additional spending and forgone revenue – as noted by the IMF, 'directly affecting government budgets' – and of liquidity support – 'such as loans, equity injections, and guarantees to firms, including through state-owned banks and enterprises', which do not have a direct effect on government budgets, but 'could add to

[31] See i.a. UN General Assembly, 'Addressing, from a human rights perspective, the debt-related problems of developing countries caused by the coronavirus disease (COVID-19) pandemic'; IMF, 'World Economic Outlook, April 2020: The Great Lockdown' (April 2020); Scali, 'Sovereign Financing during the COVID-19 Pandemic'. Besides its economic and debt implications (relevant for this chapter's analysis), the pandemic is having very acute negative consequences on employment, poverty ('revers[ing] the progress made since the 1990s in reducing global poverty'), and imposing 'a major setback in plans to achieve the Sustainable Development Goals (SDGs) by 2030', see IMF, 'World Economic Outlook, October 2020: A Long and Difficult Ascent' (October 2020), xv; IMF, 'Fiscal Monitor: Policies for the Recovery', 20) and inequality, especially in poorer countries, see e.g. World Bank, 'Impacts of COVID-19 on Poverty', www.worldbank.org/en/topic/poverty/coronavirus.

[32] Gita Gopinath, 'The Great Lockdown: Worst Economic Downturn Since the Great Depression', IMFBlog, 14 April 2020, blogs.imf.org/2020/04/14/the-great-lockdown-worst-economic-downturn-since-the-great-depression/.

[33] IMF, 'World Economic Outlook, April 2020', 9. According to IMF's classification (see IMF, 'World Economic Outlook, October 2020', Statistical Appendix, 119–124), AEs (thirty-nine countries) include i.a. the Group of Seven (G7) – that is, the United States, Japan, Germany, France, Italy, the United Kingdom and Canada – and the members of the euro area. EMMIEs (156 countries) include i.a. China, India, Russia, central and eastern European countries, Brazil, Mexico, Saudi Arabia and South Africa. Finally, LIDCs (fifty-nine countries) are countries that do not qualify as AEs or EMMIEs.

[34] IMF, 'World Economic Outlook, October 2020', 8.

[35] IMF, 'Fiscal Monitor: Policies for the Recovery'.

government debt and deficits down the road if these public interventions incur losses'.[36]

These measures have been complemented by unprecedented quantitative easing measures put in place by some advanced economies' central banks, which, as noted by the IMF, have purchased corporate bonds (Bank of England, Bank of Israel, Bank of Japan, European Central Bank, US Federal Reserve) and commercial paper (Bank of Canada, Bank of England, Bank of Japan), and implemented quasi-fiscal activities such as participation in bank loans to corporations (US Federal Reserve), or the purchase of corporate bonds in the primary (Bank of Canada, US Federal Reserve) or secondary markets (Bank of Japan).[37]

Coupled with the sharp decline in economic output and government revenue, this fiscal effort is currently projected to push public deficits up by an average 9 per cent of GDP in 2020 (14.4 per cent in AEs and 10.7 per cent in EMMIEs), and has so far been financed mostly through new debt.[38] Global public debt is, consequently, expected to reach 100 per cent of GDP in 2020 (125.5 per cent in AEs, 62.2 per cent in EMMIEs and 48.8 per cent in LIDCs)[39] (see Figure 2.1), the highest level ever reached in history, and to stabilise there until 2025 (assuming that the strong rebound in economic activity currently projected for 2021 by IMF's calculations will eventually materialise).[40] In 2020, the general government debt of Italy, Japan and Spain – among the most indebted advanced economies – will rise by 30 percentage points of GDP relative to 2019.[41] In over half of LIDCs (54 per cent of which are currently in debt distress or at high risk of debt distress, up from 51 per cent at the end of 2019), debt service relative to tax revenues will exceed 20 per cent in 2020 and 2021.[42]

The current explosion in sovereign (and private)[43] debt worldwide poses enormous financial risks for the public sector of many countries, including their central banks, and for the Eurozone and the larger international

36 IMF, 'World Economic Outlook Update, June 2020: A Crisis Like No Other, An Uncertain Recovery' (June 2020), 16; 'Fiscal Monitor: Policies for the Recovery', 5.

37 IMF, 'Fiscal Monitor: Policies for the Recovery', 5.

38 *Ibid.*, 4.

39 The lower increase in LIDCs' debt level is largely due to their restricted access to international financial markets.

40 IMF, 'World Economic Outlook, October 2020', ix.

41 Reaching, respectively, 161.8 per cent, 266.2 per cent and 123 per cent of GDP, see IMF, 'Fiscal Monitor: Policies for the Recovery', 9.

42 *Ibid.*, 8 and 10.

43 See i.a. HRC, 'Private debt and human rights'; Susanne Soederberg, *Debtfare States and the Poverty Industry: Money, Discipline and the Surplus Population* (Abingdon: Routledge, 2014).

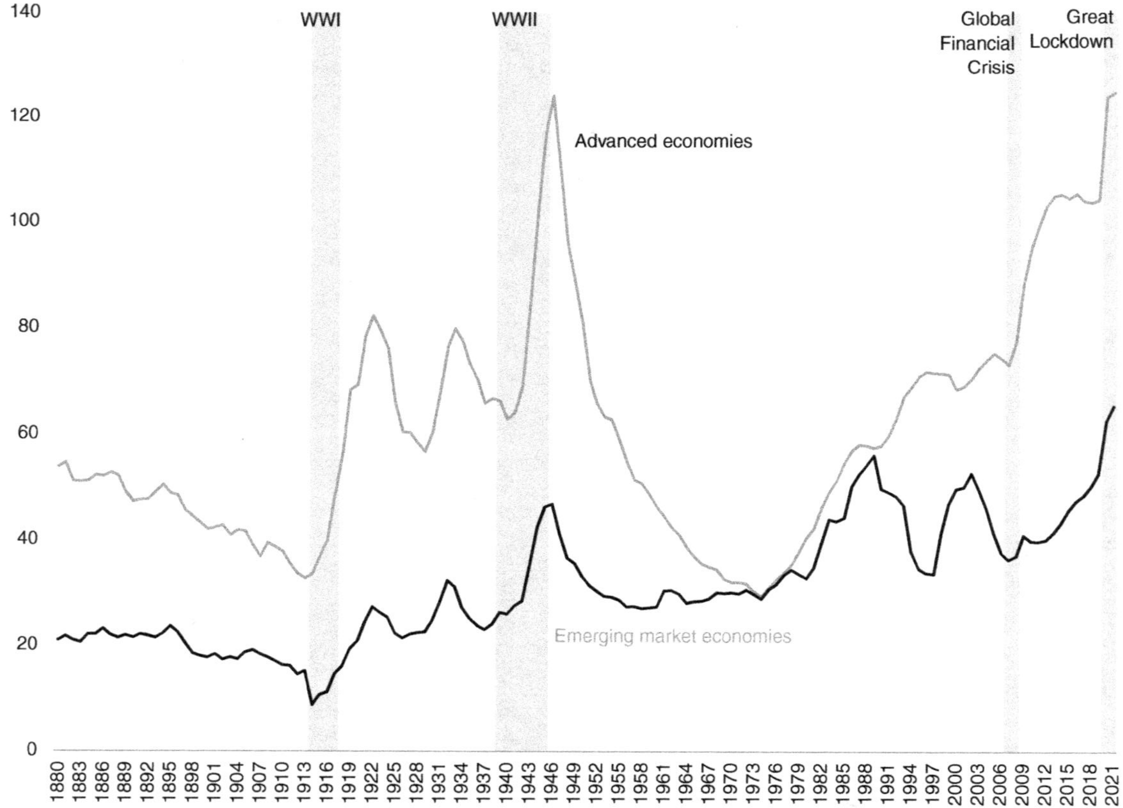

FIGURE 2.1 Historical patterns of general government debt (per cent of GDP)

Source: International Monetary Fund (IMF), 'Fiscal Monitor: Policies for the Recovery' (October 2020), 2

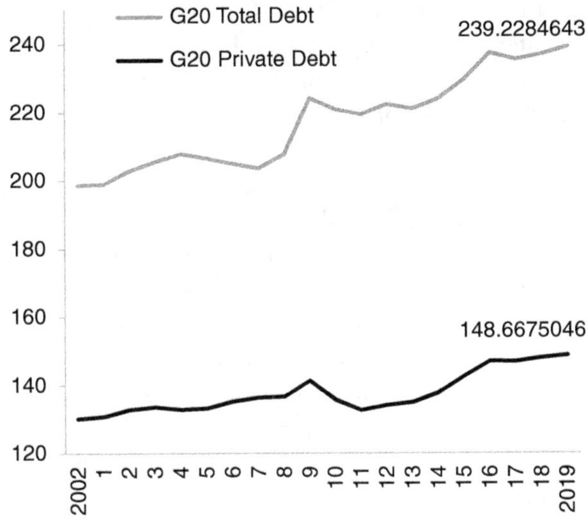

FIGURE 2.2 G20 total public and private debt, 2002–19 (per cent of GDP)
Source: International Monetary Fund (IMF), 'Fiscal Monitor: Policies for the Recovery' (October 2020), 3

financial system. As recently noted by the IMF, among other concerning prospects, 'if financial markets tighten abruptly, [...] many countries and companies could see their borrowing costs spike'; guarantees offered by governments to private economic actors (although still largely untapped) can add substantially to debt vulnerabilities, and excessive private debt can 'migrate to the public sector balance sheet';[44] and 'quantitative easing and quasi-fiscal activities by central banks could lead to a deterioration in central bank balance sheets if supported firms default on central bank holdings of their bonds or commercial paper not covered by a government guarantee'.[45]

Besides this increasingly common and gradually deeper plunge in what may eventually turn out to be, in several cases, unsustainable debt,[46] recent transformations in global debt structure and composition raise additional concerns.

44 On contingent liabilities, see i.a. Lee C. Buchheit and G. Mitu Gulati, 'Sovereign Contingent Liabilities' in Rosa M. Lastra and Lee Buchheit (eds.), *Sovereign Debt Management* (Oxford University Press, 2014), Chapter 18; Hana Polackova, 'Contingent Government Liabilities: A Hidden Fiscal Risk' (1999) 36 *Finance and Development* 1.

45 IMF, 'Fiscal Monitor: Policies for the Recovery', 14–15 and 23.

46 See i.a. Emma Luce Scali, 'Sovereign (Over)Borrowing during the COVID-19 Pandemic: Do Creditors Have a Responsibility to Prevent Unsustainable Debt Situations?', EJIL: Talk!, 17 July 2020.

Since the Latin American debt crisis of the 1980s, which marked a steep decline in syndicated lending, bonded loans have resumed as the major global source of sovereign financing.[47] Although, as has been noted, each financing method presents its own specific problems,[48] short-term and foreign currency-denominated bonds, in particular, can pose a number of fiscal risks.[49] As emphasised by Mauro Megliani, '[t]he speculative nature of short-term bond investment, backed by technological advances, subjects many [. . .] countries to the risk of arbitrary and irrational choices by a multitude of different investors', and 'may involve submitting the sovereignty of a country to the forces of private financial speculation'.[50]

In a recent report on the debt-related problems of developing countries caused by the COVID-19 pandemic, the Independent Expert on foreign debt and human rights has noted that 'since the 1990s, and especially since the 2008 global financial crisis, some countries, including low-income countries [. . .] have shifted to riskier debt', and 'external debt with short terms to maturity has been on the rise since 2010, [. . .] a very dangerous trend, resulting in greater vulnerability to rollover and solvency risk and thus potentially affecting resources available for the progressive realization of economic, social and cultural rights'.[51]

Among other possibly concerning trends, Megliani has observed that, as over-indebted central governments prefer to avoid aggravating their own fiscal budgets by taking directly new loans to finance their national entities, state-owned

[47] Previously, they had been such until the 1929 Wall Street Crash, see Mauro Megliani, 'Private Loans to Sovereign Borrowers' in Ilias Bantekas and Cephas Lumina (eds.), *Sovereign Debt and Human Rights* (Oxford University Press, 2018), pp. 69–83; Gene Frieda, 'Sovereign Debt Markets' in Lastra and Buchheit, *Sovereign Debt Management*, Chapter 20.

[48] Megliani, 'Private Loans to Sovereign Borrowers'.

[49] Short-term debt, in fact, 'can quickly re-price in the event of a rise in yields, raising the interest bill', Abbas et al., 'Sovereign Debt Composition in Advanced Economies', 3, while the inability to issue sovereign debt in domestic currency, or the so called 'original sin', has been identified as a major source of fiscal vulnerabilities in emerging market economies, *ibid.*, 4–5. See also Barry Eichengreen, Ricardo Hausmann and Ugo Panizza, 'The Pain of Original Sin', in Barry Eichengreen and Ricardo Hausmann (eds.), *Other People's Money: Debt Denomination and Financial Instability in Emerging Market Economies* (Chicago: University of Chicago Press, 2005) 13–37; Barry Eichengreen and Ricardo Hausmann (eds.), *Debt Denomination and Financial Instability in Emerging Market Economies* (University of Chicago Press, 2002); and Eduardo Borensztein, Marcos Chamon, Olivier Jeanne, Paolo Mauro and Jeromin Zettelmayer, 'Sovereign Debt Structure for Crisis Prevention' (2004) *IMF Occasional Paper* No. 237. Currently, for the Euro Area Member States, domestic currency debt is debt denominated in Euro, see Eurostat, 'Structure of Government Debt' (June 2021), ec.europa.eu/eurostat/statistics-explained/index.php/Structure_of_government_debt.

[50] Megliani, 'Private Loans to Sovereign Borrowers', pp. 78–79.

[51] United Nations, General Assembly, 'Addressing, from a human rights perspective, the debt-related problems of developing countries caused by the coronavirus disease (COVID-19) pandemic', 8–9.

enterprises and sub-national state divisions are increasingly making recourse to markets by issuing their own bonds, backed up, however, by their central governments (a trend that has grown especially since the Global Financial Crisis, and which potentially adds up to states' contingent liabilities).[52]

Explanations for the extraordinary peacetime debt surge described in this section, especially in advanced economies, vary. Low economic growth, the collapse of the Bretton Woods system, the two oil crises and the price shocks of the 1970s, as well as persistent budget deficits (due inter alia, according to different sources, to the tax reforms of the 1980s,[53] the alleged expansion of the Welfare State,[54] and high state contingent liabilities linked to population ageing-related spending pressure and weak financial systems)[55] have been listed among the causes, for instance, of the Great Accumulation in advanced economies.

However, others have argued that the long-term trend of growing public and private indebtedness that commenced in the 1970s – eventually symptomatic of an 'enduring inadequacy of government revenue compared to government spending'[56] – is instead deep-rooted in the failure of democratic capitalism,[57] notably in the 'long-term decline in the growth performance of advanced

52 Megliani, 'Private Loans to Sovereign Borrowers', p. 75. See e.g. Rajeev Syal and agencies, 'Government Finances at "Significant Risk" from Debt-Laden Councils due to Covid', The Guardian, 22 January 2021.

53 Among others, e.g. Streeck has noted how, particularly in the mid-1980s, strengthened 'tax resistance', especially from high-income earners and corporations, assisted by globalisation and the resulting international tax competition, led many countries to implement (regressive) tax reforms, Streeck, 'The Politics of Public Debt', 149. See also Piketty, *Capital in the Twenty-First Century*.

54 See e.g. Abbas et al., 'Sovereign Debt Composition in Advanced Economies', 14, footnote 30. Against accounts that emphasise the rise of the Welfare State amongst the 'causes' of rising public indebtedness (more in line with the so called 'public choice' school of institutional economics which tends to attribute the rise in public deficits and debts to 'majoritarian electoral pressure from below for redistribution through public spending'), Streeck has argued that it 'appears highly improbable, to say the least, when the increase in public debt is placed in the context of other events and developments that happened in the OECD world during the same period', notably 'because the growth of public debt was accompanied by a steady *decline* in both democratic mobilization and the distributional position of mass publics, pointing to a secular contraction of the power resources and redistributive capacities of the very democratic politics held responsible by theories of "public choice" for the rise in public indebtedness since the 1970s', Streeck, 'The Politics of Public Debt', 145–146 (emphasis in the original). See also Wolfgang Streeck, 'The Rise of the European Consolidation State' (2015) *MPIfG Discussion Paper* 15/1.

55 IMF, 'World Economic Outlook, October 2020', 101.

56 Streeck, 'The Rise of the European Consolidation State', 2.

57 Besides the above-referenced works by Wolfgang Streeck, see also his *Buying Time: The Delayed Crisis of Democratic Capitalism* (London: Verso, 2014); Maurizio Lazzarato, *Governing by Debt* (Los Angeles: Semiotext(e), 2015) and *The Making of the Indebted Man: An Essay on the Neoliberal Condition* (Los Angeles: Semiotext(e), 2012); Soederberg, *Debtfare States and the Poverty Industry*. Streeck defines 'democratic capitalism' or 'capitalist

capitalist economies and their subsequent inability to honour the promises of economic and human progress on which their legitimacy depended'.[58] In this context, the emergence of the so-called *Debt State* in the 1980s[59] – characterised by significant debt financing – must be understood 'as one element among others of a variegated response of countries and actors to declining growth and to the pressures on the politics of rich capitalist democracies that resulted from it'.[60] The escalation in sovereign indebtedness described earlier is, thus, according to this reading, an expedient of such democracies to appease the latent social conflicts generated by the 'unfulfilled promises of late postwar capitalism', essentially aimed at 'buying time' for the existing economic and social order,[61] and delaying the moment when governments 'have to do something about the increasing inadequacy of their fiscal means'.[62]

Indeed, governments across the world appear under mounting pressures to step in and level off – inter alia by recourse to public resources, a fact that, increasingly often, automatically translates into higher debt – the structural imbalances and recurring manifold crises of financialised global capitalism. Debt surges and crises, therefore, often appear as the result of the 'socialisation' of risks, failures and costs that seem intrinsic to the currently prevailing global economic order.

This is true not only of the steady increase in global debt discussed earlier but also of the more recent debt peaks linked to the 2008 Global Financial Crisis and the COVID-19 pandemic. In the case of the former, as is well- known, many

democracy' as a regime 'combining institutionalised mass participation in government with a market economy and capitalist property relations', Streeck, 'The Politics of Public Debt', 143.

58 Streeck, 'The Politics of Public Debt', 144. Consequent to this decline in growth was, according to Streeck, the progressive withdrawal of capital (identified as the 'profit-dependent' social class) from the postwar social contract of bureaucratic-political and corporatist controls, and the transition from the 'embedded liberalism' of the Keynesian political-economic regime of the postwar period to a neoliberal ('neo-Hayekian') economic order characterised by the growing role of markets in political-economic governance and by deregulation, Streeck, *Buying Time*, 36 ff.

59 Replacing the classical 'Tax State', see Streeck, 'The Rise of the European Consolidation State', 5 ff. A famous account of such displacement (not without critics, see e.g. Bonney, *Economic Systems and State Finance*) is Joseph Aloisius Schumpeter, 'The Crisis of the Tax State' (originally published in 1918 as 'Die Krise der Steuerstaates'), trans. by Stolper W. F. and Musgrave R. A. in (1954) 4 *International Economic Papers*, 5–38.

60 Streeck, *Buying Time*, p. 40 ff. The other main strategies identified in this sense by Streeck have been, so far, the inflationary monetary policy of the 1970s and the rapid increase, especially since the 1990s, of private/household debt, or the expansion of so-called 'privatised Keynesianism', on which see Colin Crouch, 'Privatised Keynesianism: An Unacknowledged Policy Regime' (2009) 11 *British Journal of Politics and International Relations* 3, 382–399.

61 Streeck, *Buying Time*, p. 40 ff.

62 Streeck, 'The Rise of the European Consolidation State', 5.

states stepped in, inter alia, to recapitalise major financial institutions at risk of collapse, absorbing private liabilities through what, in many cases, was a dramatic increase in the level of public debt. This was to some extent, for instance, also the case with Greece (see Chapter 4, Section 4.3.1) and, among other countries, significantly with the United Kingdom, whose balance sheet, as noted by the IMF, 'expanded massively during the [Global Financial C]risis', as 'the result of large-scale financial sector rescue operations that resulted in reclassification of the rescued private banks into the public sector and increased (non-central bank) public financial corporation liabilities from 0 in 2007 to 189 percent of GDP in 2008'.[63] The IMF has further observed that '[t]hese balance sheet effects drove most of the movements in net debt during the crisis period, as the government borrowed to inject funds into the banks'.[64]

In the case of the ongoing COVID-19 pandemic, the state has stepped in to assist the real economy and job markets, on which most people's livelihood depends, through the above-mentioned support measures, massively relying, also in this case, on debt, a fact that has resulted in the unprecedented surge in global debt discussed in this section.[65]

There appears to be, thus, a much deeper, *structural* link between the current economic system (its survival and the survival of some of its actors), the role and changing nature of the state, and sovereign indebtedness. This link calls into question, as mentioned in this chapter's introduction, the adequacy of (formalistic) approaches to the debt–ESR relationship that do not interrogate the current nature of sovereign financing nor the meaning and possible implications for the realisation of human rights of the widespread and growing public poverty and indebtedness that characterises our age.

Finally, Streeck has noted, as a consequence of escalating sovereign indebtedness and the resulting need of states to intensify their efforts to secure the continued confidence of their creditors, the progressive transformation, more recently also in Europe, of Debt States into 'Consolidation States'. The latter represent a state that has internalised the need to appear credible to markets, by giving precedence – also through a restructuring of politics, institutions and legal rules – to its market (debt) obligations towards creditors, over its political citizenship (and one could add also human rights) obligations towards its citizens and all persons under its jurisdiction. An established consolidation states is, according to Streeck, 'one that has managed to institutionalise

63 IMF, 'Fiscal Monitor: Managing Public Wealth' (October 2018), 9.

64 *Ibid.*

65 This public debt surge is, furthermore, more generally associated with a decrease in public wealth, *ibid.*

a political commitment and build a political capacity never to default on its debt, projecting an uncompromising determination to place its obligations to its creditors above all other obligations',[66] inter alia by rendering (also by recourse to legal means) spending increases difficult and cuts easy, or balanced budgets an enforceable constitutional requirement.[67]

In the EMU, such transformation has proceeded under and has been advanced, as Section 2.4 will argue, by the post-crisis reform of the existing regime for economic and fiscal policymaking of the Union, and it represents, according to Streeck, importantly for this book's thesis, 'the final stage of the (neo-)liberalisation process that began with the end of the "roaring seventies"'.[68]

2.3.1 *A Brief Annotation on the Social Implications of Indebtedness*

In his analysis of debt and the moral grounds of economic relations,[69] David Graeber proposed that, in any human society, economic relations can be founded on three main moral principles, coexisting everywhere and which essentially determine who has access to what sort of things under which conditions: (1) *communism*, when human relationships operate according to the principle 'from each according to their abilities, to each according to their needs'; (2) *hierarchy*, which implies a relationship between two or more parties, in which one is 'considered superior to the other', and which tends to operate by a 'logic of precedent'; and (3) *exchange*, which 'is all about equivalence[;] it's a back-and-forth process involving two sides in which each side gives as good as it gets'.[70] Commercial exchange in particular is, according to Graeber, '"impersonal": who it is that is selling something to us, or buying something from us, should in principle be entirely irrelevant'.[71] Accordingly, exchange as a moral principle implies that '[o]nce the object [of exchange] changes hands, there is no expectation that the two [parties to

66 Streeck, 'The Rise of the European Consolidation State', 11.

67 *Ibid.*, 12.

68 *Ibid.*, 20.

69 David Graeber, 'On the Moral Grounds of Economic Relations: A Maussian Approach' (2014) 14 *Journal of Classical Sociology* 1, 65–77; *Debt: The First 5,000 Years* (Brooklyn, New York: Melville House, 2011). Although Graeber's considerations originally relate to human interaction, some of the concepts he unravels can shed light on the nature of state debt alike, and the type of social relationships it sustains, both at the domestic and the international level.

70 Graeber, *Debt: The First 5,000 Years*, pp. 94, 103 and 109. As a principle of morality, communism is not just about property ownership. 'Baseline' or 'everyday communism', in particular, is, according to Graeber's approach, the raw material of all human sociability, 'a recognition of our ultimate interdependence that is the ultimate substance of social peace', *ibid.*, 98–99.

71 *Ibid.*, 103.

the transaction] will ever have anything to do with each other again'.[72] Therefore, according to this premise, debt is, in Graeber's portrayal, 'just an exchange that has not been brought to completion', it is 'what happens in between; when the two parties cannot yet walk away from each other'; it is 'strictly a creature of reciprocity [that] has little to do with other sorts of morality'[73] (i.e. communism and hierarchy).

Debt is a creature of reciprocity also in the sense that, for one even to 'feel indebted', that is, under a moral obligation to reciprocate something that they have received in the past, it is necessary that the underlying relationships are, first of all, understood in terms of exchange. In a relationship proceeding according to a different morality, for example, communism or hierarchy, one would receive something and not feel necessarily 'indebted': they would actually expect to receive what they have, based either on the knowledge that, if needed, they too would give what they can (communism), or that, according to precedent, things have always been and thus must always be this way (hierarchy). In market societies, however, we have grown used to the idea that all relationships must be based on reciprocity, and that exchange relationships are normatively superior to other forms of social bonds, since they supposedly free human beings – who, in exchange relationships, become allegedly 'equal' – from bonds that rather mean 'bondage'.[74] We are essentially used to imagining *justice as reciprocity*, and tend to perceive non-reciprocal relationships as somehow *unjust*.

While, on one side, as Graeber suggests, debt promotes social linkages, creating a 'bond' between actors who could otherwise be potentially unrelated (let us think, for instance, of foreign debt contracted by a state with a non-resident individual or commercial bank), on the other hand, this also entails that, because of the exchange nature of this interaction, debt aside, the two parts do not really need to share any further common purpose, aim or interest. Their fates can be entirely indifferent to each other; their relationship can be limited to and last for the period of indebtedness. Once the latter is written off, 'when the money changes hands, [. . .] both parties can walk away and have nothing further to do with each other'.[75] If this can be perfectly acceptable in the case of purely commercial transactions, it might be less so when the ultimate purpose of one party is the realisation of its sovereign functions.

72 *Ibid.*, 104.

73 *Ibid.*, 121–122.

74 See e.g. Nathalie Karagiannis and Peter Wagner, 'The Subject-In-Debt: Notes Towards a Sociology and Philosophy of Indebtedness' (2018), www.ub.edu/thedebt/wp-content/uploads/2018/03/Karagiannis-Wagner_The-subject-in-debt.pdf.

75 Graeber, *Debt: The First 5,000 Years*, p. 122.

The original and final *separation* between the parties in an exchange relationship is also an inherent difference between debt and other modes of state financing, in particular taxation, where there is a coincidence (at least in principle) between the interests and objectives of the taxpayers and the state, who both share a common destiny. It is true that in some cases, for instance with domestic debt, such separation is formally absent. Nonetheless, if we consider, in very abstract terms, lending as an alternative to taxpaying (as was the case, for instance, in twelfth-century Italian city-states), domestic indebtedness may imply a different, less participatory, way of conceiving one's contribution to the resources needed to realise collective aims. Clearly, since debt has to be repaid, 'debt financing is in the interest of those who have the means to lend to the government',[76] but '[f]rom the standpoint of the general interest, it is normally preferable [in terms of justice and efficiency] to tax the wealthy rather than borrow from them'.[77] The ultimate purpose of credit is some personal (financial or other) gain. Taxpaying represents, instead, a form of individual support to the achievement of the common good. Debt, even domestic debt, contributes to realising a less cohesive community, a community whose members may still be *bonded*, but ultimately in a relationship where some owe something to others, rather than everyone to everybody else per the state. This idea is partially supported by the fact that, historically, debt as a form of state financing emerged long before direct taxation, precisely because the cohesive political, social and institutional structures that were needed to implement the latter had not yet been developed. [78]

I do not intend to demonise sovereign borrowing here. In many cases, it can be a mere necessity, and under certain conditions, responsible borrowing represents an opportunity and a resource for development. It seems worthwhile, nonetheless, to reflect on its multifaceted implications, especially on the way in which indebtedness and taxation can relate and evolve side by side (and historical perspectives can offer many interesting ideas on this).[79]

A further characteristic of debt highlighted by Graeber's analysis is that

> [d]uring the time that the debt remains unpaid, the logic of hierarchy takes hold. There is no reciprocity. [. . .] [D]ebtor and creditor confront each other like a peasant before a feudal lord. The law of precedent takes hold. If you

[76] Piketty, *Capital in the Twenty-First Century*.

[77] *Ibid.*

[78] See for instance the works referenced above at n 25.

[79] See e.g. Streeck's above-mentioned considerations on the relationship between tax reforms in the 1980s and growing debt in Streeck, 'The Politics of Public Debt'.

> bring your creditor tomatoes from the garden, it never occurs to you that he would give something back.[80]

Across the world and history, indebtedness has involved (as any relationship actually does) a certain grade of dependency, be it that of the maritime republic, the medieval monarch, or the nation-state, from rich merchant and banking families, other states, supranational institutions or international financial elites of any kind. *Borrowing means depending* on someone else's resources, and with dependence comes external influence, if not actual control. In this sense, the growing indebtedness described in the previous section may be seen as a channel of oppression and domination.

Nevertheless, in order to finance its functions and no matter how it chooses to do so, any political organisation must depend on someone. Is not taxation a form of financial dependence on the taxpayers, after all? As Margaret Levi has suggested:

> rulers always depend on others for some of the resources necessary to acquire and sustain rule. They depend on the generals and even the soldiers of their armies, on the owners or managers of economic wealth, on the church officials who justify their status, or on the scientists or inventors of new technologies of force.[81]

The question at stake, then, is rather the following: *who* is in a position to influence or control, through the reins of money, what a state should or is able to achieve?

Furthermore, a fact that is often understated is that the dependency between debtor and creditor can be reciprocal as well. No political authority has ever been so powerful as not to fear the consequences of an arbitrary default; and no financial power so independent from the losses that such a default would imply. This is something to be firmly kept in mind when discussing responsibilities for and possible ways out of a sovereign debt crisis.

Finally, it has been argued that the current

> amplification and generalization of indebtedness [. . .] potentially undermines the economic meaning of debt in as far as repayment within specified periods, or even repayment at all, becomes less likely or even impossible. Generalized indebtedness is a new social situation [. . . in which] indebtedness can become 'too large to fail' the debtors, to paraphrase a term hitherto only used for banks.[82]

80 Graeber, *Debt: The First 5,000 Years*, p. 121.
81 Margaret Levi, *Of Rule and Revenue* (University of California Press, 1989), p. 43.
82 Karagiannis and Wagner, 'The Subject-In-Debt', 4.

This fact supports the always 'imminent possibility of a transformation in the meaning of debt' (something that, given the explosion of public indebtedness caused by the COVID-19 pandemic, is being currently attempted, unprecedentedly, in the European context, as some countries are advocating for the necessity of some form of debt forgiveness for the most indebted EU Member States).[83] Such transformation may lead to a contestation of indebtedness, the development of new solidarities and the redefinition of a different legal regime.

2.4 THE INCREASED NEOLIBERALISATION OF EU ECONOMIC GOVERNANCE

A first element suggesting the advanced neoliberalisation, since the crisis, in this case of EU law, which cannot be left out of consideration when discussing the debt–human rights relationship in countries that are also members of the European Union – such as Greece – is the post-crisis reform of the legal framework for economic and fiscal policy coordination in the EMU. In fact, although it nominally left fiscal policy competences to national authorities, the reform increased pressure towards greater convergence of domestic fiscal policies, further limiting the fiscal sovereignty of EU countries, with potential implications for the ability of EU Member States to realise ESRs and to comply with their obligations under the ICESCR.

After briefly introducing the core elements of the legal framework for economic governance established by EU primary and secondary law, Sections 2.4.1 and 2.4.2 will respectively present the framework's post-crisis revision and resulting increased neoliberalisation.

Since the creation of the EMU with the Treaty of Maastricht on the European Union (TEU) in 1992,[84] and especially after the Eurozone crisis, the fiscal policies of states that are members of the European Union (EU) have been increasingly subject to significant substantive and procedural constraints under EU law.

As is well known, the EMU essentially rests on an asymmetric two-pillar structure (not altered by the Treaty of Lisbon,[85] nor by post-crisis regulation),

83 See e.g. Martin Arnold, 'Soaring Eurozone Government Debt Reignites Call for Cancellation', Financial Times, 8 December 2020; Vesa Vihriälä, 'Make Room for Fiscal Action Through Debt Conversion', VoxEU.org, 15 April 2020.

84 Treaty on European Union (signed 7 February 1992, entered into force 1 November 1993) [2012] OJ C326.

85 Treaty of Lisbon amending the Treaty on European Union and the Treaty establishing the European Community (signed 13 December 2007, entered into force 1 December 2009) [2007] OJ C306/01.

constituted by a monetary union – characterised by a fully centralised, supranational monetary policy run by the European Central Bank (ECB) – and an economic union – which has taken, rather, the form of economic policy coordination. Thus, Member States have retained formal competence for the execution and, to a considerable extent, formulation of their economic policies.[86]

However, after the Eurozone crisis exposed the destabilizing effects of the 'monetary union without fiscal union', the EU adopted additional permanent legal measures (a) to strengthen the economic dimension of the EMU and increase the convergence of Member States' economic policies; and (b) to make amends for the prior lack of a legal framework to assist Eurozone countries experiencing financial difficulties (as already mentioned in Chapter 5).

At a primary law level, the fiscal policies of EU Member States are regulated under Articles 119–126 of Chapter 1 ('Economic Policy') of Title VIII ('Economic and Monetary Policy') of the TFEU;[87] and Protocol No. 12 on the Excessive Deficit Procedure, annexed to the TFEU.

Articles 119 and 120 TFEU contain general indications on the objectives and principles that should inform the activities of the Member States and the Union in the field of economic policy, while Articles 121–126 TFEU and the Protocol on the EDP lay out the key mechanisms and requirements for fiscal policy coordination under Treaty law.

EU fiscal rules have been further developed through secondary legislation, that is, the so-called Stability and Growth Pact (SGP), which fully entered into force on 1 January 1999.[88] After the crisis, this was followed by the so-called Six

86 Rosa M. Lastra, *International Financial and Monetary Law*, 2nd ed. (Oxford University Press, 2015) p. 291, para. 8.15–8.17; Alicia Hinarejos, 'Economic and Monetary Union' in Catherine Barnard and Steve Peers (eds.), *European Union Law* (Oxford University Press, 2014), pp. 567–590.

87 Treaty on the Functioning of the European Union (Consolidated version) [2012] OJ C326/49.

88 The so called SGP is actually constituted by Resolution of the European Council on the Stability and Growth Pact of 17 June 1997 [1997] OJ C236/1; Council Regulation (EC) No. 1466/97 of 7 July 1997 on strengthening of the surveillance of budgetary positions and the surveillance and coordination of economic policies [1997] OJ L209/1 as amended by Council Regulation (EC) No. 1055/2005 amending Regulation (EC) No. 1466/1997 on the strengthening of the surveillance of the budgetary positions and the surveillance and coordination of economic policies [2005] OJ L174 and by Regulation (EU) No. 1175/2011 of the European Parliament and of the Council of 16 November 2011 amending Council Regulation (EC) No. 1466/97 on the strengthening of the surveillance of budgetary positions and the surveillance and coordination of economic policies [2011] OJ L306 (see 'Six Pack' below); and Council Regulation (EC) No. 1467/97 of 7 July 1997 speeding up and clarifying the implementation of excessive deficit procedure [1997] OJ L209/6, as amended by Council Regulation (EC) No. 1056/2005 amending Regulation (EC) No. 1467/1997 on speeding up and clarifying the implementation of excessive deficit procedure [2005] OJ L174 and by Council Regulation (EU) No. 1177/2011 of 8 November 2011 amending Regulation (EC)

Pack,[89] Two Pack[90] and the Euro Plus Pact, the latter of which is a soft law instrument.[91]

In addition, on 2 March 2012, EU Member States (with the exception of the United Kingdom and the Czech Republic) concluded a new intergovernmental 'Treaty on Stability, Coordination and Governance in the Economic and Monetary Union' (TSCG), entered into force on 1 January 2013, whose fiscal part (i.e. Title III) is generally referred to as 'Fiscal Compact'.[92] Finally, the EU has introduced a new mechanism for economic policy coordination, that is, the European Semester.[93]

As defined in Article 119(1) TFEU, the economic policy of the EU under the EMU must be based on the close coordination of Members States' economic policies, on the internal market and on the definition of common objectives, and be conducted in accordance with the principle of an open market economy with free competition. It must also follow the guiding principles contained in Article 119(3) TFEU, that is, stable prices, sound

No. 1467/97 on speeding up and clarifying the implementation of the excessive deficit procedure [2011] OJ L306 (see 'Six Pack' below). For a history of the SGP, including its reform in 2005 towards a more 'flexible' and 'growth-oriented' framework, see Lastra, *International Financial and Monetary Law*, pp. 302–308.

89 Regulation (EU) No. 1173/2011 of the European Parliament and of the Council of 16 November 2011 on the effective enforcement of budgetary surveillance in the Euro Area [2011] OJ L306; Regulation (EU) No. 1174/2011 of the European Parliament and of the Council of 16 November 2011 on enforcement measures to correct excessive macroeconomic imbalances in the Euro Area [2011] OJ L306; Regulation (EU) No. 1175/2011 of the European Parliament and of the Council of 16 November 2011 amending Council Regulation (EC) No. 1466/97 on the strengthening of the surveillance of budgetary positions and the surveillance and coordination of economic policies [2011] OJ L306; Regulation (EU) No. 1176/2011 of the European Parliament and of the Council of 16 November 2011 on the prevention and correction of macroeconomic imbalances [2011] OJ L306; Council Regulation (EU) No. 1177/2011 of 8 November 2011 amending Regulation (EC) No. 1467/97 on speeding up and clarifying the implementation of the excessive deficit procedure [2011] OJ L306; and Council Directive 2011/85/EU on requirements for budgetary frameworks of the Member States [2011] OJ L306.

90 Regulation (EU) No. 473/2013 on the European Parliament and of the Council of 21 May 2013 on common provisions for monitoring and assessing draft budgetary plans and ensuring the correction of excessive deficit of the Member States in the Euro Area [2013] OJ L140; and Regulation (EU) 472/2013 of the European Parliament and of the Council of 21 May 2013 on the strengthening of economic and budgetary surveillance of Member States in the Euro Area experiencing or threatened with serious difficulties with respect to their financial stability [2013] OJ L140.

91 European Commission, 'The Euro Plus Pact: How Integration into the EU Framework can Give New Momentum for Structural Reforms in the Euro Area' (8 May 2015), https://ec.europa.eu/epsc/publications/strategic-notes/euro-plus-pact_en.

92 Out of the 25 Contracting Parties to the TSCG, 22 are formally bound by the Fiscal Compact (the 19 Euro Area Member States plus Bulgaria, Denmark and Romania).

93 European Commission, 'The European Semester', https://ec.europa.eu/info/strategy/european-semester_en.

public finances and monetary conditions and a sustainable balance of payments. Article 120 TFEU reiterates the point that the economic policies of Member States must be conducted in accordance with the principle of an open market economy with free competition, favouring an efficient allocation of resources, with a view to contributing to the achievement of the objectives of the Union, as defined in Article 3 of the TEU and in the context of the broad guidelines referred to in Article 121(2) TFEU (further in the text).

As revealed by the language of these articles, economic policy coordination within the EMU is bound by treaty law to comply with the operating principles of a 'market economy' (whose major defining characteristic could be taken to be that decisions regarding investment, production and distribution are to be exclusively based on the interplay of market forces, i.e. supply and demand, and competition, rather than political intervention). Instead, Article 3 TEU – recalled by Article 120 TFEU – makes reference to a different economic system: among the objectives of the Union to which the coordinated economic policies of EU Member States should be directed, Article 3 TEU indicates, in fact, 'a highly competitive *social market economy*, aiming at full employment and social progress'.[94]

'Social market economy' is a concept with a long (German) history. The invention of the term, in the mid-1940s, is ascribed to Alfred Müller-Armack, a German Professor of Economics, who was state secretary of the German Minister of Economic Affairs, Ludwig Erhard, in 1958–63, and chief negotiator on behalf of Germany for the Treaty of Rome on the European Economic Community. He presented the social market economy (sometimes called 'Rhine capitalism') as a 'third way' between laissez-faire liberalism and planned economy.[95]

It is an economic system that combines market economy with a 'system of social and societal measures, geared to market requirements',[96] thus promoting interventionist state measures and policies to serve the social balance in

94 The inclusion of a 'social market economy' among the 'objectives' of the Union was first proposed by the European Convention in Article 3(3) of the Draft Treaty establishing a Constitution for Europe of 2003, but it was incorporated into Article 3 TEU only with the Treaty of Lisbon.

95 See i.a. Christian Joerges and Florian Rödl, '"Social Market Economy" as Europe's Social Model?' (2004) *EUI Working Paper Law 2004/8*; Hans F Zacher, 'Social Market Economy, Social Policy, and the Law' (1982) 138 *Zeitschrift für die gesamte Staatswissenschaft/Journal of Institutional and Theoretical Economics* 367–388.

96 Alfred Müller-Armack, 'Wirtschaftslenkung und Marktwirtschaft' (1946) reprinted in *Wirtschaftsordnung und Wirtschaftspolitik. Studien und Konzepten zur sozialen Markwirtschaft und zur europäischen Integration* (Freiburg: Rombach Verlag, 1966).

society.[97] It must be noted, however, that, although they may pursue similar social goals, there is an important difference between the distinctive notion of social market economy and other mixed economy systems, in terms of the instruments deemed plausible for the realisation of such goals. In a social market economy, in fact, 'all social state policies [are] subordinated to the functionality of market mechanisms. Social policies which threaten to distort market competition and its core, the price mechanism, are excluded from the socio-political agenda.'[98]

Some commentators have remarked that the appeal to a social market economy, at first presumably as a 'constitutional principle' in the failed Draft Constitutional Treaty, may have been related 'to a desire to anchor the claim to develop and extend policies of social balance [...] [and was] directed against a strong bias towards free markets and undistorted competition at the EU level'.[99] Nonetheless, they have contested the adequacy of such an appeal, on the basis that to make the intended social character of the EU explicit with reference to 'the key concept of an influential but still specific line of thought in the young Federal Republic of Germany [...] may implicitly and possibly involuntary exclude [...] alternative conceptions of how the state, the sphere of society and their reciprocal interference should be understood in general'.[100]

Beyond this reasonable concern, however, it must be noted that, despite the reference in Article 3 TEU to the notion of social market economy, any indication in favour of a 'social balance' of market mechanisms has disappeared in relation to economic policy coordination within the EMU, where reference is made by Articles 119 and 120 only to an open market economy with free competition. Moreover, while the coordinating competence of the EU in this

97 Among these measures are, according to Müller-Armack's notion of social market economy, policies aimed at preventing economic fluctuations and at 'approximating' full employment, as well as redistributive policies for those in need, such as welfare, pensions, subsidies for homeowners and tenants, etc., to be implemented through taxation and subsidies, *ibid.* In a 'second phase' of the social market economy, Müller-Armack envisaged also the adoption of broader social measures, such as investments in higher education, public services, currency stability to protect employees' savings, and several other forms of state intervention, see Alfred Müller-Armack, 'Die zweite Phase der sozialen Marktwirtschaft. Ihre Enrgänzung durch das Leitbild einer neuen Gesellschaftspolitik' (1906) reprinted in *Wirtschaftsordnung und Wirtschaftspolitik*.

98 *Ibid.* This characteristic is the reason why the term 'social market economy' has also been used to describe the use of market mechanisms to increase the efficiency of the social functions of the state, see 'Social Market' in 'Economics A-Z', *The Economist*, www.economist.com/economics-a-to-z/s#node-21529660.

99 Joerges and Rödl, '"Social Market Economy" as Europe's Social Model?', 20.

100 *Ibid.*, 12.

area was strengthened after the crisis, it appears to have been generally inspired by a different, neoliberal, economic model, on which more will be said later.

A second element worth highlighting, and to which I will return, is that, as outlined by Article 119(2) and (3) and noted by various commentators,[101] the fiscal policies of EU Member States (and, indirectly, their social policies, central to this book's discussion) are subordinated to the objectives and requirements of monetary stability.

2.4.1 *The Post-Crisis Reform of the Legal Framework for Economic and Fiscal Policy in the EMU*

Post-crisis regulation has (1) strengthened fiscal policy coordination and surveillance (via a more stringent SGP and the Fiscal Compact), as well as general economic policy coordination (i.a. via the Integrated Guidelines, on which more will be said shortly); (2) introduced a new macroeconomic surveillance mechanism, underpinned by sanctions; and (3) synchronised all the mechanisms of economic policy coordination under the European Semester.

The economic and fiscal policies of EU Member States are currently disciplined both in 'quantitative' and 'qualitative' terms, with the asserted aim to ensure prudent fiscal behaviour and to improve economic competitiveness and growth.

In quantitative terms, the 'post-crisis' SGP and the Fiscal Compact have introduced stricter deficit rules. They reiterate the so-called Balanced Budget Rule (already established by the 'pre-crisis' SGP and going beyond the simple prohibition of excessive deficits contained in Article 126 TFEU), that is, the requirement that Member States' budgets are balanced or in surplus. In order to achieve this aim, Members States are under an obligation to reach or to be heading towards country-specific medium-term budgetary objectives (MTOs) – that is, country-specific numerical values for the structural balance.[102] These can

101 Lastra, *International Financial and Monetary Law*, para. 8.02. See also Section 2.4.2, for further references.

102 The structural or underlying fiscal balance is the difference between government revenues and expenditures corrected by the effects that could be attributed to the economic cycle and one-off events. Eliminating possible economic fluctuations (which have an impact on government revenues and expenditures), this indicator aims to capture the underlying structural fiscal trends of a country that are associated with the sustainability of public finances in the long run, see OECD, 'Government at a Glance 2015: General Government Structural Balance' (6 July 2015), www.oecd-ilibrary.org/governance/government-at-a-glance-2015/general-government-structural-balance_gov_glance-2015-9-en. MTOs are updated every 3 years, or more frequently in the case of a country that has undergone a structural reform which significantly impacted on its public

vary, depending on the assumed trend growth and debt level, between a surplus of 1 per cent and a deficit of 1 per cent of GDP. Members are also under an obligation to respect a newly introduced 'expenditure benchmark' that essentially demands that net expenditure grows at a rate equivalent to or lower than the rate of potential GDP growth.[103]

This new benchmark could have critical implications for states' 'available resources' and the duty to take continuous forward steps in the realisation of ESR. For instance, it potentially represents a first contradiction with the requirement by the CESCR that where there is an increase in the availability of resources in a country, which could be presumed in the case of GDP growth, such a country is expected to proportionally increase its allocation of resources for the realisation of ESR.[104]

Article 3(1)(e) TSCG requires that, in the event of a significant observed deviation[105] from the MTO or the adjustment path towards it, a correction mechanism must be triggered *automatically*, and this must include the obligation of the state concerned to implement measures to correct the deviations over a defined period of time. A deviation will not be considered significant only under specific circumstances. These include the situation when there is an unusual event beyond the Member State's control that has a major impact on its budgetary position or in the case of a severe overall economic downturn. Further leniency is offered to a Member State that has undertaken structural reforms, especially pension reforms or reforms to enhance potential economic growth, having a short-term negative impact on the country's budgetary position, but improving the long-term sustainability of its public finances.[106] Very reduced margins of deviation from the above-mentioned criteria exist, thus, for purposes that cannot be justified in terms of economic performance.

The Fiscal Compact introduced an obligation for the contracting parties to the TSCG to incorporate, within a year after the Treaty's entry into force, the Balanced Budget Rule, MTO rules and the correction mechanism within their national legislation, 'through provisions of binding force and permanent

finances, see European Commission, 'Medium-term Budgetary Objectives (MTOs)', https://ec.europa.eu/info/business-economy-euro/economic-and-fiscal-policy-coordination/eu-economic-governance-monitoring-prevention-correction/stability-and-growth-pact/preventive-arm/medium-term-budgetary-objectives-mtos_en.

103 The expenditure benchmark requires that, for Member States at MTO, net expenditure growth does not exceed the medium-term potential GDP growth, while, for Member States not at MTO, net expenditure grows at a lower rate.

104 See Chapter 4.

105 I.e. a deviation of at least 0.5 per cent of GDP over a given year, or at least 0.25 per cent of GDP per annum average over two consecutive years.

106 Lastra, *International Financial and Monetary Law*, p. 316, para. 8.127.

character, preferably constitutional, or otherwise guaranteed to be fully respected and adhered to throughout the national budgetary processes' (Article 3(2) TSCG).[107] These rules must be monitored at the national level by an independent institution. To corroborate this obligation, Article 8(1) TSCG also contains an 'indirect threat' of sanction, providing that one or more contracting parties may call upon the Court of Justice of the European Union (CJEU) to verify (with a binding ruling) compliance with this obligation.[108]

The requirement to transpose the new fiscal rules into national law has encountered severe criticism both in terms of its legitimacy – as an externally imposed legislative and in many cases constitutional reform – and in terms of its content. In Greece, for instance, during the debates on its implementation, which mainly took place during the parliamentary session of 28 March 2012, the parties of the opposition (at the time, mainly LA.O.S., SY.RIZ.A., DIM. AR. and K.K.E.) raised objections. They stated that 'by imposing balanced and exceeding budgets and sanctions in case of noncompliance, the Fiscal Compact was imposing neoliberal policies [entailing] austerity, infringement of labor and social rights, and cuts on public services, for the profit of business groups and the capital in general'.[109] Despite criticism, however, EU countries enacted specific legislation, in many cases of a constitutional character, to incorporate these fiscal rules in their domestic frameworks.[110]

Greater 'consistency' between national and European fiscal rules has also been promoted through Council Directive 2011/85/EU (part of the Six Pack).

107 See also European Commission, 'Communication from the Commission: Common Principles on National Fiscal Correction Mechanisms', COM(2012) 342 final (20 June 2012); Xenophon Contiades (ed.), *Constitutions in the Global Financial Crisis: A Comparative Analysis* (Abingdon: Routledge, 2016); Kaarlo Tuori and Klaus Tuori, *The Eurozone Crisis: A Constitutional Analysis* (Cambridge University Press, 2014).

108 Lastra, *International Financial and Monetary Law*, p. 316, para. 8.129.

109 See European University Institute (EUI), 'Constitutional Change through Euro Crisis Law: A Multi-Level Legal Analysis of Economic and Monetary Union', Greece – IX. Fiscal Compact – IX.5. Debate Balanced Budget Rule, http://eurocrisislaw.eui.eu/country/greece/topic/fiscal-compact/.

110 In Greece this has occurred through Law No. 4270 of 28 June 2014 on Fiscal Management and Supervision Principles, as amended by Law No. 4336 of 14 August 2015. In Italy, for instance, among other EU countries, this requirement led to a revision of Article 81 of the Constitution with Constitutional Law No. 1 of 20 April 2012, 'Introduzione del principio del pareggio di bilancio nella Carta Costituzionale', GU No. 95 of 23 April 2012 and to the adoption of Law 243/2012 of 24 December 2012 on Provisions for implementation of the balanced budget principle pursuant to Article 81 paragraph 6 of the Constitution, as amended by Law No. 164 of 12 August 2016. For country-specific reports from the Commission in this regard, see European Commission, 'The Fiscal Compact – Taking Stock' (22 February 2017), https://ec.europa.eu/info/publications/fiscal-compact-taking-stock_en.

In addition to laying down detailed rules on the characteristics of Member States' public accounting systems, including bookkeeping, internal control, financial reporting and auditing, the Directive also requires Member States to introduce strong numerical fiscal rules in their budgetary frameworks. These must be 'based on the reliable and independent analysis carried out by independent bodies or bodies endowed with functional autonomy *vis-à-vis* the fiscal authorities of the Member States'.[111]

In qualitative terms, convergence of the fiscal policies of EU Member States is achieved, first of all, through the broad economic policy guidelines (BEPGs) foreseen in Article 121(2) TFEU.[112] These are, in principle, non-binding recommendations formulated and adopted by the Council, based on a proposal from the Commission and the conclusions of the European Council. They are meant to instruct the national reform programmes that, each spring, Member States have to submit to the Commission as part of the multilateral surveillance mechanism provided for in Article 121(3)–(6) TFEU. In 2010, the BEPGs were brought together with the Employment Guidelines under the single heading of the Integrated Guidelines (IGs), as part of the adoption of the Europe 2020 Strategy.[113] The BEPGs remain valid for an indefinite period and the most recent BEPGs were adopted in July 2015.[114]

As has been remarked, the BEPGs largely mirror the (predominantly neoliberal) economic prescriptions of the IMF or the Organisation for Economic Co-operation and Development (OECD).[115] The 2015 BEPGs contain four Guidelines, respectively, on boosting investment; increasing growth via structural reforms in EU countries; eliminating the main obstacles to sustainable growth and employment in the EU; and making public finances more sustainable and growth friendly.

The TSCG also contains an obligation for the contracting parties to report ex ante on their public debt issuance plans to the Council and the Commission (Article 6), and to discuss ex ante and, where appropriate, coordinate among them all the major economic policy reforms that they plan to undertake (Article 11 TSCG).

111 Council Directive 2011/85/EU, Preamble 16 and Chapter IV.

112 European Parliament, 'At a Glance: Broad Economic Policy Guidelines and Employment Guidelines' (2015), www.europarl.europa.eu/RegData/etudes/ATAG/2015/542652/IPOL_ATA(2015)542652_EN.pdf.

113 European Commission, 'Europe 2020: Integrated Guidelines for the Economic and Employment Policies of the Member States' (27 April 2010).

114 Council Recommendation (EU) 2015/1184 of 14 July 2015 on broad guidelines for the economic policies of the Member States and of the European Union [2015] OJ L192, 27–31.

115 Lastra, *International Financial and Monetary Law*, p. 294, para. 8.27.

Two of the legislative texts of the Six Pack,[116] furthermore, establish a new macroeconomic surveillance framework, aimed at identifying, preventing and addressing the emergence of potentially harmful macroeconomic imbalances that could adversely affect economic stability in a particular EU country, the Euro Area, or the EU as a whole.[117] The macroeconomic imbalance procedure (MIP) starts around November, when the Commission issues an 'alert mechanism report' (AMR), in conjunction with the annual growth survey.

The AMR uses a scoreboard of selected indicators to screen EU Member States for potential economic imbalances needing policy action, and to identify countries that need an in-depth review (IDR) by the Commission. A country may be found to have 'no imbalances', 'imbalances', 'excessive imbalances' or 'excessive imbalances with corrective action', which may trigger the excessive imbalance procedure (EIP).

Lastly, the excessive deficit procedure (EDP), provided for by Article 126 TFEU, was strengthened under the post-crisis rules, particularly for Euro Area Member States. It would be beyond the scope of this section to go through the various stages of the procedure in detail, so I will only briefly report the most relevant innovations introduced after the crisis.

Similar to the previous system, an EDP can be launched if a country's deficit exceeds or risks exceeding the threshold of 3 per cent of GDP, or if its public debt exceeds 60 per cent of GDP and is not diminishing at a satisfactory pace (i.e. the gap between the debt level and the 60 per cent reference must be reduced by 1/20th annually, on average over three years). The new governance framework has introduced the possibility to gradually impose financial sanctions already from the so-called preventive arm of the SGP (i.e. before an EDP is actually launched, which is a possibility not foreseen under the previous system) to the latest stages of the EDP. Sanctions may eventually reach 0.5 per cent of GDP. Furthermore, Member States subject to an EDP procedure must set a 'fiscal and economic partnership programme', entailing, in practice, the implementation of reforms similar to the structural reforms implemented by countries under the EU/IMF financial adjustment programmes.

A new fine has also been introduced against the statistical misrepresentation of budgetary data on deficit and debt which are relevant for the application of Articles 121 and 126 TFEU, or for the EDP Protocol.[118] Finally, in order to limit the Council's discretion in following the Commission's recommendations

116 Regulation (EU) No. 1174/2011 and Regulation (EU) No. 1176/2011.

117 European Commission, 'Macroeconomic Imbalance Procedure', https://ec.europa.eu/info/business-economy-euro/economic-and-fiscal-policy-coordination/eu-economic-governance-monitoring-prevention-correction/macroeconomic-imbalance-procedure_en.

118 Lastra, *International Financial and Monetary Law*, p. 320.

(especially in the EDP), the 2011 reforms introduced a reverse qualified majority voting mechanism has been introduced for the imposition of most sanctions, whereby a qualified majority of Member States is needed to reject, rather than to adopt, a Commission proposal for a Council decision.

Under the EIP, countries with macroeconomic imbalances or excessive imbalances may receive policy recommendations for reducing them, and, depending on the nature and severity of their imbalances, their policy commitments will be monitored through specific monitoring. In addition to increased monitoring, countries in the Euro Area can also face sanctions. As with the EDP, the Council takes the decision in these cases by means of reverse qualified majority voting.[119]

2.4.2 *The Neoliberal Character of the Post-Crisis Reform and the Consolidation of the Neoliberal State in Europe*

The main elements of the post-crisis reform of the EU legal framework for economic and fiscal policy coordination just outlined reveal a strengthening of EU fiscal rules that goes temporally and substantially beyond the crisis and responses thereto, with potential implications for the ability of EU member states to comply with their international human right obligations, including under the ICESCR. Although EU institutions still have no formal legislative competence over national fiscal policies, as this has been nominally left to the Member States, the rules introduced especially after the crisis enable stricter economic and fiscal policy coordination, surveillance and ultimately 'direction'/'control' by EU institutions (especially for Euro Area countries). Thus, the fiscal sovereignty of EU Member States has become considerably limited, although 'voluntarily' so.

This can be, of course, beneficial for the prevention, in theory, of irresponsible state conduct, including irresponsible borrowing and lending practices and the accumulation of unsustainable debt burdens, which can be a threat to the realisation of ESR. Nonetheless, the new rules stand in potential contradiction with the requirements of social policy/ESR both because, together with their fiscal policies, the social policies of EU Member States have been made increasingly contingent upon the objectives of financial stability, and because of the specific, neoliberal character of the required qualitative adjustments (e.g. social expenditure cuts, labour markets 'flexibilisation'[120] and privatisations).

[119] *Ibid.*, 320–321.

[120] See i.a. Report of the Independent Expert on the effects of foreign debt and other related international financial obligations of states on the full enjoyment of all human rights, particularly economic, social and cultural rights, UN Doc. A/HRC/34/57 (2016); Report of

There is no qualitative difference, in this sense, between the broad economic policy objectives pursued by the EU in the EMU or through the MoUs agreed with EU Member States in financial difficulties (on which, see Chapter 4).

The new arrangements appear to preserve and enhance in particular the stabilisation function of fiscal policymaking, while restricting, to say the least, its redistributive function. Accordingly, the only social policies de facto allowed by the new rules are those that satisfy the economic condition of enhancing the sustainability of EU members states' public finances, or at least of being compatible with the economic objectives of the EMU (first and foremost, monetary stability).[121]

Furthermore, as has been remarked, one of the key aims of the regulatory changes introduced after the crisis was to make fiscal (and social) policy convergence more 'automatic',[122] that is, less politically manoeuvrable. This has occurred, inter alia, through the requirement to transpose EU fiscal rules (including an automatically activating corrective mechanism) into domestic legislation, and the introduction of reverse qualified majority voting in the corrective arm of the EU framework, in order to limit the discretion of the Council in following the Commission's recommendations in the EDP and EIP.

Fiscal policy decision-making has, thus, not only been partially isolated from the control and authority of Member States but also from the political process itself, in a successful attempt to make it – and, consequently, social policy decision-making – *appear* as a purely technical/regulatory exercise, ostensibly devoid of political and social significance. This idea has been eloquently summarised as follows:

> Fiscal rules are explicitly pitched as devices to constrain the sovereignty of democratic institutions. 'Such rules', according to one analyst, 'remove legislators' discretion in making spending and taxation decisions.'[123] [...]

the Independent Expert on the effects of foreign debt and other related international financial obligations of states on the full enjoyment of all human rights, particularly economic, social and cultural rights on his mission to institutions of the European Union, UN Doc. A/HRC/34/57/Add.1 (2016).

121 See i.a. Francesco Costamagna, 'National Social Spaces as Adjustment Variables in the EMU: A Critical Legal Appraisal' (2018) 24 *European Law Journal* 163–190, at 164 (noting how 'these reforms have converted national social spaces into adjustment variables whose main function is to contribute to the pursuit of EMU-related objectives'); Violeta Ruiz Almendral, 'The European Fiscal Consolidation Legal Framework: Its Impact on National Fiscal Constitutions and Parliamentary Democracy' in Thomas Beukers, Bruno de Witte and Claire Kilpatrick (eds.), *Constitutional Change through Euro-Crisis Law* (Cambridge University Press, 2017), p. 27 ff.

122 Lastra, *International Financial and Monetary Law*, 319.

123 Marion Wrobel, *Fiscal Rules for the Control of Government* (Ottawa: Research Branch, Library of Parliament, 1993).

> The ideal rule was one that constrained 'successive governments [. . .] over a reasonably long period of time'. Limiting discretion seemed reasonable because it was understood that this discretion was usually abused. 'The main underlying cause' of fiscal indiscipline, an IMF study reported in 2007, is 'the injudicious use of discretion [. . .] in the context of competing electoral constituencies and political and redistributive conflicts'. [. . .] Fiscal rules [. . .] shared the purpose of restraining democratic processes, on the premise that those processes were prone to misbehaviour. [. . .] A well-designed fiscal rule could establish 'a depoliticized framework for fiscal policy' just as central bank reforms appeared to depoliticize monetary policy.[124]

The current phase of EU fiscal and social policymaking has been, thus, defined as 'authoritarian', because 'it understands the market and social policies as structurally distinct from political and representative processes, and suggests that EU social policy is something to be managed by technocrats rather than decided by political actors'.[125] This trend clearly reflects one of the main manifestations of neoliberalisation mentioned in Chapter 1.

Nonetheless, the purported de-politicisation of fiscal and social policy is deceptive. As has been observed, '[t]he purpose of these rules is clear: they serve to force Member States into adjusting their social and economic policies towards a specific model',[126] that of neoliberalism and the neoliberal state. This model has precise normative and distributive implications that, inter alia, undermine the capacity of states to comply with their ESR obligations.

2.5 CONCLUSIONS

After briefly introducing existing legal definitions of sovereign debt and outlining a general definition for this book's purposes, this chapter has described and discussed global trends in sovereign borrowing since the Second World War. It has noted how, especially since the 1970s, states have been increasingly relying on debt, global financial markets and international institutions to fund their ordinary sovereign functions, and sovereign debt has become a routine, market-based state-financing practice, with a pronounced transnational dimension. Furthermore, this chapter has noted, over the same period,

[124] Alasdair Roberts, *The Logic of Discipline: Global Capitalism and the Architecture of Government* (Oxford University Press, 2011), p. 57.

[125] Floris de Witte, 'The Architecture of a "Social Market Economy"' (2015) *LSE Law Society and Economy Working Papers* 13/2015, 17. See also Matthias Goldmann, 'Human Rights and Democracy in Economic Policy Reform: The European COVID-19 Response under Scrutiny' (2020) 24 *The International Journal of Human Rights* 9, 1290–1310.

[126] De Witte, 'The Architecture of a "Social Market Economy"', 15.

a steady and significant increase in global public debt levels, a trend that has been exacerbated by the 2008 Global Financial Crisis and the COVID-19 pandemic. For the first time since the Second World War, in 2020 global debt has reached again wartime levels. The chapter has further noted some concerning changes in the structure and composition trend of current sovereign debt.

In discussing the possible reasons for this extraordinary peacetime surge in global debt, this chapter has placed particular emphasis on more systemic analyses, in particular that of Wolfgang Streeck, which considers growing indebtedness and the emergence of the debt state as a political strategy adopted by capitalist democracies to (temporarily) cope with (and delay the effects of) the failure of democratic capitalism's promise of economic and human progress (a failure evidenced, inter alia, by the unrelenting expansion of poverty and inequality across the world). In this sense, debt surges and crises increasingly often are the results of the socialisation of risks, failures and costs that are rather inherent to the currently prevailing global economic order. This has been the case, for instance, not only of the steady expansion of global public debt since the 1970s but also of the Global Financial Crisis, and the debt explosion that is currently accompanying the COVID-19 pandemic.

Increasing indebtedness is also at the roots of the emergence, inter alia in Europe, of the so-called Consolidation State, that is, one that has managed to institutionalise – including by legal means – the primacy of its market (debt) obligations over its other political (including human rights) ones. In Europe, such transformation has been advanced by the post-crisis reform of the legal framework of the EMU, a reform that has reinforced – as this chapter has argued – its neoliberalisation. The new European economic rules stand in potential contradiction with the requirements of the international ESR regime, something that will be discussed in the Chapter 3. More generally, the present chapter intended to emphasise that any consideration of the debt–ESR relationship, and of relevant international law, should proceed from a different understanding of the meaning of contemporary sovereign debt in the global economy, and its actual implications for the realisation of ESR.

3

Economic and Social Rights and Neoliberalism

3.1 INTRODUCTION

Today, economic and social rights (ESR) are an established component of the international human rights framework, on a par, at least in principle, with civil and political rights. Over the years, the distinctions between 'generations' and 'dichotomies' of rights that were brought into the international human rights discourse by the ideological frictions of the Cold War – inter alia, between positive/negative, progressive/immediate, expensive/cost-free, vague/precise rights – have gradually faded in favour of a comprehensive human rights approach that acknowledges the indivisibility, interdependence and interrelatedness of all human rights.[1] It is now generally accepted, especially since the publication of Henry Shue's previously mentioned seminal work,[2] that if any distinctions exist, they are between duties rather than rights.

Despite developments in theory, law and practice, however, the inexorable regression in the enjoyment of ESR that has been registered in Europe and elsewhere as a consequence of the recent financial, economic and sovereign debt crises, together with the fact that human rights did not have a significant role (if any) in the remedies devised by states and international institutions, rehabilitates timeworn allegations that ESR are mere 'interests', 'preferences', 'aspirations' or, worse, subjective and unjustified 'demands', rather than human rights enjoying legal protection under international law.

[1] Among several international declarations reaffirming such 'leading axiom' of human rights, see the Proclamation of Teheran, Final Act of the International Conference on Human Rights (Teheran, 22 April to 13 May 1968) A/CONF. 32/41 at 3 (1968), para. 13; Vienna Declaration and Programme of Action, adopted by the World Conference on Human Rights in Vienna on 25 June 1993, para. 5; UNGA, Res 60/1 of 16 September 2005, '2005 World Summit Outcome', A/RES/60/1 (24 October 2005), para. 13; UNGA, Res 60/251 of 15 March 2006, 'Human Rights Council', A/RES/60/251 (3 April 2006), Preamble.

[2] Shue, *Basic Rights*.

This chapter aims at introducing and critically reviewing the existing international legal framework on ESR and sovereign debt, specifically the nature and scope of states parties' obligations under the International Covenant on Economic, Social and Cultural Rights (ICESCR), and the more recent Guiding Principles elaborated by various human rights monitoring bodies and experts, to direct inter alia the debt-related conduct of states and other relevant actors in accordance with their existing human rights obligations. Considering their relevance for public budgets and sovereign financing, including state borrowing and lending, special attention will be paid, in Section 3.2, to the legal concepts of 'maximum available resources', 'non-retrogression' and 'international cooperation and assistance', and the clarification of their normative content by human rights monitoring bodies, in particular the Committee on Economic, Social and Cultural Rights (hereinafter, the CESCR).

This chapter essentially argues that, despite attempts at formally asserting the 'neutrality' of the ICESCR in respect of the economic system possibly needed to fully realise ESR, the economic policy measures recommended over the years particularly by the CESCR suggest that, to further the realisation of ESR, human rights bodies in effect still largely presume and promote a generally 'Keynesian'/'pro-cyclical' approach to economic and fiscal policy, and the implementation of a 'mixed' economy, characterised by the substantial participation of the state, also through the mobilisation and allocation of public resources for the realisation of social (and not exclusively economic) objectives (Section 3.3). This approach seems, therefore, destined to clash with the more neoliberal 'economic philosophy of governance'[3] currently embedded in, and after the crisis also more stringently enforceable under the existing global and European economic orders (as discussed in Chapter 2). To the contrary, some of the key post-crisis, especially austerity-related developments in the international ESR framework seem to point towards its increased neoliberalisation: an alignment with, rather than a counterweight to – as conventionally assumed – a neoliberalised conception of the economic and social order.

3.2 STATE OBLIGATIONS UNDER THE INTERNATIONAL COVENANT ON ECONOMIC, SOCIAL AND CULTURAL RIGHTS

Before embarking on the analysis of the normative content of the ICESCR, it is essential to briefly introduce the different categories of states' obligations

3 Report of the Special Rapporteur on Extreme Poverty and Human Rights, UN Doc. A/73/396 (26 September 2018), para. 67.

contained in the Covenant, as well as the role of the CESCR, particularly in relation to the clarification of the Covenant's normative content.

The Covenant includes thirty-one provisions divided into five parts. Part I is constituted of only one provision, article 1, recognising the right to self-determination. Part II, articles 2 to 5, covers states parties' general (or basic) obligations. These discipline state conduct with regard to the Covenant as a whole, and apply to all the substantive rights recognised in Part III, articles 6 to 15, which contain states' specific (or rights-based) obligations.

In particular, article 2(1) ICESCR describes the general legal obligations of states parties under the Covenant, while the remaining articles of Part II contain, respectively, a prohibition of discrimination (art. 2(2)), the duty to treat men and women equally in the enjoyment of the Covenant's rights (art. 3), a limitation clause (art. 4) and the Covenant's interpretation rules (art. 5).

In addition to the right to self-determination (art. 1), the other substantive rights recognised in the Covenant are the rights to equality for men and women (art. 3); to work and to just and favourable conditions of work (arts. 6 and 7); to form and join trade unions, and to strike (art. 8); to social security, including social insurance (art. 9); to protection and assistance for the family, and the prohibition of child labour (art. 10); to an adequate standard of living for oneself and one's family, including adequate food, clothing and housing, and to the continuous improvement of living conditions (art. 11); to the highest attainable level of physical and mental health (art. 12); to education (art. 13); to free and compulsory primary education (art. 14); to take part in cultural life, to benefit from scientific progress, and to benefit from the protection of scientific, literary or artistic production of which one is the author (art. 15).

Part IV of the Covenant, articles 16 to 25, establishes the supervisory system, and, lastly, Part V, articles 26 to 31, contains miscellaneous provisions relating to matters such as ratification and entry into force.

3.2.1 *The Committee on Economic, Social and Cultural Rights and the Interpretation of the ICESCR*

As is well known, the International Covenant on Civil and Political Rights (ICCPR)[4] and the ICESCR were initially equipped with very different supervisory systems. Differently from the ICCPR – which provided for three monitoring procedures, that is, state reporting, inter-state complaints and

[4] International Covenant on Civil and Political Rights (adopted 16 December 1966, entered into force 3 January 1976) 999 UNTS 3.

individual communications,[5] and established the Human Rights Committee (art. 28 ICCPR) – the ICESCR devised only vague state reporting obligations and did not establish a special supervisory body but assigned the task of supervision of states' compliance with the Covenant's provisions to the Economic and Social Council (ECOSOC).[6] In 1976, however, the ECOSOC laid down more specific implementation procedures and set up a subsidiary organ – the Sessional Working Group on the Implementation of the ICESCR – to *assist* the Council in the consideration of state reports.[7] In 1982, the Working Group was partially reorganised and renamed as the Sessional Working Group of Governmental Experts on the Implementation of the International Covenant,[8] before being eventually renamed, in 1985, as the CESCR.[9] The latter started its work with independent experts in 1987.

It must be noted that, formally speaking, the CESCR is a subsidiary organ of the ECOSOC. It is, therefore, a sui generis treaty-body, which differs quite significantly from other human rights committees. Its mandate and authority do not derive from the Covenant itself, but from an ECOSOC resolution. Hence, differently from other human rights monitoring bodies, which are directly responsible before the states parties for their supervisory activities, the CESCR is formally responsible before the ECOSOC.[10] This special legal

5 The latter mechanism is provided under the Optional Protocol to the International Covenant on Civil and Political Rights (adopted 16 December 1966, entered into force 23 March 1976) 999 UNTS 171.

6 ICESCR, Part IV, Articles 16 to 21.

7 ECOSOC Res 1988 (LX) (11 May 1976), 'Procedures for the Implementation of the International Covenant on Economic, Social and Cultural Rights', E/C.12/1989/4 (27 October 1988), and ECOSOC Decision 1978/10 (3 May 1978), 'Composition of the Sessional Working Group on the Implementation of the International Covenant on Economic, Social and Cultural Rights', E/C.12/1989/4 (27 October 1988).

8 ECOSOC Res 1982/33 (6 May 1982), 'Review of the composition, organization and administrative arrangements of the Sessional Working Group (of Governmental Experts) on the Implementation of the International Covenant on Economic, Social and Cultural Rights', E/C.12/1989/4 (27 October 1988).

9 ECOSOC Res 1985/17 (28 May 1985), 'Review of the composition, organization and administrative arrangements of the Sessional Working Group of Governmental Experts on the Implementation of the International Covenant on Economic, Social and Cultural Rights', E/C.12/1989/4 (27 October 1988).

10 In 2014, the UN General Assembly recommended, in the context of the intergovernmental process on strengthening and enhancing the effective functioning of the human rights treaty body system, that the ECOSOC 'consider replacing the existing procedure for the election of experts to the Committee on Economic, Social and Cultural Rights with a meeting of states parties to the International Covenant on Economic, Social and Cultural Rights, while preserving the current structure, organization and administrative arrangement of the Committee as set forth in [ECOSOC] resolution 1985/17', UNGA Res 68/268, 'Strengthening and enhancing the effective functioning of the human rights treaty body

status has admittedly placed it, to some extent, in a vulnerable situation, the CESCR being strongly dependent on the ECOSOC – and 'sea changes' within it – for its existence.[11] Until now, however, this peculiar legal standing does not seem to have affected the work of the Committee nor, more importantly, the legitimacy with which it is perceived by states and other human rights monitoring bodies.[12]

Furthermore, in 2008, the Human Rights Council adopted an Optional Protocol to the International Covenant on Economic, Social and Cultural Rights (OP-ICESCR),[13] which entered into force on 5 May 2013 and, as of 2020, has been ratified by 26[14] of the 171 states parties to the ICESCR.

The OP-ICESCR establishes three new monitoring procedures, this time formally entrusted to the CESCR. Firstly, an individual complaints procedure, largely mirroring the one foreseen by the ICCPR, although with some differences, among which the possibility to submit communications by or on behalf of groups of individuals is certainly remarkable.[15] Secondly, an inter-state complaints procedure, allowing a state party claiming that another state party is not fulfilling its obligations under the Covenant to refer the matter to

system', Resolution adopted by the General Assembly on 9 April 2014, UN Doc. A/RES/68/268 (21 April 2014), para. 11.

11 Matthew C. R. *Craven, The International Covenant on Economic, Social and Cultural Rights: A Perspective on its Development* (Oxford: Clarendon Press, 1998), p. 51; Magdalena Sepúlveda, *The Nature of the Obligations under the International Covenant on Economic, Social and Cultural Rights* (Cambridge: Intersentia, 2003), p. 90. Craven has noted that the 'indirect' mandate of the CESCR could potentially raise a conflict of competence with the ECOSOC similar to that experienced by the Committee of Independent Experts to the European Social Charter vis-à-vis the Governmental Committee, although in practice the ECOSOC has manifested very little interest in the work of the Committee. However, to bring the Committee formally in line with the other human rights treaty bodies would require an amendment to the ICESCR, an arduous endeavour whose outcome would eventually bind only the states parties that will accept it, *The International Covenant on Economic, Social and Cultural Rights*, p. 51.

12 Riedel, Giacca and Golay, *Economic, Social and Cultural Rights in International Law*, p. 7; Philip Alston, *The United Nations and Human Rights: A Critical Appraisal* (Oxford: Clarendon Press, 1992), pp. 488–489; Craven, *The International Covenant on Economic, Social and Cultural Rights*, p. 51. For an extensive analysis of the legitimacy of the Committee and its work, particularly its interpretation of the Covenant, see Sepúlveda, *The Nature of the Obligations*, p. 87 ff.

13 Optional Protocol to the International Covenant on Economic, Social and Cultural Rights (adopted 10 December 2008, entered into force 5 May 2013) A/RES/63/117.

14 I.e. Argentina, Armenia, *Belgium*, Bolivia, Bosnia and Herzegovina, Cabo Verde, Central African Republic, Costa Rica, Ecuador, El Salvador, *Finland*, *France*, Gabon, Honduras, *Italy*, *Luxemburg*, Maldives, Mongolia, Montenegro, Niger, *Portugal*, San Marino, *Slovakia*, *Spain*, Uruguay and Venezuela (countries in italics are members of the European Union). Greece has not yet ratified the Protocol, hence it has only state reporting obligations.

15 Art. 2 OP-ICESCR.

the CESCR (only, though, where both states have expressly declared that they recognise the competence of the CESCR to receive and consider such communications).[16] Thirdly, an enquiry procedure, which can be initiated by the CESCR, on its own initiative, upon receipt of reliable information on serious, grave or systematic violations by a state party to the Covenant (in this case as well, enquiries may only involve states parties who have explicitly recognized the specific competence of the Committee, and states can at any time withdraw their declaration, by notification to the secretary general).[17]

The OP-ICESCR potentially represents an historic step forward for the effective protection of ESR, offering additional means to the CESCR to strengthen its interpretation of the Covenant. However, given its recent entry into force and the limited number of ratifications, the jurisprudence of the Committee is still limited compared to that of other human rights treaty monitoring bodies. Although, especially since 2017, it has experienced a significant increase in the average number of communications received,[18] as of March 2020 the Committee has adopted views only on seven cases.[19]

Immediately after its creation, however, and well before the proposal of an Optional Protocol had even come into existence, the Committee had substantially moved beyond the 'advisory' role assigned to it by the ECOSOC, gradually emerging as 'the principal forum in which the implications of the concept of ESR are being explored'.[20] Especially through the practice of its General Comments,[21] as well as the adoption of Concluding Observations, Statements and Letters addressed to the states parties, the Committee has had a critical role in generating interpretative clarity on the normative content of

16 Art. 10 OP-ICESCR.

17 Art. 11 OP-ICESCR. As of 2017, only Belgium, El Salvador, Finland, San Marino and Portugal have made declarations under arts. 10 and 11 OP-ICESCR.

18 UNGA, 'Status of the human rights treaty body system', Report of the Secretary-General, UN Doc. A/74/643 (10 January 2020), para. 16.

19 Views adopted by the Committee in the cases *Rosario Gómez-Limón Pardo* (Spain), 5 March 2020, communication No. 052/2018, UN Doc. E/C.12/67/D/52/2018; *López Albán and others* (Spain), 11 October 2019, communication No. 037/201, UN Doc. E/C.12/66/D/37/2018; *S.C. and G.P.* (Italy), 7 March 2019, communication No. 022/2017, UN Doc. E/C.12/65/D/22/2017; *Trujillo Calero* (Ecuador), 26 March 2018, communication No. 010/2015, UN Doc. E/C.12/63/D/10/2015; *Ben Djazia and others* (Spain), 21 July 2017, communication No. 005/2015, UN Doc. E/C.12/61/D/5/201; *López Rodríguez* (Spain), 20 April 2016, communication No. 001/2013, UN Doc. E/C.12/57/D/1/2013; and *I.D.G.* (Spain), 13 October 2015, communication No. 002/2014, UN Doc. E/C.12/55/D/2/2014.

20 Philip Alston and Bruno Simma, 'Second Session of the UN Committee on Economic, Social and Cultural Rights' (1988) 82 *American Journal of International Law* 3, 604; Sepúlveda, *The Nature of the Obligations*, p. 32.

21 To date, the CESCR has adopted 25 General Comments.

the Covenant.[22] It must be emphasised, however, that the Committee's observations, comments and views and, consequently, the interpretations of the Covenant therein expressed, are not per se binding upon states parties. They have, nonetheless, considerable legal weight[23] and seem to be widely accepted, as reflected in the states parties' practice before the Committee, as well as by a plethora of resolutions and decisions adopted by states in international fora.[24] With regard to the Committee's Concluding Observations, it has been noted, for instance, that

> while the Committee's concluding observations, in particular suggestions and recommendations, may not carry legally binding status, they are indicative of the opinion of the only expert body entrusted with and capable of making such pronouncements. Consequently, for states parties to ignore or not act on such views would be to show bad faith in implementing their Covenant-based obligations. In a number of instances, changes in policy, practice and law have been registered at least partly in response to the Committee's concluding observations.[25]

Over the years, key academics and civil society actors have also contributed to the elucidation of the normative content of the ICESCR, through the adoption of international expert opinions. Prominent among these are, in ascending chronological order, the 1986 Limburg Principles on the Implementation of the International Covenant on Economic, Social and Cultural Rights (hereinafter, the Limburg Principles);[26] the 'basic postulates' on the nature of state obligations with respect to economic, social and cultural rights, proposed in 1992 by Danilo Türk, then Special Rapporteur of the Sub-Commission on Prevention of Discrimination and Protection of Minorities;[27] the 1997 Maastricht Guidelines on Violations of Economic, Social and Cultural Rights (hereinafter, the 'Maastricht Guidelines');[28] and the 2011 Maastricht Principles on Extraterritorial

22 Craven, *The International Covenant on Economic, Social and Cultural Rights*, p. 57.

23 Carlo Focarelli, *Trattato di Diritto Internazionale* (Torino: UTET, 2015), p. 1017 ff.

24 Sepúlveda, *The Nature of the Obligations*, pp. 88 and 110; Craven, *The International Covenant on Economic, Social and Cultural Rights*, pp. 91–92.

25 OHCHR, 'Fact Sheet No.16 (Rev.1), The Committee on Economic, Social and Cultural Rights' (May 1996), www.ohchr.org/Documents/Publications/FactSheet16rev.1en.pdf (last accessed March 2017).

26 'The Limburg Principles on the Implementation of the International Covenant on Economic, Social and Cultural Rights' (1987) 9 *Human Rights Quarterly* 122.

27 Commission on Human Rights, Sub-Commission on Prevention of Discrimination and Protection of Minorities, 'The realization of economic, social and cultural rights', Second progress report prepared by Mr Danilo Türk, Special Rapporteur, E/CN.4/Sub.2/1991/17 (18 July 1991).

28 'The Maastricht Guidelines on Violations of Economic, Social and Cultural Rights' (1998) 20 *Human Rights Quarterly* 691.

Obligations of States in the Area of Economic, Social and Cultural Rights (hereinafter, the 'Maastricht Principles').[29] Reference to these documents, which, according to their authors, predominantly reflect the state of international law at the time of their adoption,[30] will be made throughout the following sections. However, it must be emphasised that, being interpretative guidelines and principles adopted by groups of experts, these instruments do not, as such, represent legally binding norms, although they are frequently recalled by other human rights monitoring bodies.

3.2.2 *States Parties' General Obligations under Article 2(1) ICESCR, Economic Policy and Post-Crisis Interpretative Developments: A Neoliberalised Approach?*

Article 2(1) ICESCR describes the nature of the general legal obligations undertaken by states parties and, according to the CESCR, it 'must be seen as having a dynamic relationship with all of the other [Covenant's] provisions'.[31] It provides that

> Each State Party to the present Covenant undertakes to take steps, individually and through international assistance and co-operation, especially economic and technical, to the maximum of its available resources, with a view to achieving progressively the full realization of the rights recognized in the present Covenant by all appropriate means, including particularly the adoption of legislative measures.

The main elements of article 2(1) will be presented here in brief general terms while, in the following subsections, I will more extensively discuss the three elements that have a special bearing in relation to the issue of sovereign debt, that is the prohibition on non-retrogression, the notion of maximum available resources and the duty of international assistance and cooperation.

Firstly, article 2(1) requires states to take steps *with a view to achieving progressively the full realization of the Covenant's rights*. The concept of 'progressive realisation' is considered to be in many ways the linchpin of the

29 Other important expert contributions are the 1995 Bangalore Declaration and Plan of Action on the realisation of economic, social and cultural rights (specifically examining the role of lawyers with regard to ESR) in 'Special Issue' (1995) *ICJ Review* 55, 219–227; and, at the Latin American level, the 1998 Quito Declaration on the Enforcement and Realisation of Economic, Social and Cultural Rights in Latin America and the Caribbean (1999) 2 *Yale Human Rights and Development Law Journal* 6.

30 Sepúlveda, *The Nature of the Obligations*, p. 64.

31 CESCR, General Comment No. 3, 'The nature of states parties' obligations (art. 2, para. 1)', E/1991/23 (1 January 1991) (hereinafter, 'GC3').

whole Covenant.[32] It was deployed by the drafters as a 'necessary flexibility device, reflecting the realities of the real world and the difficulties involved for any country in ensuring full realization of economic, social and cultural rights',[33] in line with their persuasion that such full realisation cannot be achieved in a short period of time, that progress towards that goal cannot be universal but only relative to states' available resources, and hence that economic circumstances must be taken into account in determining the scope of states parties' obligations.[34]

Although the concept of progressive realisation has been often mistakenly taken to imply that ESR can be realised only when a country reaches a certain level of economic development, it must be stressed that this is neither the intent nor the legal interpretation of this provision.[35] As the language of article 2(1) makes clear, states parties have voluntarily committed to the *full realisation* of economic, social and cultural rights, which is the ultimate goal of the ICESCR (although the exact meaning of this goal – when is an economic, social or cultural right 'fully realised'? – remains elusive). Thus, progressive realisation is essentially a means to this end.[36] states cannot use the notion as a pretext for failing to comply with or for indefinitely deferring their efforts to ensure the enjoyment of the Covenant's rights; nor can they justify limitations of or derogation from ESR on that basis.[37] As the OHCHR has usefully explained, the standard of progressive realisation 'must be viewed, used and acted upon by States in a positive way to prevent or reverse any regressive policies, laws or practices negatively affecting the full enjoyment of economic, social and cultural rights'.[38]

Bearing this qualification in mind, states parties' obligations under article 2(1) ICESCR, according to the subsequent interpretations of the Committee, can be outlined as follows: (a) states must take steps, immediately and continuously, towards the progressive achievement of the full realisation of ESR,

32 Philip Alston and Gerard Quinn, 'The Nature and Scope of States Parties' Obligations under the International Covenant on Economic, Social and Cultural Rights' (1987) 9 *Human Rights Quarterly* 173.

33 CESCR, GC3, para. 9.

34 Alston and Quinn, 'The Nature and Scope of States Parties' Obligations', 172 ff; Aoife Nolan and Mira Dutschke, 'Article 2(1) ICESCR and States Parties' Obligations: Whither the Budget?' (2010) 3 *European Human Rights Law Review*, 280–289, p. 282.

35 OHCHR, *Economic, Social and Cultural Rights: Handbook for National Human Rights Institutions* (United Nations, 2005), p. 10.

36 Nolan and Dutschke, 'Article 2(1) ICESCR', 282.

37 Limburg Principles, principle 21; Maastricht Guidelines, guideline 8; OHCHR, *Economic, Social and Cultural Rights*, p. 11.

38 OHCHR, *Economic, Social and Cultural Rights*, 12.

(a)(1) to the maximum of their available resources, and (a)(2) individually and through international cooperation and assistance; (b) states must immediately ensure the satisfaction, at the very least, of minimum essential levels of each substantive right (minimum core obligation); (c) states must protect, at any time and regardless of available resources, the most vulnerable and disadvantaged members or groups of society; and (d) states must not take any deliberately retrogressive measures.

I will now briefly outline the obligations under the points (a), (b) and (c), while reserving the following sections to analyse those under the points (d), (a) (1) and (a)(2).

States parties have *(a)* an obligation to take, 'within a reasonably short time after the Covenant's entry into force' (and continuously thereafter), steps that must be 'deliberate, concrete and targeted as clearly as possible towards meeting the obligations recognized in the Covenant'.[39] This is, therefore, an *immediate* obligation. 'Steps' should engage 'all appropriate means', including (but not limited to) the adoption of legislative measures, the provision of judicial remedies, as well as 'administrative, financial, educational and social measures'.[40] Furthermore, as suggested by the ordinary meaning of the adjective 'progressive' (i.e. 'to make continuous forward movement'),[41] progressive realisation has been interpreted as requiring states parties to *continuously* take 'forward' steps, both in 'qualitative' and 'quantitative' terms (i.e. improving the implementation of the rights as well as gradually expanding both the number and the range of people who can access the rights), towards the full realisation of ESR.[42]

Rooted in the immediate obligation to take steps are also other immediate obligations, first of all *(b)* an obligation to ensure the satisfaction of, at the very least, minimum essential levels of each of the Covenant's rights, or the so called 'minimum core' obligation.[43] In General Comment No. 3, in fact, the Committee underlined that 'if the Covenant were to be read in such a way as not to establish such a minimum core obligation, it would be largely deprived of its raison d'être'.[44]

What is to be meant by 'minimum essential levels' in relation to each of the substantive rights recognised in the ICESCR has been further clarified by the

39 CESCR, GC3, para. 2.

40 *Ibid.*, paras. 4–5 and 7; Limburg Principles, principles 16–20.

41 Sepúlveda, *The Nature of the Obligations*, p. 319.

42 OHCHR, *Economic, Social and Cultural Rights*, p. 12; Nolan and Dutschke, 'Article 2(1) ICESCR', 284; Sepúlveda, *The Nature of the Obligations*, pp. 319–323.

43 CESCR, GC3, para. 10; Maastricht Guidelines, guideline 9.

44 CESCR, GC3, para. 10.

Committee in its General Comments on the specific rights,[45] and in some of the Concluding Observations.

The minimum core obligation consequently entails, according to the Committee, that a 'State party in which any significant number of individuals is deprived of essential foodstuffs, or essential primary health care, of basic shelter and housing, or of the most basic forms of education is, prima facie, failing to discharge its obligations under the Covenant'.[46]

Also rooted in the duty to take immediate and continuous steps to progressively achieve the full realisation of ESR is *(c)* an obligation to protect at any time, even and especially in times of severe resources constraints, the most vulnerable and disadvantaged members and groups of society through the adoption of relatively low-cost targeted programmes.[47]

3.2.2.1 Retrogressive Measures

The obligation for states parties *not to take any deliberately retrogressive measures* is, instead, rooted in the idea of progressive realisation. A retrogressive measure has been usefully defined by Magdalena Sepúlveda as

45 For instance, with regard to the right to the highest attainable standard of physical and mental health (article 12), the CESCR has explained that '[. . .] these core obligations include at least the following obligations: (a) To ensure the right of access to health facilities, goods and services on a non-discriminatory basis, especially for vulnerable or marginalized groups; (b) To ensure access to the minimum essential food which is nutritionally adequate and safe, to ensure freedom from hunger to everyone; (c) To ensure access to basic shelter, housing and sanitation, and an adequate supply of safe and potable water; (d) To provide essential drugs, as from time to time defined under the WHO Action Programme on Essential Drugs; (e) To ensure equitable distribution of all health facilities, goods and services; (f) To adopt and implement a national public health strategy and plan of action, on the basis of epidemiological evidence, addressing the health concerns of the whole population; the strategy and plan of action shall be devised, and periodically reviewed, on the basis of a participatory and transparent process; they shall include methods, such as right to health indicators and benchmarks, by which progress can be closely monitored; the process by which the strategy and plan of action are devised, as well as their content, shall give particular attention to all vulnerable or marginalized groups', see CESCR, General Comment No. 14, 'The right to the highest attainable standard of health (art. 12)', E/C.12/2000/4 (11 August 2000), para. 43 (hereinafter, 'GC14').

46 CESCR, GC3, para. 10.

47 *Ibid.*, para. 12; General Comment No. 5, 'Persons with disabilities' (1 January 1995), para. 10; General Comment No. 6, 'The economic, social and cultural rights of older persons' (7 October 1996), para. 17; General Comment No. 12, 'The right to adequate food (art. 11)', E/C.12/1999/5 (12 May 1999), para. 28; GC 14, para. 18; General Comment No. 17, 'The right of everyone to benefit from the protection of the moral and material interests resulting from any scientific, literary or artistic production of which he or she is the author (article 15, paragraph 1 (c), of the Covenant)', E/C.12/GC/17 (12 January 2006), para. 20; General Comment No. 18, 'The right to work (art. 6)', E/C.12/GC/18 (6 February 2006), para. 12 (hereinafter, respectively, 'GC5', 'GC6', 'GC12', 'GC17' and 'GC18').

> any measure that implies a step back in the level of protection accorded to the rights contained in the Covenant which is the consequence of an intentional decision by the State.[48]

Examples of retrogressive measures could be the introduction of a legislation or policy with a direct collateral negative effect on the enjoyment of ESR, or containing discriminatory provisions, or abrogating ESR-favourable legislation (unless outdated) without replacing it with equally or more consistent law or with compensatory measures; or an unjustified reduction in public expenditures devoted to implementing ESR, in the absence of adequate compensatory measures aimed to protect the injured individuals.[49]

Retrogressive measures are prima facie prohibited and amount to a violation of the ICESCR,[50] so that states have the burden of proving their compatibility with the Covenant.

To that aim, the CESCR has outlined, in its General Comments No. 3 and No. 19, the requirements that states must fulfil for a retrogressive measure to be considered permissible under the Covenant. These included the need for a state to prove that any such measure received 'the most careful consideration' and was 'fully justified', 'by reference to the totality of the rights provided for in the Covenant', and 'in the context of the full use of the maximum available resources'.[51] Furthermore, the CESCR noted that, in assessing the compatibility of retrogressive measures with the Covenant, it

> will look carefully at whether: (a) there was reasonable justification for the action; (b) alternatives were comprehensively examined; (c) there was genuine participation of affected groups [...]; (d) the measures were directly or indirectly discriminatory; (e) the measures will have a sustained impact on the realization of the right to social security, an unreasonable impact on acquired social security rights or whether an individual or group is deprived of access to the minimum essential level of social security; and (f) whether there was an independent review of the measures [...].[52]

48 Sepúlveda, *The Nature of the Obligations*, p. 323, on the basis of CESCR's General Comment No. 4, 'The right to adequate housing (art. 11, para. 1)', E/1992/23 (13 December 1991), para. 1 (hereinafter, 'GC4').

49 Sepúlveda, *The Nature of the Obligations*, p. 324.

50 Statements concerning the presumption of the impermissibility of retrogressive measures can be found, inter alia, in General Comment No. 13, 'The right to education (art. 13)', E/C.12/1999/10 (8 December 1999), para. 45 (hereinafter, 'GC13') and GC14, para. 32; Maastricht Guidelines, guideline 14(e).

51 CESCR, GC3, para. 9.

52 CESCR, General Comment No. 19, 'The right to social security (art. 9)', E/C.12/GC/19 (4 February 2008), para. 42 (hereinafter, 'GC19').

Several commentators have noted that, so far, the CESCR has not seriously monitored the adoption of deliberately retrogressive measures by states parties and that, in the few cases where the Committee has actually engaged with measures of this kind, it has been far too permissive.[53] Hence, when, on the occasion of the more recent economic and debt crises, the prohibition of retrogressive measures could have assumed exceptional relevance in containing the negative ESR impacts of the fiscal consolidation measures adopted by several countries, the Committee had not yet developed clear-enough benchmarks to urge states effectively to comply with this prohibition.

3.2.2.1.1 POST-CRISIS DEVELOPMENTS: A NEOLIBERALISED APPROACH TO NON-RETROGRESSION? In 2012, the CESCR addressed to states parties an important Letter on austerity measures,[54] spelling out some rather different criteria to assess the compatibility with the Covenant of the retrogressive measures in the meanwhile increasingly adopted by a growing number of states parties in the context of their fiscal consolidation efforts. While acknowledging that 'states parties have, of course, a margin of appreciation within which to set national economic, social and cultural policies that respect, protect, and fulfil the Covenant'[55] and that 'some adjustments in the implementation of some Covenant rights are at times inevitable',[56] the Committee emphasised that, to be compatible with the ICESCR, any proposed adjustment has to meet the following requirements: (1) it must be a *temporary* measure covering only the period of crisis; (2) the measure must be *necessary and proportionate*, in the sense that the adoption of any other policy, or failure to act, would be more detrimental to ESR; (3) the measure must *not be discriminatory* and must comprise all possible measures, including tax measures, to support social transfers to mitigate inequalities that can grow in times of crisis and to ensure that the rights of the disadvantaged and marginalized individuals and groups are not disproportionately affected and (4) it must identify the minimum core content of rights or a social protection floor, as developed by the International Labour Organization, and *ensure the protection of this core content at all times*.[57]

53 Sepúlveda, *The Nature of the Obligations*, pp. 324–325, attributing the Committee's flexible approach to the fact that an assessment of whether states have actually adopted such measures, would require to undertake complex analyses and consider a wide range of information that are usually out of the Committee's reach.

54 Letter dated 16 May 2012 addressed by the Chairperson of the Committee on Economic, Social and Cultural Rights to states parties to the International Covenant on Economic, Social and Cultural Rights (hereinafter, '2012 Letter on austerity measures').

55 *Ibid.*, 1.

56 *Ibid.*

57 *Ibid* (emphasis added).

The same criteria were later reiterated by the Committee in a 2016 Statement on Public Debt, Austerity Measures and the International Covenant on Economic, Social and Cultural Rights.[58]

As it has been correctly observed, with its 2012 Letter the CESCR has established a new 'emergency regime' for the implementation of ESR obligations, which amounts to a 'near-suspension of some key obligations'[59] and which may pose serious dangers for the realisation of ESR.

In fact, the pre-2012 approach to non-retrogression granted significant everyday discretion and flexibility to states in the fulfilment of their obligations under the Covenant through the combination of article 2(1), article 4, the less prescriptive formulation of individual rights and the doctrine of non-retrogression as formulated in the General Comments No. 3 and 19, while denying, to the contrary – in accordance with the more general formulation of the ICESCR – the need for derogations, special powers or the suspension of legal frameworks. This quality was particularly apt to ensure consistency of outcomes, the value of consistent protection of ESR, and, since obligations remained intact also in emergency situations, the preservation of avenues for contesting retrogressive measures.[60]

The 2012 Letter, on the contrary, has produced a substantial alteration of the doctrine of non-retrogression, towards a more 'adaptive approach' grounded on 'emergency accommodation'.[61] It now provides only four criteria (compared with the previous eight), two of which, that is, non-discrimination and the protection of the minimum core, 'cannot even properly be described as conditions specific to the taking of retrogressive measures [. . .] [but] are general, longstanding and immediate obligations that exist beyond the circumstances of retrogression'.[62] Hence, the non-retrogression test is de facto reduced to two criteria, largely mirroring the derogations regimes provided for by the International Covenant on Civil and Political Rights (ICCPR), the European Convention of Human Rights (ECHR) and the American Convention of Human Rights (ACHR): to be justified under the Covenant, retrogressive measures must be *temporary*, and *necessary and proportionate*.[63]

58 CESCR, 'Statement on Public Debt, Austerity Measures and the International Covenant on Economic, Social and Cultural Rights', E/C.12/2016/1 (22 July 2016) (hereinafter, '2016 Statement on Public Debt'), para. 4.

59 Ben T. C. Warwick, 'Socio-Economic Rights During Economic Crises: A Changed Approach to Retrogression' (2016) 65 *International and Comparative Law Quarterly* 1, 250.

60 *Ibid.*, 254.

61 *Ibid.*, 257.

62 *Ibid.*

63 *Ibid.*, 257–258.

Besides the substantive concerns and uncertainties raised by these new standards, the 2012 Letter and 2016 Statement require further attention as they seem to have adopted, and transposed into international human rights law, neoliberal assumptions.

As it has been noted, the Committee's Letter strongly 'relie[d] on rhetorical devices to show deference to states and inflate the importance of (neo-liberal) market-based idea(l)s'.[64] When asked to address the then intensifying adoption of austerity by the states parties, the Committee passively ingested a characterisation of the situation, at the time, as one of crisis that automatically demanded responses of a specific economic nature.[65] The Committee never questioned that austerity measures were the most appropriate means to cope with the crisis, despite their admittedly negative impact on ESR, nor whether states were actually in good faith when maintaining that austerity was their only option. On the contrary, the Committee endorsed the neoliberal idea that 'a lack of growth [...] can lead to regression in the enjoyment of [ESR]', and that 'some adjustments in the implementation of some Covenant rights are at times inevitable',[66] without questioning, however, the possible sources and reality of such 'inevitability'. In its 2016 Statement, the Committee even asserted that conditionality is not necessarily detrimental to ESR and that, on the contrary, 'the adoption of fiscal consolidation programmes may be necessary for the implementation of economic and social rights'.[67]

The Letter and following Statement de facto seem to attempt at reconciling austerity with socio-economic rights, by accommodating the requirements of ESR, notably the prohibition of retrogression, to neoliberal market imperatives, rather than the other way around. This approach is visible, for instance, in the following statement of the Committee:

> Decisions to adopt austerity measures are always difficult and complex, and the Committee is acutely aware that this may lead many States to take decisions with painful effects, especially when these austerity measures are taken in a recession.[68]

Portraying state conduct that could actually constitute a violation of a legal right, as a decision with 'painful' but seemingly 'inculpable' consequences, inevitably undermines the legal standing and protection of socio-economic rights.

64 *Ibid.*, 256.
65 *Ibid.*
66 CESCR, '2012 Letter on austerity measures'.
67 CESCR, '2016 Statement on Public Debt', para. 2 (emphasis added).
68 CESCR, '2012 Letter on austerity measures' (emphasis added).

3.2.2.2 Maximum Available Resources

As mentioned earlier, the obligation of states parties to take steps under article 2(1) ICESCR is qualified by the same article's reference *to the maximum of their available resources.*[69] As it is well known, a similar specification was not deployed in the ICCPR, owing to the idea, prevalent at the time of the Covenants' drafting, that ESR imposed positive and expensive obligations, while civil and political rights were essentially negative and 'cost-free'. It is plausible that, anchored in this perception, the limitation to the maximum of available resources was presented by some states' representatives, at the time, as a means to exclude that the ICESCR could be interpreted as requiring states to devote all their resources, without exception, to the realisation of ESR.[70]

Today, however, it is well established that the realisation of all human rights, not just ESR, necessitates resources. At the very least, in fact, resources are needed to establish an institutional structure to secure compliance also with civil and political rights.[71] Nonetheless, the distinct legal weight assigned to the concept of maximum available resources in relation to ESR obligations remains, as this represents an 'important qualifier'[72] to the obligation to take steps: although it does not alter the immediacy of this obligation, as the CESCR has clarified,[73] it inevitably restricts its scope.

3.2.2.2.1 AVAILABLE RESOURCES Neither the Covenant nor the CESCR has expressly defined what is meant by the expression 'available resources'. It seems plausible, however, as some commentators have noted, that the Covenant's drafters intended to refer not only to financial, but to other resources as well, broadly interpreted; and to the 'real' resources of a country, of which budgetary allocations are not necessarily an authoritative description.[74] The Committee, on

69 Similar provisions are included, with specific regard to ESR, in the Convention on the Rights of the Child (20 November 1989), art. 4, and the Convention on the Rights of Persons with Disabilities (13 December 2006), art. 4(2).

70 This view is supported, for instance, by a Statement by Mrs. Roosevelt emphasising that 'in a legal instrument it should be clear that a State was not required to use all its resources without exception but only the maximum which could be expended for a particular purpose without sacrificing essential services', 8 U.N. ESCOR C.4 (271st mtg.) at 12, UN Doc. E/CN.4/SR.271 (1952) (Mrs. Roosevelt, USA) 3, quoted in Alston and Quinn, 'The Nature and Scope of States Parties' Obligations', 178.

71 Sepúlveda, *The Nature of the Obligations*, p. 127. Sigrun Skogly, 'The Requirement of Using the "Maximum of Available Resources" for Human Rights Realisation: A Question of Quality as Well as Quantity?' (2012) 12 *Human Rights Law Review* 3, 395–396.

72 CESCR, '2016 Statement on Public Debt', para. 4.

73 *Ibid.*

74 Skogly, 'The Requirement of Using the "Maximum of Available Resources"', 398; Alston and Quinn, 'The Nature and Scope of States Parties' Obligations', 178.

its part, has repeatedly observed that 'available resources' refer to both the resources existing within a state and those available from the international community through international cooperation and assistance (on which see later, Section 3.2.2.3).[75]

Interestingly, in the matter of sovereign debt, it has been contended that funds that are necessary to service debt would be excluded from a state's available resources, as the state would be under a contractual obligation to use these funds to repay its debts, so that they would be in fact 'creditor property'.[76] However, it has been more convincingly observed that if funds owed as debt were excluded from the notion of available resources, many developing countries would simply not have any resources available to meet their ESR obligations. Moreover, states could then 'easily contract out of their [ESR] obligations by simply entering into financial transactions by which the country's resources would be bound',[77] without having to eventually provide any justification for giving precedence to debt repayment over social programmes. Hence, it has been correctly argued that

> being under a contractual obligation does not mean that the funds that need to be dedicated to its fulfilment are therefore not at the free disposition of the debtor. Instead, while it might give rise to claims for breach of contract if a debtor State does not fulfil its contractual obligations, the State is nevertheless, in principle, free to decide how to use these funds.[78]

3.2.2.2.2 RESOURCE ALLOCATION: THE ECONOMIC AND FISCAL POLICY MEASURES CALLED FOR UNDER THE ICESCR States parties maintain considerable discretion in determining both what their available resources are and how to allocate and use them.[79]

At the time of the Covenant's drafting, various states' representatives expressed their concern that attempts to dictate how states should allocate their resources for the realisation of ESR would have been 'unrealistic', considering that in drawing up their budgets, governments have to make very difficult choices of economic policy, a domain 'closely related to national sovereignty'[80]

75 CESCR, GC3, para. 13; CESCR, '2016 Statement on Public Debt', para. 5; Limburg Principles, principle 26.

76 Sabine Michalowski, 'Sovereign Debt and Social Rights: Legal Reflections on a Difficult Relationship' (2008) 8 *Human Rights Law Review* 1, 48.

77 *Ibid.*

78 *Ibid.*

79 Alston and Quinn, 'The Nature and Scope of States Parties' Obligations', 180.

80 *Ibid.*, quoting the Inter-American Commission on Human Rights on the issue of governmental discretion, *Annual Report of the Inter-American Commission on Human Rights 1979–1980*, OEA/Ser. G/CP/doc. 110/80 (1980), 151.

(this assertion clashes, today, with the reality of the increased supranational coordination of economic policies implemented both de jure and de facto under the current European and international economic regimes). Therefore, the Covenant remained silent on the matter.

More recently, the Committee has reiterated that it 'always respects the margin of appreciation of a state party to determine the optimum use of its resources and to adopt national policies and prioritize certain resource demands over others',[81] bearing in mind 'its own role as an international treaty body and the role of the State in formulating or adopting, funding and implementing laws and policies concerning economic, social and cultural rights'.[82] Nevertheless, states' discretion on the allocation and use of their available resources is not unlimited, nor is their conduct in this respect completely immune from scrutiny by the CESCR.[83] Over the years, the Committee has outlined, particularly in its General Comments and Concluding Observations, and in a 2007 Statement on the Evaluation of the obligation to take steps to the maximum available resources under the OP-ICESCR,[84] some indications on the conduct that is *required* or, more generally, *recommended* (the difference among the two notions is important, as will be discussed further below) to States Parties under the Covenant in relation to the use of their maximum available resources. These indications clearly have some significant budgetary and economic policy implications.

With regard to asserted *obligations*, the General Comments contain very limited and general indications, establishing only minimal standards, aimed, in effect, at excluding that states could deem themselves completely free in their resource allocation, or use resource constraints as a way out of their obligations under the Covenant. States parties are, in fact, required: (a) to *use their maximum available resources* in order to realise ESR, both the resources existing within the country and those available through international cooperation and assistance. States' unwillingness to do so amounts to a violation of the Covenant.[85] In this regard, states are also under a procedural obligation, inferred from the obligation to work out and adopt a detailed plan of action for the progressive implementation of each

81 CESCR, '2016 Statement on Public Debt', para. 12.

82 *Ibid.*, para. 11.

83 Alston and Quinn, 'The Nature and Scope of States Parties' Obligations', 180; Sepúlveda, *The Nature of the Obligations*, p. 315.

84 CESCR, 'An evaluation of the obligation to take steps to the "maximum of available resources" under an optional protocol to the Covenant', E/C.12/2007/1 (21 September 2007) (hereinafter, '2007 Statement on Maximum Available Resources').

85 CESCR, GC12; General Comment No. 15, 'The right to water (arts. 11 and 12)', E/C.12/2002/11 (20 January 2003) (hereinafter, 'GC15'); GC17; and GC18.

of the rights contained in the Covenant (principled policymaking), to give adequate consideration to the possible resources available to satisfy each of the Covenant's requirements.[86] (b) To *ensure the widest possible enjoyment* of the relevant rights under the prevailing circumstances, even where the available resources are demonstrably inadequate.[87] (c) To *protect the more vulnerable members of society* by the adoption of relatively low-cost targeted programmes, at any time, even and especially in times of severe resources constraints, whether caused by a process of adjustment, or economic recession or by other factors (prioritisation of the most vulnerable).[88] This requires, inter alia, the allocation by the state of adequate financial resources (e.g. for the effective implementation of poverty reduction programmes, or for social housing and rental subsidies),[89] and that resources should not be allocated to benefit already advantaged social groups at the expense of other, more vulnerable segments of society. (d) Where states are claiming to be unable to carry out even their minimum core obligations for reasons behind their control, to *demonstrate that every effort has been made* to use all the resources that are at their disposition in an effort to satisfy, as a matter of priority, such obligations (prioritisation of minimum core, and burden of proof).[90]

The relationship between the notion of maximum available resources and the minimum core obligation deserves to be addressed briefly in greater detail. In fact, whether minimum core obligations are (or not) completely 'resource-independent' is not entirely clear from the Committee's work, which also seems to contradict the Maastricht Guidelines on the point. In addition to the provision mentioned earlier at point (d), in its General Comment No. 3 the Committee acknowledged that 'any assessment as to whether a State has discharged its minimum core obligation must also take account of resource constraints applying within the country concerned'.[91] The Maastricht Guidelines, on the contrary, provide that 'minimum core

86 CESCR, General Comment No. 1, 'Reporting by States Parties', E/1989/22 (27 July 1981), para. 4 (hereinafter, 'GC1'); Alston and Quinn, 'The Nature and Scope of States Parties' Obligations', 181; Nolan and Dutschke, 'Article 2(1) ICESCR', 288.

87 CESCR, GC3, para. 11; 2007 Statement on Maximum Available Resources, para. 4 (the language here is the following: '[. . .] the obligation remains for a State party to ensure the widest possible enjoyment [. . .]', while in GC3 it was 'to strive to ensure').

88 CESCR, GC3, para. 12; 2007 Statement on Maximum Available Resources, para. 4.

89 CESCR, 'Concluding observations on the second periodic report of Greece', E/C.12/GRC/CO/2 (27 October 2015), paras. 30 and 34.

90 CESCR, GC3, para. 10; GC12, para. 17; GC17; GC18; GC19, para. 60.

91 CESCR, GC3, para. 10.

obligations apply irrespective of the availability of resources of the country concerned or any other factors and difficulties',[92] and 'resource scarcity does not relieve states of certain minimum obligations in respect of the implementation of ESR'.[93] Actually, in later interpretations of the Covenant, for example in General Comment No. 14, the Committee has affirmed that 'a State party cannot, under any circumstances whatsoever, justify its non-compliance with the core obligations [...], which are non-derogable'.[94] Furthermore, several commentators seem to agree on the view that minimum core obligations apply irrespective of available resources, based on the (rebuttable) presumption that all states have the resources necessary to give effect to minimum core obligations if they define resources broadly enough and are sufficiently aggressive in resource acquisition.[95]

Nevertheless, in further General Comments, the Committee seems to leave the door open to the idea that resource constraints still matter in the assessment of states parties' compliance with their minimum core obligations. In fact, several more recent General Comments reiterate the provision mentioned at point (d).[96] This seems to imply that, where states are able to demonstrate that such effort has been made and, yet, they are unable to ensure minimum essential levels of ESR, they will not be considered in breach of their minimum core obligation. This would exclude, in particular, that this obligation is to be automatically considered as 'resource-independent', with evident implications for the assessment of states parties' compliance (it creates, in fact, a legal loophole through which the non-realisation of minimum levels of ESR could still be justified).

Secondly, the Committee's *recommendations* on the use of the maximum available resources, notably expressed in its Concluding Observations, touch upon a wide range of de facto economic and fiscal policy issues.

The Committee has, at times, recommended specific economic policy measures, such as 'diversification of the economy' (drawing the attention away from certain industries, for example, the oil industry, towards other industries and business models, such as local small and medium-scale enterprises);[97]

[92] Maastricht Guidelines, guideline 9. See also guideline 10: 'As established by the Limburg Principles 25–28 and confirmed by the developing jurisprudence of the CESCR, resource scarcity does not relieve States of certain minimum obligations in respect of the implementation of economic, social and cultural rights.'

[93] Maastricht Guidelines, guideline 10.

[94] CESCR, GC14, para. 47.

[95] Robert E. Robertson, 'Measuring State Compliance with the Obligation to Devote the "Maximum Available Resources" to Realizing Economic, Social, and Cultural Rights' (1994) 156 *Human Rights Quarterly* 702; Nolan and Dutschke, 'Article 2(1) ICESCR', 288.

[96] CESCR, GC3, para. 10; GC12, para. 17; GC17; GC18; GC19, para. 60.

[97] CESCR, Concluding Observations, Azerbaijan, para. 345.

increases in real salaries of certain categories of workers (e.g. teachers and nurses),[98] or upwards adjustments of minimum wage levels.[99]

Furthermore, with regard to fiscal policy, the following are some of the guidelines developed by the CESCR: (a) the allocation of significantly more funds to non-Covenant-related expenditures (e.g. military defence or business subsidies), rather than Covenant-related items, is considered by the Committee as an indicator of non-compliance by the state with its obligation to use the maximum available resources. In such cases, the CESCR has recommended the state to increase the proportion of the national budget devoted to Covenant-related expenditures.[100] (b) If the percentage of the national budget allocated by a state for the realisation of a specific right is significantly lower than the percentage devoted to the realisation of the same right by another state with a similar level of development, the Committee has considered this an indication of non-compliance with the obligation to use the maximum of available resources.[101] (c) Likewise, depending on the level of development of a state (advanced economies generally go under higher scrutiny), the Committee has considered the allocation of scarce resources for the realisation of specific rights (e.g. only 1 per cent of budget allocated to health, or only primary education provided free of charge, where the economic circumstances of a country would allow higher spending) as an indication of non-compliance with the obligation to use the maximum of available resources.[102] The Committee has, thus, often recommended states to

98 CESCR, Concluding observations on the second periodic report of Uruguay, in CESCR, 'Report on the Sixteenth and Seventeenth Sessions (28 April–16 May 1997, 17 November–5 December 1997)', E/1998/22 (1998), para. 378.

99 CESCR, Concluding observations on the second periodic report of Portugal, in CESCR, 'Report on the Twelfth and Thirteenth Sessions (1–19 May 1995, 20 November–8 December 1995)', E/1996/22 (1996), paras. 95 and 98; Concluding observations on the third periodic report of Mexico, in CESCR, 'Report on the Twentieth and Twenty-first Sessions (26 April–14 May 1999, 15 November–3 December 1999)', E/2000/22 (2000), para. 382.

100 Sepúlveda, *The Nature of the Obligations*, pp. 316–317; *inter alia*, CESCR, Concluding observations on the initial report of the Philippines, in CESCR, 'Report on the Twelfth and Thirteenth Sessions (1–19 May 1995, 20 November–8 December 1995)', E/1996/22 (1996), paras. 121–123; Concluding observations on the initial report of Azerbaijan, in CESCR, 'Report on the Sixteenth and Seventeenth Sessions (28 April–16 May 1997, 17 November–5 December 1997)', E/1998/22 (1998), para. 345.

101 Sepúlveda, *The Nature of the Obligations*, p. 317; *inter alia*, CESCR, Concluding observations on the second periodic report of the Dominican Republic, in CESCR, 'Report on the Twelfth and Thirteenth Sessions (1–19 May 1995, 20 November–8 December 1995)', E/1996/22 (1996), para. 228.

102 Sepúlveda, *The Nature of the Obligations*, pp. 317–318; *inter alia*, CESCR, Concluding observations on the initial report of the Republic of Korea, in CESCR, 'Report on the Twelfth and Thirteenth Sessions (1–19 May 1995, 20 November–8 December 1995)', E/1996/22 (1996), paras. 26 and 29.

progressively increase their expenditure on a certain right as a proportion of their gross domestic product (GDP).[103] The CESCR has also considered the existence of serious problems with the implementation of a right (e.g. high numbers of homeless people) in a developed country (e.g. Canada) sufficient to indicate that it has not devoted the maximum of its available resources to the realisation of ESR.[104] (d) The non-utilisation or the diversion (e.g. due to inefficient administration or corruption) of budget items already allocated to social expenditure is considered by the Committee another indicator of non-compliance with the Covenant.[105] The CESCR has, thus, recommended to combat the practice of non-utilisation of budget items earmarked for social expenditure and to ensure that such appropriations are used for the purposes for which they were budgeted.[106] (e) Where there is an increase in the availability of resources in a country, the Committee expects and has recommended that states proportionally increase their allocation of resources for the realisation of ESR (also in accordance with their obligation to continuously take steps towards the progressive achievement of full ESR).[107] (f) It must be also recalled that, as mentioned earlier (Section 3.2.2.1), an unjustified reduction in ESR expenditure, resulting in the non-enjoyment of such rights, would constitute a deliberately retrogressive measure and a potential violation of the Covenant.[108]

Similar economic and fiscal policy recommendations have been promoted also in the context of the more recent initiatives (addressed in Section 3.3) to direct the sovereign financing (including borrowing/lending) practice of states in terms of their international human rights obligations.

The Committee has clarified that, in assessing the adequacy and reasonableness of the measures taken by a state party in light of the maximum available resources criterion, in the context of the monitoring procedures provided by the OP-ICESCR, it may take into account, inter alia, whether the state party's decision to allocate available resources was in accordance with

103 Inter alia, CESCR, Concluding Observations, Greece, para. 36(a).

104 Sepúlveda, *The Nature of the Obligations*, p. 318; CESCR, Concluding observations on the third periodic report of Canada, in CESCR, 'Report on the Eighteenth and Nineteenth Sessions (27 April–15 May 1998, 16 November–4 December 1998)', E/1999/22 (1999), para. 399.

105 See also, Maastricht Guidelines, guideline 14.

106 Sepúlveda, *The Nature of the Obligations*, p. 315; inter alia, CESCR, Concluding observations on the third periodic report of Colombia, in CESCR, 'Report on the Twelfth and Thirteenth Sessions (1–19 May 1995, 20 November–8 December 1995)', E/1996/22 (1996), para. 181.

107 Sepúlveda, *The Nature of the Obligations*, p. 322.

108 *Ibid.*, 324; Maastricht Guidelines, guideline 14 (f).

international human rights standards, although the Committee provides no further indication as to what these standards are supposed to be.[109]

Finally, the Committee has explained that, where a state party uses resource constraints as an explanation for any retrogressive steps taken, it will consider such information on a country-by-country basis, in the light of objective criteria such as: (a) the country's level of development; (b) the severity of the alleged breach, in particular whether the situation concerned the enjoyment of the minimum core content of the Covenant; (c) the country's current economic situation, in particular whether the country was undergoing a period of economic recession; (d) the existence of other serious claims on the state party's limited resources, for example, resulting from a recent natural disaster or from recent internal or international armed conflict; (e) whether the state party had sought to identify low-cost options; and (f) whether the state party had sought cooperation and assistance or rejected offers of resources from the international community for the purposes of implementing the provisions of the Covenant without sufficient reason.[110]

3.2.2.3 International Assistance and Cooperation

As mentioned earlier, according to article 2(1) ICESCR, states parties must take steps towards the full realisation of ESR both individually and *through international assistance and cooperation, especially economic and technical.*[111]

The CESCR has emphasised that

> in accordance with Articles 55 and 56 of the Charter of the United Nations, with well-established principles of international law, and with the provisions of the Covenant [on Economic, Social and Cultural Rights, particularly Article 2.1], international cooperation for development and thus for the realization of economic, social and cultural rights is an obligation of all States [...] [that] is particularly incumbent upon those [among them] which are in a position to assist others in this regard.[112]

Compliance with this obligation shall have in view, as a matter of priority, the realisation of all human rights and fundamental freedoms, must be directed towards the establishment of a social and international order in which the rights and freedoms set forth in the Covenant can be fully realised (in

[109] CESCR, 2007 Statement on Maximum Available Resources, para. 8 (c), (d) and (f).
[110] *Ibid.*, para. 10.
[111] Alston and Quinn, 'The Nature and Scope of States Parties' Obligations', 190. The essential role of international cooperation in facilitating the full realisation of the relevant rights is further underlined by the specific provisions contained in articles 11, 15, 22 and 23 ICESCR, see CESCR, GC3, para. 13.
[112] CESCR, GC3, para. 14; OHCHR, *Economic, Social and Cultural Rights*, p. 14.

accordance also with art. 28 UDHR) and shall be based on the sovereign equality of states.[113] Notwithstanding, the detailed legal implications of an obligation of international assistance and cooperation under the ICESCR and more generally under international law remain imprecise. To an extent, the existence of a legally binding obligation of states in this sense (which, in fact, is often referred to as a duty) is still significantly debated, even more so where *economic* or *financial* assistance is involved, and state practice does not appear to contradict this statement (consider, for instance, the nature and extent of the financial assistance so far provided by states and international organisations, for example, in the European context, to respond to the unprecedented economic crisis triggered by the COVID-19 pandemic).[114]

3.3 SOVEREIGN DEBT AND HUMAN RIGHTS

As recently reaffirmed by the Independent Expert on Foreign Debt and Human Rights (on which, see later), debt is not 'per se a human rights problem, even less a violation',[115] but 'depending on a variety of factors, such as responsible lending and borrowing, the loan terms and conditions, prudent use of loans and proper debt management, debt financing can contribute to countries' economic development and the establishment of conditions for the realization of human rights'.[116] However, unsustainable debt burdens,[117] and the costs associated with their servicing, can reduce the amount of resources available, especially to poorer countries, for the realisation of human rights, hinder the achievement of development goals and pose a more general threat to economic, social and political stability and to democratic regimes.[118] The

113 CESCR, GC3, para. 14; Limburg Principles, principles 29–34.

114 See i.a. Scali, 'Sovereign Financing during the COVID-19 Pandemic'.

115 UN Human Rights Council (HRC) (2020) 'Private debt and human rights', Report of the Independent Expert on the effects of foreign debt and other related international financial obligations of states on the full enjoyment of human rights, particularly economic, social and cultural rights, A/HRC/43/45, para. 20.

116 HRC 2011, 3.

117 On human rights-oriented (re)definitions of sustainability, see HRC (2018) 'Guiding Principles on human rights impact assessments of economic reforms', Report of the Independent Expert on the effect of foreign debt and other related international financial obligations of states on the full enjoyment of human rights, particularly economic, social and cultural rights, A/HRC/40/57, 13; HRC (2012) 'Guiding principles on foreign debt and human rights', Report of the Independent Expert on the effects of foreign debt and other related international financial obligations of states on the full enjoyment of human rights, particularly economic, social and cultural rights, Cephas Lumina, A/HRC/20/23, 18.

118 Cephas Lumina, 'Sovereign Debt and Human Rights: Making the Connection' in Bantekas and Lumina, *Sovereign Debt and Human Rights*, pp. 169–185.

above-discussed recent debt trends are particularly alarming in this regard. In addition to excessive debt levels, the harmful consequences of the (neoliberal) policy conditions generally attached to loans, emergency assistance and debt relief on a wide range of human rights and on specific individuals and groups, have now been extensively documented[119] (on this aspect, see Section 4.4.1 on conditionality in Chapter 4).

The potentially adverse impacts of sovereign debt on human rights have, thus, preoccupied the international community and various UN bodies since the 1990s, particularly the United Nations Conference on Trade and Development (UNCTAD) and the Human Rights Commission (the latter superseded, in 2006, by the Human Rights Council). In 1997, it was also decided to address the issue of foreign debt and human rights through the establishment of a thematic mandate, which, in 2008, after several transformations, developed into the mandate of the current Independent Expert on the effects of foreign debt and other related international financial obligations of states on the full enjoyment of all human rights, particularly economic, social and cultural rights (hereinafter, the Independent Expert on Foreign Debt and Human Rights).[120]

It seems important to briefly mention that, despite the fact that the adverse impacts of debt and related policies on the enjoyment of human rights, particularly ESR, are now well established and abundantly evidenced, the mandate of the Independent Expert and, more generally, the consideration of the topic by the Human Rights Council (and the Commission on Human Rights before it) has met considerable opposition from developed (mainly creditor) countries which are members of the Human Rights Council. These have contended that to treat the issue of sovereign debt as a human rights problem would be 'inappropriate', and likewise would be the attention

[119] OHCHR (2013) 'Report on austerity measures and economic and social rights'.

[120] The current Independent Expert is Ms Yuefen Li. As mentioned, since the 1990s, the mandate of the Independent Expert has undergone several changes. In 1997 and 1998, the Commission on Human Rights had established the two mandates, respectively, of the Independent Expert on structural adjustment policies, and of the Special Rapporteur on the effects of foreign debt on the full enjoyment of economic, social and cultural rights. In 2000, the two mandates were discontinued, and replaced with an Independent Expert on the effects of structural adjustment policies and foreign debt on the full enjoyment of all human rights, particularly economic, social and cultural rights, which, in 2005, was renamed as Independent Expert on the effects of economic reform policies and foreign debt on the full enjoyment of all human rights, particularly economic, social and cultural rights. Finally, in 2008, the mandate of the Independent Expert was redefined and the title reformulated in its current form, see Human Rights Council, Res 7/4 of 27 March 2008, Mandate of the Independent Expert on the effects of foreign debt and other related international financial obligations of states on the full enjoyment of all human rights, particularly economic, social and cultural rights.

devoted to the issue by the Human Rights Council and the continuation of the mandate of the Independent Expert,[121] since other international *fora* – presumably the international financial institutions and the Paris Club – would be better equipped to deal with this issue. Developing (mainly borrower) countries, on the contrary, have always overwhelmingly supported the involvement of the Human Rights Council.[122]

The Independent Expert has eventually reaffirmed the competence of UN human rights bodies on the matter, by emphasising, inter alia, that 'rules other than human rights law and other international forums [. . .] have thus far failed to deliver an equitable and lasting solution to the sovereign debt problem in line with the various commitments made by the international community', nor have those other fora 'explicit mandates to promote and protect human rights'.[123] On the contrary, as creditors, they 'cannot realistically be expected to focus on finding a solution to the debt crisis that prioritizes social and economic justice over debt repayment'.[124]

Perhaps also as a consequence of the limitations of the existing international ESR regime (and the apparent impossibility, at present, to overcome such limitations), in the last couple of decades, several human rights organisations, scholars and monitoring bodies have increasingly directed their efforts to instruct and assess the process, contents and outcomes of public budgets (including debt-related aspects) and, more generally, of economic policy-making, in terms of states' substantive human rights obligations.[125] Besides

121 HRC (16th Session) 'US Explanation of Vote on Foreign Debt as a Human Rights Problem' (23 March 2011) quoted in Cephas Lumina, 'Sovereign Debt and Human Rights: The UN Approach' in Juan Pablo Bohoslavsky and Jernej Letnar Černič (eds.), *Making Sovereign Financing and Human Rights Work* (Oxford: Hart Publishing, 2014) 251–268.

122 Report of the independent expert on the effects of foreign debt and other related international financial obligations of states on the full enjoyment of all human rights, particularly economic, social and cultural rights, A/63/289 (14 August 2008), para. 8 (hereinafter, 'IE 2008 Report').

123 Report of the Independent Expert on the effects of foreign debt and other related international financial obligations of states on the full enjoyment of all human rights, particularly economic, social and cultural rights, Cephas Lumina: Guiding principles on foreign debt and human rights, A/HRC/20/23 (10 April 2011), para. 7, endorsed by HRC, Res 20/10 of 18 July 2012, 'The effects of foreign debt and other related international financial obligations of states on the full enjoyment of all human rights, particularly economic, social and cultural rights', A/HRC/RES/20/10, para. 7 (hereinafter, 'UN Guiding Principles on Foreign Debt and Human Rights').

124 HRC, Report of the Independent Expert on the effects of foreign debt and other related international financial obligations of states on the full enjoyment of all human rights, particularly economic, social and cultural rights, Cephas Lumina, A/HRC/25/50 (7 March 2014), para. 9.

125 See i.a. Aoife Nolan and Juan Pablo Bohoslavsky, 'Human Rights and Economic Policy Reforms' (2020) 24 *The International Journal of Human Rights* 1247–1267 (and more generally the entire Issue 9/24 of the Journal, on 'Human Rights and Economic Policy Reforms); OHCHR and International Budget Partnership, 'Realizing Human Rights Through

the guidance provided in specific statements or General Comments (GC) – for example, the Committee on the Rights of the Child's 2016 GC No. 19 on budgeting for children's rights, or the Committee on Economic, Social and Cultural Rights' 2016 Statement on public debt and 2012 Letter on austerity measures – these efforts have led, as far as sovereign debt is particularly concerned, to the elaboration of the UNCTAD Principles on responsible sovereign borrowing and lending (2012),[126] the UN Guiding Principles on foreign debt and human rights (2012)[127] and the Basic Principles on sovereign restructuring processes (2015).[128] Furthermore, attention has been increasingly

Government Budgets', 2017; Zhora Khan and Nalini Burn (eds.), *Financing for Gender Equality: Realising Women's Rights through Gender Responsive Budgeting* (London: Palgrave Macmillan, 2017); Rory O'Connell, Aoife Nolan, Colin Harvey, Mira Dutschke and Eoin Rooney, *Applying an International Human Rights Framework to State Budget Allocations: Rights and Resources* (Abingdon: Routledge, 2014) (providing also a review of selected existing guidance and case studies on ESR-based budget analysis, pp. 38–60); Ann Blyberg and Helena Hofbauer, 'Article 2 and Governments' Budgets' (International Budget Partnership, 2014); OHCHR, 'Promoting a Rights-Based Approach to Economic Stabilization, Recovery and Growth', Background paper, April 2013; Aoife Nolan, Rory O'Connell and Colin Harvey (eds.), *Human Rights and Public Finance: Budgets for the Promotion of Economic and Social Rights* (Oxford: Hart Publishing, 2013); QUB Budget Analysis Project, 'Budget Analysis and Economic and Social Rights: A Review of Selected Case Studies and Guidance', Queen's University Belfast, 2010; Andy Norton and Diane Elson, 'What's Behind the Budget? Politics, Rights and Accountability in the Budget Process' (London: Overseas Development Institute, 2002); Fundar-Center for Analysis and Research, International Budget Project and International Human Rights Internship Program, 'Dignity Counts: A Guide to Using Budget Analysis to Advance Human Rights', 2004.

126 UNCTAD, Principles on Promoting Responsible Sovereign Lending and Borrowing (10 January 2012). In 2009, the UNCTAD launched the Project to Promote Responsible Sovereign Lending and Borrowing, with the aim to develop a set of internationally recognised principles to promote and reinforce responsible sovereign lending and borrowing practices. These could, in the intentions of UNCTAD, eventually lead to the establishment of criteria to assess whether the contracting of sovereign debt has been performed in accordance with commonly accepted principles.

127 UN Guiding Principles on Foreign Debt and Human Rights.

128 UNGA, Res 69/319 of 10 September 2015, 'Basic Principles on Sovereign Debt Restructuring Processes', A/RES/69/319 (29 September 2015). Based on the principles previously identified by an UNCTAD working group (UNCTAD, *Sovereign Debt Workouts: Going Forward. Roadmap and Guide*, http://unctad.org/en/PublicationsLibrary/gdsddf2015misc1_en.pdf), the Basic Principles propose an incremental approach to sovereign debt workouts that relies on the continuous, progressive development of sovereign debt restructuring practice. Of major importance is also the fact that the Basic Principles explicitly affirm that the principle of sustainability must include respect for human rights, see Report of the Independent Expert on the effects of foreign debt and other related international financial obligations of states on the full enjoyment of all human rights, particularly economic, social and cultural rights, A/71/305 (5 August 2016), para. 53 (hereinafter 'IE 2016 Annual Report'). On the incremental approach and the economic and legal implications of the Basic Principles, see the Special Edition on Sovereign Debt of the *Yale Journal of International Law* (2016) vol. 41.

directed towards 'procedural obligations' and the promotion of methods – in particular, human rights impact assessments (HRIAs) –[129] aimed at integrating human rights considerations and emerging principles in economic decision-making (a solution, in essence, akin to human rights 'mainstreaming').[130]

It must be remarked, also in this case, that these instruments are not per se legally binding upon states and other international actors.

While the 2012 UNCTAD Principles on responsible sovereign borrowing and lending and the 2015 Basic Principles on sovereign debt restructuring practices concern the identification and recommendation of 'responsible' behaviour in relation to, respectively, borrowing/lending and debt restructuring practices, the Guiding Principles on foreign debt and human rights specifically address the scope of the *human rights obligations* of states, international financial institutions and other non-state actors in relation to sovereign debt and related policies. They attempt to articulate 'a universally applicable framework on foreign debt and human rights [...] to ensure that the obligations assumed by States under debt and other international financial arrangements do not undermine their capacity to create the conditions for the realization of all human rights, particularly ESR and the right to development'.[131]

For this reason, the Guiding Principles will be included, together with the above-cited Statement of the CESCR on Public debt, austerity measures and the ICESCR,[132] and with other relevant documents produced by the Independent Expert on foreign debt and human rights, in the next subsection which, based on the normative contribution of these documents, attempts at systematising the existing international standards on sovereign debt and ESR.

3.3.1 *ESR Obligations and Sovereign Debt*

As already mentioned earlier, international human rights bodies have recognised the constraints that states may face due to their debt arrangements, especially during a crisis. Nonetheless, there are limits to the extent to

129 See i.a. the Guiding Principles on human rights impact assessments of economic reforms (2018); Report of the Special Rapporteur on the right to food, Olivier De Schutter: Addendum, Guiding Principles on human rights impacts assessment for trade and investment agreements, UN Doc. A/HRC/19/59/Add.5 (2011); and references to HRIAs in the Guiding principles on foreign debt and human rights, in the OHCHR Guiding Principles on Extreme Poverty and Human Rights (2012), in CESCR, GC24, and in CRC, GC19.

130 Martti Koskenniemi, 'Human Rights Mainstreaming as a Strategy for Institutional Power' (2010) 1 *Humanity* 1, 47–58; Christopher McCrudden, 'Mainstreaming Human Rights' (2004) *Public Law & Legal Theory Research Papers* No. 47, University of Michigan School of Law.

131 UN Guiding Principles on Foreign Debt and Human Rights, para. 14.

132 CESCR, '2016 Statement on Public Debt'.

which states may deviate from their obligations to realise ESR. The aim of the Guiding Principles, as well as of further guidance provided by the CESCR and the IE, is to 'balance a debtor and creditor state's contractual obligations arising from external debt arrangements and both debtor and creditor's international legal obligations to respect, protect and fulfil all human rights, particularly economic, social and cultural rights'.[133]

3.3.1.1 The Primacy of Human Rights and the Human Rights Obligations of States also as Members of International Organisations

The Guiding Principles reassert that all states, when acting individually or collectively, including through international and regional organisations of which they are members, have to respect, protect and fulfil human rights.[134] Furthermore, the Independent Expert on foreign debt and human rights has explicitly affirmed that states' human rights obligations have primacy over many other types of legal obligations under international law.[135]

Consequently, all state actions should be consistent with international human rights law. This means, inter alia, that states should ensure that

> any and all of their activities concerning their lending and borrowing decisions, those of international or national public or private institutions to which they belong or in which they have an interest, the negotiation and implementation of loan agreements or other debt instruments, the utilization of loan funds, debt repayments, the renegotiation and restructuring of external debt, and the provision of debt relief when appropriate, do not derogate from these obligations.[136]

When making decisions in their capacity as members of international financial institutions (such as the IMF, the World Bank or regional development banks) or other international organisations, states parties to the ICESCR retain their ESR obligations,[137] nor would they be absolved of their responsibility, even where, in that capacity, they would be acting in full accordance with the rules of the

[133] UN Guiding Principles on Foreign Debt and Human Rights, principle 2.

[134] *Ibid.*, principle 6.

[135] HRC, IE 2008 Report, para. 14. This pre-eminence would be confirmed, according to the Independent Expert, by Article 103 of the UN Charter: '[i]n the event of a conflict between the obligations of the Members of the United Nations under the present Charter and their obligations under any other international agreement, their obligations under the present Charter shall prevail'. As remarked by the IE, the obligations under the Charter include the duty to cooperate with the United Nations in its quest to promote universal respect for human rights (art. 56 UN Charter), *ibid.*

[136] UN Guiding Principles on Foreign Debt and Human Rights, principle 6.

[137] CESCR, '2016 Statement on Public Debt', para. 9; Report of the Independent Expert on the effects and foreign debt and other related international financial obligations of states on the full enjoyment of all human rights, particularly economic, social and cultural rights on his

organisation.[138] Furthermore, when the lender is an international organisation of which the borrowing state is a member, it would not be acceptable for the borrowing state to circumvent its international obligations under the ICESCR by transferring certain competencies relating to the subject matter of the Covenant to an organisation, thus causing the organisation to commit an act that, if committed by the state party, would be in breach of its obligations under the Covenant.[139] States parties to the ICESCR would, thus, be acting in violation of the obligations if they were to delegate powers to the IMF, for instance, or to other agencies, and allowed such powers to be exercised without ensuring that they do not infringe on human rights. Similarly, they would be acting in breach of their obligations if they were to exercise their voting rights within such agencies without taking human rights into account (according to the CESCR, the same duty applies to states that are not parties to the Covenant, under human rights law as part of general international law). States parties to the ICESCR, as well as the relevant UN agencies, should, thus, make a particular effort to ensure that the protection of the most basic ESR is, to the maximum extent possible, built into programmes and policies designed to promote adjustment.[140]

3.3.1.2 The Human Rights Obligations of International Organisations

International financial institutions and, more generally, international organisations have to act in accordance with any human rights obligations incumbent upon them on the basis of the general rules of international law, their foundational treaties and the human rights treaties to which they are parties.[141]

With regard to the general international law obligations of EU institutions, the Independent Expert of foreign debt and human rights has recently reasserted the principle that 'international organisations and international financial institutions have certain obligations under international human rights law based on customary law and general principles of international law',[142]

mission to institutions of the European Union, A/HRC/34/57/Add.1 (28 December 2016), para. 34 (hereinafter, 'IE 2016 Report on mission to the EU').

138 CESCR, '2016 Statement on Public Debt', para. 9.

139 *Ibid.*, para. 5; Report of the International Law Commission, 'Articles on the Responsibility of International Organizations', A/66/10 (2011).

140 CESCR, '2016 Statement on Public Debt', para. 9; see also GC2, para. 9. These requirements have been also reiterated also in Olivier De Schutter and Margot E. Salomon, 'Economic Policy Conditionality, Socio-economic Rights and International Legal Responsibility: The Case of Greece 2010–2015' (15 June 2015) *Legal Brief for the Special Committee of the Hellenic Parliament on the Audit of the Greek Debt* 14–15.

141 ICJ, *Interpretation of the Agreement of 25 March 1951 between the WHO and Egypt*, Advisory Opinion of 20 December 1980 [1980] ICJ Rep 73, para. 37; 'IE 2016 Report on mission to the EU', para. 19.

142 'IE 2016 Report on mission to the EU', para. 28.

recalling in particular the Statement of the CESCR on Public debt, austerity measures and the International Covenant on Economic, Social and Cultural Rights.[143] Here, the CESCR has made explicit reference only to 'human rights, as listed in particular in the Universal Declaration of Human Rights, that are part of customary international law or of the general principles of law, both of which are sources of international law'. Although this is correct in principle, neither the Independent Expert nor the CESCR have provided further clarifications on which specific economic and social rights possibly belong to such category, an issue that has not been yet conclusively resolved. Some authors include among general international law some of the core obligations contained in the ICESCR, or the minimum core rights.[144]

However, the CESCR also disagrees with interpretation by the IMF and International Bank for Reconstruction and Development (IBRD), in particular, that the relevant Articles of Agreement are not requiring them to include human rights considerations in their decision-making. According to the Committee, in fact, it is in the exercise of the powers that have been delegated to them by their Member States that these organisations should refrain from adopting measures that would result in human rights violations. Moreover, as specialised agencies of the United Nations,[145] they are obligated to act in accordance with the principles of the UN Charter (arts 1(3) and 55(c)), which sets the realisation of human rights and fundamental freedoms as one of the purposes of the organisation.[146]

The Guiding Principles reiterated that international financial organisations and private corporations too have an obligation to respect international human rights, which implies a duty to refrain from 'formulating, adopting, funding and implementing policies and programmes which directly or indirectly contravene the enjoyment of human rights'.[147]

3.3.1.3 Retrogressive Measures and Conditionality-Related Duties

The CESCR has clearly affirmed that any conditions attached to a loan that would imply an obligation on the (borrowing) state to adopt retrogressive measures in the area of ESR that are unjustifiable would be a violation of

143 CESCR, '2016 Statement on Public Debt', paras. 7–8.

144 Bruno Simma and Philip Alston, 'The Sources of International Human Rights Law: Custom, *Jus Cogens*, and General Principles' (1992) 12 *Australian Yearbook of International Law* 82; Riedel, Giacca and Golay, *Economic, Social and Cultural Rights in International Law*, p. 21.

145 Charter of the United Nations (26 June 1945), Articles 57 and 63; UNGA, Res 124 (II) of 15 November 1947, 'Agreements with specialized agencies'.

146 CESCR, '2016 Statement on Public Debt', para. 8.

147 UN Guiding Principles on Foreign Debt and Human Rights, para. 9.

the ICESCR. The borrowing state should therefore ensure that such conditions do not unreasonably reduce its ability to respect, protect and fulfil the Covenant's rights.[148]

If the adoption of retrogressive measures is unavoidable, the criteria outlined in the Committee's Letter of 2012 apply[149] (these have been further developed in the United Nations High Commissioner for Human Rights' report to the ECOSOC of 2013).[150] As already mentioned, retrogressive measures are justifiable, according to the Committee's interpretation, only if they are unavoidable, necessary and proportionate, in the sense that the adoption of any other policy or failure to act would be more detrimental to ESR (states bear, thus, the burden of ensuring that retrogressive measures are introduced only after the most careful consideration of all other less restrictive alternatives).[151] Retrogressive measures should remain in place only insofar as they are necessary; they should not result in discrimination; they should mitigate inequalities that can grow in times of crisis and ensure that the rights of disadvantaged and marginalised individuals and groups are not disproportionately affected and they should not affect the minimum core content of the rights protected under the Covenant.[152]

According to the Independent Expert on foreign debt and human rights, these criteria should also inform the assessment by EU institutions of whether adjustment measures that may encroach on ESR are justifiable.[153]

Furthermore, when exiting financial assistance programmes, states parties are also required to review their policies so as to enhance the effective protection of the Covenant's rights, in line with the progress achieved in the post-crisis economic recovery.[154] For instance, in its Concluding Observations on the situation in Cyprus, the Committee recommended the state party to

148 CESCR, '2016 Statement on Public Debt', para. 4.

149 CESCR, '2012 Letter on austerity measures'.

150 ECOSOC, Report of the United Nations High Commissioner for Human Rights, E/2013/82 (7 May 2013), paras. 15–21, also recalled in HRC, Report of the Independent Expert on the effects of foreign debt and other related international financial obligations of states on the full enjoyment of all human rights, particularly economic, social and cultural rights, Cephas Lumina, Addendum: Mission to Greece (22–27 April 2013), A/HRC/25/50/Add.1 (7 March 2014), para. 10 (hereinafter, 'IE 2014 Report on first mission to Greece').

151 HRC, Report of the Independent Expert on the effects of foreign debt and other related international financial obligations of states on the full enjoyment of all human rights, particularly economic, social and cultural rights on his mission to Greece, A/HRC/31/60/Add.2 (21 April 2016), para. 17 (hereinafter, 'IE 2016 Report on second mission to Greece').

152 CESCR, '2016 Statement on Public Debt', para. 4; 'IE 2016 Report on mission to the EU', paras. 32–33; IE 2016 Annual Report, paras. 62–63; 'IE 2016 Report on second mission to Greece', para. 17; 'IE 2014 Report on first mission to Greece', para. 9.

153 'IE 2016 Report on mission to the EU', para. 33.

154 CESCR, '2016 Statement on Public Debt', para. 6.

'ensure that austerity measures are gradually phased out and that the effective protection of the rights under the Covenant is enhanced in line with the progress achieved in the post-crisis economic recovery', and to 'restore the pre-crisis levels of public services and social benefits'.[155]

3.3.1.4 Coercion

All states, whether parties to the ICESCR or not, that coerce other states into violating their own obligations under either the Covenant or other rules of international law are responsible for that act under international law. Both as lenders of bilateral loans and as members of international organisations providing financial assistance, all states should therefore ensure that they do not impose obligations on borrowing states that would lead them to breach their duties, for example, adopting retrogressive measures in violation of their obligations under the Covenant.[156]

3.3.1.5 Procedural Obligations: (a) Human Rights Impact Assessments

The Committee is of the view that the above-cited obligations imposed under the ICESCR require both lending and borrowing states seeking loans with certain conditionalities, to carry out a human rights impact assessment prior to the provision of the loan, in order to ensure that the conditionalities do not disproportionately affect ESR nor lead to discrimination. The CESCR drew attention to the Guiding Principles on foreign debt and human rights[157] and the 2012 Guiding Principles on extreme poverty and human rights,[158] both of which call for human rights impact assessment of conditionalities attached to loans or of measures which create a foreseeable risk of impairing the enjoyment of human rights by persons living in poverty beyond their national territory.[159]

Principle 12 of the Guiding Principles on foreign debt and human rights enjoins states to analyse policies and programmes, including those relating to external debt, macroeconomic stability, structural reform and investment, with respect to their impact on poverty and inequality, social development and the enjoyment of human rights as well as their gender implications, and adjust them as appropriate to promote a more equitable and non-discriminatory distribution

155 CESCR, Concluding observations on the sixth periodic report of Cyprus (28 October 2016) E/C.12/CYP/CO/6, para. 12(b) and (c).

156 CESCR, '2016 Statement on Public Debt', para. 10.

157 UN Guiding Principles on Foreign Debt and Human Rights, para. 40.

158 HRC, Res 21/11 of 18 October 2012, 'Guiding Principles on Extreme Poverty and Human Rights', A/HRC/RES/21/11, para. 92.

159 CESCR, '2016 Statement on Public Debt', para. 11. See also the Human Rights Council, 'Guiding Principles for Human Rights Impact Assessments for Economic Reform Policies', A/HRC/40/57 (19 December 2018).

of the benefits of growth and services. Principle 13 specifies that such impact analyses should pay special attention to certain groups in society that may be particularly vulnerable, including children, women, persons with disabilities, older persons, persons belonging to minorities, and migrant workers and members of their families.[160]

In addition, in accordance with principles 40 and 41, it is incumbent upon lenders to conduct a credible human rights impact assessment as a prerequisite to providing new loans.[161]

According to the Guiding Principles on foreign debt and human rights,

> [l]enders should not finance activities or projects that violate, or would foreseeably violate, human rights in the Borrower States. To avoid this eventuality, it is incumbent upon lenders intending to finance specific activities or project in Borrower States to conduct a credible Human Rights Impact Assessment [...] as a prerequisite to providing a new loan.[162]

Similarly, also the Guiding Principles on extreme poverty and human rights require human rights impact assessments.[163]

3.3.1.6 Procedural Obligations: (b) Transparency, Participation and Accountability

The Guiding Principles on foreign debt and human rights underline that transparency, participation and accountability are core values that should be observed in lending and borrowing decisions by states, international financial institutions and other actors. Transparency requires the full disclosure of all relevant information regarding loan agreements; participation means ensuring effective and meaningful input from all stakeholders in loan policy and resource utilisation decisions; and accountability requires that decision-makers be answerable and held accountable, if warranted, for their actions regarding external debt agreements and external debt policies and strategies. Meaningful participation goes beyond ensuring that adjustment policies are subject to approval by national parliaments; it also requires that individuals and groups affected by policy decisions be consulted and able to provide meaningful input to decisions affecting them.[164]

160 'IE 2016 Report on mission to the EU', para. 38; UN Guiding Principles on Foreign Debt and Human Rights, principles 12–13 and 40–41.

161 'IE 2016 Report on mission to the EU', para. 38.

162 UN Guiding Principles on Foreign Debt and Human Rights, para. 40.

163 UN Guiding Principles on Extreme Poverty and Human Rights, paras. 61 and 92; 'IE 2016 Report on second mission to Greece', para. 26.

164 'IE 2016 Report on mission to the EU', para. 39; UN Guiding Principles on Foreign Debt and Human Rights, principles 28–31.

3.4 IS INTERNATIONAL HUMAN RIGHTS LAW 'NEUTRAL' IN TERMS OF ECONOMIC SYSTEMS? SOME REMARKS ON THE ECONOMIC AND FISCAL POLICIES RECOMMENDED BY THE CESCR

There are some important considerations that can be inferred from the description so far outlined of states parties' general obligations under article 2(1) ICESCR.

First of all, as it has been repeatedly noticed, due to the ideological contentions that affected the drafting process, the provisions of the ICESCR are formulated in vague and general terms.[165] As one commentator has duly remarked, article 2(1) is 'a fairly unsatisfactory article', whose 'convoluted phraseology' makes it 'virtually impossible to determine the precise nature of the obligations'.[166]

By reason of the same contentions, the Covenant was also initially equipped with an extremely weak (and uncertain) supervisory mechanism, and this fact delayed for several years any useful clarification of the Covenant's normative content. Later, the Committee began essentially to work, formally, ultra vires, although its authority as an interpretive body, as mentioned before, has not been so far challenged by the states parties, and has been certainly strengthened by the adoption of the OP-ICESCR. It might be argued, though, that the hesitant commitment of states towards ESR, reflected in the protracted and elusive formulation of both the Covenant and its supervisory mechanism, has created a constant tension for and against the legal assertion of ESR, which strongly influenced the work of the Committee. It has, in fact, often found itself in the position of rather having to reassure the states parties about the limitations of its role, often adopting a cautious stance when outlining the Covenant's requirements, or the criteria the Committee intends to apply to assess states parties' compliance. This happened, for instance, when the Committee was requested by the states parties to clarify how it would apply the obligation under article 2(1) to take steps 'to the maximum of the available resources' in the context of an individual communications procedure, when such communications procedure was, at the time, still in the drafting.[167] Without detracting from the other several factors that impacted on the Committee's work – such as the initial absence of a complaints procedure, the scarcity of information (often belatedly) provided by states' reports or the limited technical expertise of the CESCR on matters, for instance, of

[165] Sepúlveda, *The Nature of the Obligations*, p. 132.

[166] Craven, *The International Covenant on Economic, Social and Cultural Rights*, p. 151.

[167] CESCR, 2007 Statement on Maximum Available Resources, paras. 1–2.

economic policy[168] – the wavering commitment of states towards ESR, perhaps more than limited scholarly attention itself,[169] may be the main reason why the normative content of the Covenant, despite the important efforts of the Committee, remains quite elusive, and the legal protection of ESR under international law, de facto, relatively weak, as responses to the Eurozone sovereign debt crisis have revealed.

If we consider, first of all, what general state conduct is actually required – as a matter of legal obligation – under the Covenant, this could be summarised as follows: states parties are under an immediate obligation to take steps to progressively achieve the full realisation of ESR, which entails (i) a minimum core obligation, (ii) an obligation to protect at any time the most vulnerable and disadvantaged members of society, and (iii) a prima facie prohibition to adopt deliberately retrogressive measures. As mentioned earlier, these general obligations apply to all the substantive rights recognised in articles 6–15 of the Covenant. Nonetheless, they are – with the exception of the protection of the most vulnerable – further qualified, to a greater or lesser extent, by the availability of resources. As a result, it could be argued that the Covenant recognises and protects as a legal human right, at least, the right to minimum subsistence levels of ESR for all (or, in the jargon of political analyses, the 'right' to a minimal Welfare State).[170] The prohibition of retrogressive measures could be read, in this sense, as a 'safety clause' to preserve the basic welfare function of the state, although its force has been put into question by more recent crises. Whether and to what extent the legal protection of ESR under the ICESCR goes beyond that essentially depends on the still uncertain interpretation of the notion of available resources.

As discussed earlier, the interpretation of this notion has been developed, over the years, through the work of the Committee, in the form, mostly, of recommendations. These can reveal, as I attempted to describe before, some of the different fiscal and economic policies that the Committee seems to pursue, in effect, when guiding states parties in the use of their maximum available resources. To identify and make these policies explicit, can be, in my

168 Sepulveda, *The Nature of the Obligations*.

169 Aoife Nolan, 'Not Fit for Purpose? Human Rights in Times of Financial and Economic Crisis' (2015) 4 *European Human Rights Law Review* 368–369.

170 It might be worth recalling, here, Robert Goodin's definition of a 'minimal welfare State': a state which, at least, attempts to relieve palpable distress of those in desperate circumstances, through programs of general social assistance, as a matter of right, i.e. 'in a way that [its] agents [. . .] are bound by a legal duty to provide those in distress with certain resources that they need [. . .] [and] must have no discretionary power over those resources that the State allocates for the relief of people in distress', Robert E. Goodin, *Reasons for Welfare: The Political Theory of the Welfare State* (Princeton University Press, 1988), pp. 6–7.

opinion, extremely revealing, firstly, about the relationship between ESR and (different) economic systems or, better, between the economic system that has so far (at least implicitly) been considered to underpin ESR and other economic systems; and, secondly, about the relationship between, on one side, the economic and fiscal policy measures promoted by the CESCR for the protection of ESR and, on the other side, the policy measures required of states by the market, especially in the context of sovereign debt arrangements (as will be discussed in the next chapter). Is the Committee actually promoting *neutral* policies in terms of the economic system that is deemed functional to the realisation of ESR? Are these policies incompatible with other political economy approaches?

During the travaux préparatoires for the Covenant (which – it seems worth recalling – took place during the Cold War period and under the exceptional influence of the United States), there was an intense debate over whether the obligations assumed under the Covenant were inherently incompatible with one or more systems of political economy and would thus necessitate the adoption of a radically different economic system by at least some states.[171] In fact, as has been reported, the proponents of ESR were not 'unaware of the Pandora's Box that was being opened',[172] that is, 'of the reforms or, indeed, upheavals that were sometimes necessary to implement certain ESR which had not yet been recognised for the reason that a number of diverse measures had to be adopted involving changes in the country's economic and social equilibrium'.[173] Nonetheless, most probably for reasons of 'diplomatic' necessity – existing at the time of the Covenant's drafting and until the end of the Cold War, given the fragile compromise that had been reached over ESR in the Covenant – several authors and the Committee itself have made extensive efforts to affirm the idea that such inherent incompatibility does not exist. In its General Comment No. 3 (drafted in 1990), the CESCR has clarified that the Covenant

> neither requires nor precludes any particular form of government or economic system being used as the vehicle for the steps in question, provided only that it is democratic and that all human rights are thereby respected. Thus, in terms of political and economic systems the Covenant is neutral and its principles cannot accurately be described as being predicated exclusively upon the need for, or the desirability of a socialist or a capitalist system, or a mixed, centrally planned, or laissez faire economy, or upon any other

171 Alston and Quinn, 'The Nature and Scope of States Parties' Obligations', 181.

172 *Ibid.*, 168.

173 *Ibid.*, 168, quoting René Cassin, the representative of France during the drafting of the ICESCR, 7 U.N. ESCOR C.4 (232d mtg.) at 11, E/CN.4/SR.232 (1951).

> particular approach. In this regard, the Committee reaffirms that the rights recognized in the Covenant are susceptible of realization within the context of a wide variety of economic and political systems, provided only that the interdependence and indivisibility of the two sets of human rights, as affirmed inter alia in the preamble to the Covenant, is recognized and reflected in the system in question.[174]

Indeed, the Covenant itself does not explicitly dictate any particular economic system. states parties' obligations under the ICESCR are formulated in such a way as to leave governments, in principle, a considerable degree of discretion to determine for themselves how best to promote the realisation of the relevant rights.[175] However, the concerns of the drafters (and, later, of the CESCR) were, quite understandably, directed towards excluding that the realisation of ESR could be understood by some states (essentially, the Western bloc) as requiring them to adopt a different (non-market) economic system. Those historical circumstances, though, have disappeared, and we must now re-contextualise the Covenant, and re-open the debate on its possible relationship with different economic systems, in light of the current settings.

In fact, although the Covenant may have been kept *formally* 'neutral' in respect of the economic system that states might be required to adopt, if we consider, on one hand, the specific economic and fiscal policy measures that have been recommended by the Committee over the years in its Concluding Observations (described earlier), it might be argued that these seem to promote, de facto, a generally 'Keynesian'/'pro-cyclical' approach to economic and fiscal policy, and the implementation of a 'mixed economy',[176] characterised by the substantial participation of the state in the economy – also through the mobilisation and allocation of public resources – for the realisation of social (and not exclusively economic) objectives. In this sense, the measures recommended by the Committee seem inevitably destined to clash with neoliberal economic prescriptions[177] and, more generally, with the neoliberal 'economic philosophy of governance'[178] currently embedded in, and after the crisis also more stringently

174 CESCR, GC3, para. 8.

175 Alston and Quinn, 'The Nature and Scope of States Parties' Obligations', 182–183.

176 On which see Chapter 2.

177 Nolan, 'Not Fit for Purpose', 370; Wyn Grant and Graham K. Wilson, 'Introduction' in Wyn Grant and Graham K. Wilson (eds.), *The Consequences of the Global Financial Crisis: The Rhetoric of Reform and Regulation* (Oxford University Press, 2012), p. 6; Colin Crouch, *The Strange Non-Death of Neoliberalism* (Cambridge: Polity, 2011); Margot E. Salomon, 'Of Austerity, Human Rights and International Institutions' (2015) 21 *European Law Journal* 4, 543.

178 Report of the Special Rapporteur on Extreme Poverty and Human Rights, UN Doc. A/73/396 (26 September 2018), para. 67.

enforceable under the existing global and especially European economic orders.[179]

On the other hand, the Committee has been generally reluctant to engage more purposefully (and critically) with issues of economic and fiscal policy,[180] and with the possible structural causes of its concerns. This has caused, I believe, the Committee to adopt, at times, an ambiguous attitude towards economic paradigms which have been proved to have a negative impact on the realisation of ESR, in primis fiscal austerity,[181] with the result that its instructions have remained inevitably weak. This happened for instance when, as mentioned earlier, the Committee maintained that '[t]he adoption of fiscal consolidation programmes may be *necessary* for the implementation of economic and social rights'.[182] By not critically engaging with such economic paradigms, the Committee has de facto reiterated, in the circumstances addressed earlier, the subordination of ESR to the requirements of global capitalism.

The possible struggle is not anymore, as it was historically, between 'blocs' of countries with different economic ideologies, but between different political economic approaches themselves, and it manifests, this time, as a struggle to redefine the notion and typical functions of the state. It is time, I believe, to openly and methodically engage with such approaches. My hesitations are, thus, directed to persisting attempts at preserving the asserted economic 'neutrality' of international human rights law, while demanding, at the same time, an improved, more comprehensive definition of state obligations under the ICESCR. I doubt that this could be achieved without an honest, explicit consideration of the economic and social arrangements that are actually needed to realise the 'values' that underpin and should be protected through ESR.

Finally, what is the relationship between the economic and fiscal policy measures that states are 'recommended' or 'required' to adopt by the CESCR, on one side, and in the context of their other supranational economic (including debt-related) arrangements, on the other?

In addition to the fact that they are not per se legally binding (state reporting is in effect a mechanism of political supervision), the economic and fiscal policies encouraged by the Committee are also usually expressed in cautious and extremely general terms. Moreover, as has been observed, the Committee

179 See Chapter 2.

180 Nolan, 'Not Fit for Purpose', 368.

181 Jonathan D. Ostry, Prakash Loungani and Davide Furceri, 'Neoliberalism: Oversold?' (2016) 53 *Finance and Development* 2, www.imf.org/external/pubs/ft/fandd/2016/06/ostry.htm.

182 CESCR, '2016 Statement on Public Debt', para. 2 (emphasis added).

has not always been consistent and equally strict in its recommendations. On the contrary, the fiscal and economic policy requirements currently promoted in the context of international economic coordination and financial assistance arrangements (inter alia, within the European Economic and Monetary Union) are expressed in clear and detailed terms, within instruments which have a legally binding nature. These will be the object of analysis in Chapters 4 and 5.

3.5 CONCLUSIONS

This chapter has examined the existing international legal standards on ESR and sovereign debt, particularly the 1966 International Covenant on Economic, Social and Cultural Rights – especially states' general obligations relating to the use of the maximum available resources and the prohibition of non-retrogression – and the 2012 UN Guiding Principles on foreign debt and human rights, with the aim to present a useful background discussion on the nature, scope and potential limitations of the existing international legal framework applicable to the issue of sovereign debt and ESR.

Despite the efforts of the CESCR, the normative content of the ICESCR remains quite elusive, offering relatively limited protection to ESR under international law. Among the key reasons for this weakness is the legal weight assigned to the notion of available resources, as an important qualifier which inevitably restricts the scope of states' obligations under article 2(1) ICESCR to take steps to progressively achieve the full realisation of ESR. As a result, the ICESCR certainly offers legal protection, at least, to a 'human right' to a minimal welfare state – that is, to minimum subsistence levels of ESR for all – but whether and to what extent the legal protection of ESR under the Covenant goes beyond that depends on the uncertain interpretation of the notion of available resources.

Furthermore, the new emergency regime introduced by the CESCR since 2012 with regard to the prohibition of non-retrogression has been accused of further endangering the legal protection of ESR, by reducing the non-retrogression test to just two criteria (temporariness, and necessity and proportionality). Although the Committee has been generally reluctant to deliberately engage with issues of economic and fiscal policy, it has adopted a rather ambiguous stance towards economic paradigms whose negative effects on ESR have become apparent. At times, this attitude has actually reinforced the subordination of ESR to the requirements of the market.

This chapter has challenged the idea that the ICESCR can be really 'neutral' in respect of the economic system that is needed to realise ESR.

The economic and fiscal policy measures specifically recommended, over the years, by the CESCR, especially in its Concluding Observations, have de facto promoted a mixed economy system, which is seemingly contradicted by the more recent global economic developments and the neoliberal prescriptions endorsed especially by supranational institutions, including in the context of the Eurozone debt crisis.

4

Sovereign Debt and ESR in Greece (2009–)

4.1 INTRODUCTION

The outbreak of the Greek sovereign debt crisis is conventionally dated back to the famous announcement made, at the meeting of the Eurozone finance ministers on 19 October 2009, by Georgios Papaconstantinou, former Greek Minister of Finance under the then incoming socialist government of Georgios Papandreou, that Greece had significantly underreported its deficit and debt figures.[1] On that occasion, Papaconstantinou revealed that the country's deficit for 2009 would have more than doubled the estimates provided by the former conservative government (which had already revised its figures more than once, during the course of the year), amounting to 12.7 per cent of GDP, more than four times the maximum allowed by EU rules.[2] Similarly, the figure for public debt at the end of that year was revised from 113 per cent to 127–130 per cent of GDP,[3] or

[1] For timelines of the Greek debt crisis up to 2015, see Graeme Wearden, 'Greece Debt Crisis: Timeline' (2001–2010), The Guardian, 5 May 2010; Phillip Inman, 'Greek Debt Crisis: Timeline' (2009–2012), The Guardian, 9 March 2012; and Katie Allen, 'Greece Crisis Timeline: The Rocky Road to Another Bailout', The Guardian, 20 August 2015. For a history of the crisis in charts, see Matt Phillips, 'The Complete History of the Greek Debt Drama in Charts', Quartz, 30 June 2015.

[2] Greece, Ministry of Finance, 'Update of the Hellenic Stability and Growth Programme including an Updated Reform Programme', January 2010, ec.europa.eu/economy_finance/economic_governance/sgp/pdf/20_scps/2009-10/01_programme/el_2010-01-15_sp_en.pdf, p. 16.

[3] Tony Barber, 'Greece Vows Action to Cut Budget Deficit', Financial Times, 20 October 2009. Different sources report different figures, see e.g. HRC, 'IE 2014 Report on first mission to Greece', para. 22; Truth Committee on Public Debt, 'Preliminary Report', 18 June 2015, cadtm.org/Preliminary-Report-of-the-Truth, 11 and 18; Arturo C. Porzecanski, 'Behind the 2012 Greek Default and Restructuring' in Eugenio Bruno (ed.), *Sovereign Debt and Debt Restructuring: Legal, Financial and Regulatory Aspects* (London: Globe Business, 2013), pp. 34–35. This Chapter attempts to report the most accredited figures, indicating ranges whenever those are not univocal.

approximately €300 billion.[4] As is now a well-known story, the announcement plunged Greece into a destructive spiral of growing market scepticism over the country's solvency, constant increases of yields on Greek bonds, intensifying talks with other Eurozone members (who feared that the crisis could spread to other countries and destabilise the Euro Area as a whole) and mounting social unrest in Greece. Despite the attempts of the Greek government to preserve some trust from its creditors,[5] in December 2009, Fitch downgraded the country's credit rating from A– to BBB+, marking the first time in ten years that Greece had seen its rating falling below an A grade. Downgrading by Standard & Poor's and Moody's followed shortly,[6] and in the spring of 2010, the Hellenic Republic had de facto lost access to financial markets.[7] However, the prosaic version of the story tends to omit that on the other side of Greece's solvency troubles in 2009 there were mostly European banks, heavily exposed to the country. French and German banks in particular had lent to Greece, respectively, €60 and €35 billion.[8] These same banks were concurrently exposed for more than €620 billion to other countries of the Eurozone's periphery, that is, Portugal, Ireland and Spain,[9] at a time when several German banks (as those of other European countries) were already being bailed out by the government for their US losses, through a €500 billion Financial Market

4 Rosa M. Lastra, *International Financial and Monetary Law*, 2nd ed. (Oxford University Press, 2015), p. 310. Eventually, the actual figures of Greece's deficit and debt for 2009 were, respectively, 15.1 per cent and 126.7 per cent of GDP, see Eurostat data, 'Government Finance Statistics' (GFS), ec.europa.eu/eurostat/web/government-finance-statistics/overview.

5 Helena Smith, 'Papandreou Unveils Radical Reforms to Salvage Greece's Public Finances', The Guardian, 14 December 2009.

6 Helena Smith and Ashley Seager, 'Financial Markets Tumble after Fitch Downgrades Greece's Credit Rating', The Guardian, 8 December 2009; 'Greece is Downgraded by a Second Credit Rating Agency', BBC News, 16 December 2009; and 'Greece Debt Rating Downgraded by Third Agency', BBC News, 22 December 2009.

7 Richard Wachman and Nick Fletcher, 'Standard & Poor's Downgrade Greek Credit Rating to Junk Status', The Guardian, 27 April 2010.

8 Figures about the actual exposure of EU banks to Greek public debt vary. The numbers reported here are from the Bank for International Settlements, 'Consolidated positions on counterparties resident in Greece', Q4 2009, http://stats.bis.org/statx/srs/table/B4?c=GR&p=20094, and correspond also to data from the Truth Committee on Public Debt, 'Preliminary Report', 15 and 19. See also HRC, 'IE 2014 Report on first mission to Greece', para. 21, footnote 22. According to Yanis Varoufakis – Greece's Finance Minister between January and June 2015 – who has reported slightly higher figures, in the years preceding the crisis, French and German banks had lent to Greece up to €102 billion each, see Yanis Varoufakis, *Adults in the Room: My Battle with Europe's Deep Establishment* (London: Bodley Head, 2017).

9 Vanessa Fuhrmans and Sebastian Moffett, 'Exposure to Greece Weighs on French, German Banks', The New York Times, 17 February 2010.

Stabilization Fund.[10] As the saying goes, 'for every irresponsible borrower there must be an irresponsible lender'.

What followed in the Greek story, as this chapter will illustrate, were three consecutive adjustment programmes, all accompanied by harsh conditionality. They were supposed to restore – in line with consolidation narratives – Greece's fiscal sustainability, market access and economic competitiveness.[11] Instead, in 2019 Greece's debt stood at 180.5 per cent of GDP or €331.1 billion, well above its 2009 level, and at the time of writing it is projected to reach 205.2 per cent of GDP in 2020 as a consequence of the COVID-19 crisis.[12] In 2017, its already shrunken economy fell back into recession, while ten years since the outbreak of the crisis the country still had reduced access to international financial markets.[13] Economically speaking, Greece is stuck – as other highly indebted, especially developing, countries – in a debtors' prison of Dickensian memory.[14] Meanwhile, conditionality has radically transformed the country's labour market and enforced a permanent restructuring/downsizing of its welfare system. The realisation of economic, social and cultural rights in Greece has suffered an appalling setback that shows no signs of reversing, while human rights law has been almost irrelevant throughout the process.[15]

Through a comprehensive and contextualised examination of the specific, but paradigmatic, Greek debt crisis, this chapter aims at providing a further illustration of the debt trends and dynamics discussed in the previous chapters. Section 4.2 will provide background historical context for the outbreak of the crisis in 2009, zooming out from the circumstances of latter to encompass the possible structural determinants of Greece's prior fiscal vulnerability. This retrospective stems from the assumption that the economic decisions of

10 Christian Reiermann and Wolfgang Reuter, 'The State's Silent Takeover: Germany's Big Banking Bailout', Spiegel Online, 2 February 2009.

11 See e.g. HRC, 'IE 2014 Report on first mission to Greece', para. 24; IMF, 'Greece: 2013 Article IV Consultation' (5 June 2013) *IMF Country Report No. 13/154* 5; IMF, 'Greece: Request for Stand-By Arrangement' (10 May 2010) *IMF Country Report No. 10/111* 4.

12 Eurostat data, 'Government Deficit/Surplus, Debt and Associated Data', online data set code: GOV_10DD_EDPT1 (last visited 31 December 2020); IMF, 'Fiscal Monitor: Policies for the Recovery', 75.

13 'Greek Economy Sinks Back into Recession', BBC News, 16 May 2017; Elaine Moore, 'What is the Message from Greece's Bond Market?', Financial Times, 21 February 2017; Dhara Ranasinghe, Abhinav Ramnarayan and Lefteris Papadimas, 'Pariah No More? Greece Needs Big Bond Investors to Seal Its Comeback', Reuters, 30 April 2019.

14 Varoufakis, *Adults in the Room*.

15 On this issue, see in particular Nolan, 'Not Fit for Purpose?', 360; Mary Dowell-Jones, 'The Sovereign Bond Markets and Socio-Economic Rights: Understanding the Challenge of Austerity' in Riedel, Giacca and Golay (eds.), *Economic, Social and Cultural Rights in International Law*, p. 51 ff; Margot E. Salomon, 'Europe's Debt to Greece', EJIL: Talk!, 25 August 2015.

a country do not happen in a vacuum, especially in a globalised economic system, and even more so in a monetary union. Afterwards, Section 4.3 will examine the three programmes of economic adjustment undertaken by Greece since 2010, as well as the 2012 restructuring of the Greek debt. This section will not merely provide a descriptive account of facts and data. On the contrary, a critical discussion of these initiatives and of the deferential approach adopted in their regard by some human rights monitoring bodies (especially the European Court of Human Rights) will bring to light the neoliberal character of responses to the Greek debt crisis. Section 4.4 will, then, proceed to examine conditionality as a controversial tool of economic governance, and its incorporation under EU law, before illustrating the main conditionalities implemented in Greece since 2010 and their impacts on the rights to work/labour rights, health, education, adequate housing and social security (including pensions).[16] The chapter will, finally, conclude with an overall assessment of the implications of the sovereign debt crisis and responses thereto for socio-economic rights in Greece and, possibly, in the other (especially European) countries that may find themselves in a similar predicament in the future.

4.2 BEFORE THE CRISIS: GREEK ECONOMY AND DEBT AFTER THE DICTATORSHIP

Several narratives exist on the causes of the Greek sovereign debt crisis, and to try to separate the different accounts from political agendas can be a challenging task. Undoubtedly, Greece confronted the economic crisis that reached Europe in 2008 from a position of pre-existing economic and fiscal vulnerability, as this section will illustrate shortly. Nonetheless, against those who have argued that responsibility for the latter lies entirely on the Greeks, being a consequence of the country's long-standing fiscal mismanagement, others have acknowledged the importance of concurrent exogenous

[16] A brief methodological premise is, nonetheless, necessary: with the exception of more specific monitoring bodies, e.g. the Independent Expert on Foreign Debt and Human Rights, which have continued to observe the impacts of conditionality and more generally of economic/fiscal policymaking on socio-economic rights in Greece and elsewhere, after 2015 the attention of many civil society organisations and human rights bodies has increasingly shifted to other issues (e.g. the extraordinary increase in the inflow of refugees towards the EU in recent years, of which Greece itself is a foremost witness, or, lately, the effects of the COVID-19 crisis on human rights). This fact entails that, for instance, post-2015 austerity-related legislative developments in Greece have been relatively less monitored, especially by international actors. As a consequence, less data has been gathered on the impacts of conditionality on socio-economic rights, so that available reports usually reference data up to 2014/2015.

factors, particularly the architecture of the Economic and Monetary Union (EMU) and the resulting divergence in competitiveness trends among its Member States.[17] Indeed, Greece's fiscal behaviour in the years preceding the crisis and its predicament at the end of 2009 cannot be fully evaluated in isolation from the broader institutional and economic context. To this end, it seems necessary to review in brief the main elements of Greece's economic history after the end of the seven-year military dictatorship in 1974 and its transition to parliamentary democracy.

Most sources agree that the high level of the Greek debt at the onset of the debt crisis was essentially the main heir to debts accumulated during the period 1980–1993, in line with the more general upward trend of public indebtedness discussed in Chapter 2. During those thirteen years, in fact, the debt-to-GDP ratio of the country increased by 70.4 percentage points, compared to an increase of 11.9 percentage points in the fourteen years between 1993 and 2007.

Until the mid-1970s, Greek governments had followed the 'golden rule' of allowing fiscal deficits only for public investment purposes, so that, until 1980, the country's deficit had remained below 3 per cent of GDP. However, confronted with a stagnating economic situation and high unemployment rates after that the Greek 'economic miracle' of the 1960s had been brought to an end by the energy crises of the 1970s, the socialist governments that ruled for two consecutive terms, between 1981 and 1989, responded with the adoption of expansionary fiscal policies. These were aimed at the protection of income and employment, mostly by means of social transfers and bailouts of insolvent firms by state-owned banks.[18] The period 1981–1993 witnessed also in Greece

[17] Costas Lapavitsas, Annina Kaltenbrunner, Duncan Lindo, Jo Michell, Juan Pablo Painceira, Eugenia Pires, Jeff Powell, Alexis Stenfors and Nuno Teles, 'Euro-zone Crisis: Beggar Thyself and Thy Neighbour' (2010) 12 *Journal of Balkan and Near Eastern Studies* 4, 321–373; Costas Simitis, *The European Debt Crisis: The Greek Case* (Manchester University Press, 2014); Heiner Flassbeck and Costas Lapavitsas, *Against the Troika: Crisis and Austerity in the Eurozone* (London: Verso, 2015); Lastra, *International Financial and Monetary Law*, p. 311; Andrew Yianni and Nikita Aggarwal, 'Eurozone Financial Rescue and Stabilization Measures, and Their Legal Foundations' in Lastra and Buchheit, *Sovereign Debt Management*, paras. 26.06–26.19.

[18] Stavros B. Thomadakis, 'Growth, Debt and Sovereignty Prolegomena to the Greek Crisis', GreeSE Paper No. 91, LSE Hellenic Observatory Papers on Greece and Southeast Europe, May 2015, 5–7. The 1980s have been described by some commentators as a period, in many countries, of 'redistribution without growth' and 'macroeconomic populism', when, according to this view, macroeconomic policy was essentially used for the attainment of mass political outcomes. The concept of 'macroeconomic populism' is attributed to Rudiger Dornbusch and Sebastian Edwards (eds.), *The Macroeconomics of Populism in Latin America* (University of Chicago Press, 1991).

the emergence of strong electoral-fiscal cycles, where systemic fiscal expansions occurred shortly before election periods. It was estimated that each one of the seven electoral contests held in Greece over the period 1974–1993 increased the public deficit by 1.83 per cent of GDP on average. Pre-election populism alone translated into cumulative deficits of about 13 per cent of GDP.[19]

Consequently, in 1981 the country's deficit rose to 9 per cent of GDP and lingered at almost 10 per cent of GDP on average until 1990.[20] As a result, public debt exploded. Whilst before 1981 the country's debt-to-GDP ratio had been fluctuating under 20 per cent, between 1981 and 1993, it rose to 94 per cent of GDP, bequeathing the country the high debt burden that has threatened its stability ever since.[21]

On the contrary – thanks to a combination of fiscal stabilisation, modest tax reforms, increased foreign investments,[22] lower interest rates, and the inflow of European funds[23] – the period 1990–2007 was for Greece one of impressive economic growth, large public investments and an import boom.[24] The rate of GDP growth at market prices went from negative at the beginning of the 1980s to an average 3.7 per cent per year between 1996 and 2006, with peaks of 5.9 per cent and 5.5 per cent respectively in 2003 and 2006.[25] Consequently, the years 1993–2007 saw the quasi-stabilisation of the Greek debt, from 94 per cent to 103 per cent of GDP (see Figure 4.1).

In economic terms, before the 2007 financial crisis and the ensuing economic downturn, Greece was considered a 'star performer' in Europe, compared to countries that had started in a similar economic position, such as Spain or Portugal, but had grown at lower annual average rates (over 1996–2006, Spain and Portugal grew, respectively, at 3 per cent and

19 Thomadakis, 'Growth, Debt and Sovereignty Prolegomena to the Greek Crisis', 9; Stavros B. Thomadakis, 'The Greek Economy: Performance, Expectations and Paradoxes' in Graham Allison and Kalïpso Nicolaidis (eds.), *The Greek Paradox* (Cambridge, MA: MIT Press, 1997), pp. 39–60; George Alogoskoufis, 'Greece's Sovereign Debt Crisis: Retrospect and Prospect', GreeSE Paper No. 54, Hellenic Observatory Papers on Greece and Southeast Europe, January 2012, 16–17.

20 Alogoskoufis, 'Greece's Sovereign Debt Crisis', 17.

21 *Ibid.*

22 The 1990s were characterised by an important reform of the domestic financial sector and the liberalisation of capital movements, which led to large-scale capital inflows especially after the stabilisation of the drachma in 1998, Alogoskoufis, 'Greece's Sovereign Debt Crisis', 14.

23 EU transfers have amounted regularly to 4–5 per cent of GDP per year, *ibid.*, 11, footnote 10.

24 *Ibid.*, 10–11; Simitis, *The European Debt Crisis*, p. 3.

25 Eurostat data, 'GDP and Main Components, Volumes: GDP at Market Prices, Percentage Change on Previous Period', ec.europa.eu/eurostat/data/database. See also OECD data, 'Aggregate National Accounts, SNA 2008 (or SNA 1993): Gross Domestic Product', www.oecd-ilibrary.org/economics/data/aggregate-national-accounts/gross-domestic-product_data-00001-en.

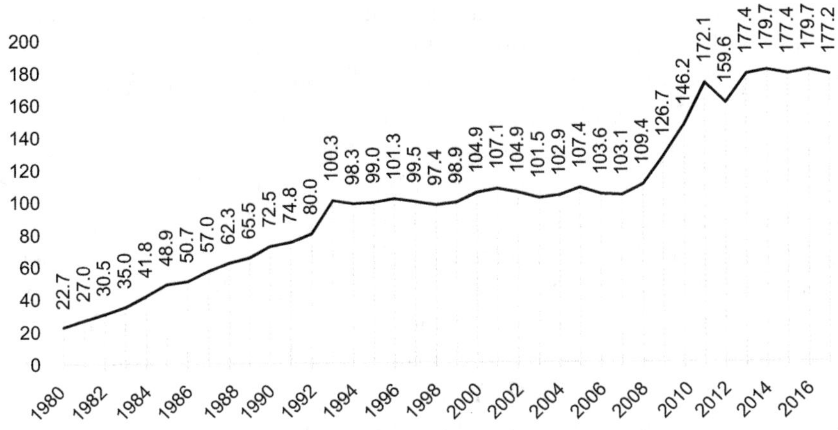

FIGURE 4.1 Greece – general government debt, 1980–2017 (per cent of GDP)
Source: AMECO (2017) Database

2 per cent).[26] However, as will be mentioned shortly, economic growth in Greece, especially since 2001, was essentially debt-driven.

Greece's entry in the Eurozone, effective as of 2001, was approved in 1999 with, allegedly, public debt at around 100 per cent of GDP and deficit below 3 per cent of GDP. In 2004, these statistical data were contested by Eurostat and revised upward, and the European Commission launched an infringement procedure against Greece.[27] The country effectively accessed the EMU without meeting the necessary fiscal requirements.

In addition, participation in the Eurozone marked for Greece, as for the other Member States of the Euro Area,[28] a qualitative change in the sovereignty of debt.[29] With the transfer of monetary sovereignty to the European Central Bank, monetisation of debts and currency devaluations were removed from the government's debt management toolkit, and debt sovereignty restricted to servicing, refinancing or defaulting on debts.[30]

26 *Ibid.*

27 Eurostat, 'Report on the Revision of the Greek Government Deficit and Debt Figures' (22 November 2004). The infringement procedure was dismissed in 2007, when the Commission concluded that the measures adopted in the meantime by the Greek authorities had annulled the procedure's specific grounds, see European Commission, 'Report on Greek Government Deficit and Debt Statistics' (COM(2010)) 1 Final, 8 January 2010, 16.

28 See e.g. IMF, 'World Economic Outlook, October 2020', 116 ff.

29 Thomadakis, 'Growth, Debt and Sovereignty', 16.

30 *Ibid.* Monetisation of government debt is prohibited under Article 123(1) TFEU and Article 21 of the Statute of the European System of Central Banks and of the European Central Bank,

Accession to the Euro Area was also accompanied by the ability to issue debt without exchange risk, borrowing in the common currency. If this, on one hand, removed a previous barrier to market access for both the government and private agents in Greece, on the other, it intensified opportunities to (over) borrow, especially since the interest rates at the time were favourably low.[31] Most importantly, in the early years of the euro, financial markets did not evaluate the difference in sovereign assets across the EMU, so that Eurozone countries of actually different creditworthiness all received similar, very low interest rates for their bonds.[32] This fact entailed that, although in the meantime the economic and fiscal performance of Greece had started deteriorating, as will be said shortly, until 2007 Greek bonds enjoyed the same market conditions of German bonds.[33] The absence of market discipline, attributed by some to the optimism of financial markets, reassured by Greece's persisting high growth rates, has been credited among the causes of the 'fiscal fatigue' that contributed to the Eurozone crisis.[34] In fact, since 2001, Greece had relaxed its fiscal management, with a crucial turnaround in 2002 towards primary fiscal deficit (–0.5 per cent of GDP), opposite to the surplus trend of the period 1995–2001.[35] It also experienced a considerable worsening of its external current account deficit,[36] by some considered in no small part a consequence of the design of the Euro Area itself. In fact, with the adoption of the single currency, the mostly southern economies of the Eurozone struggled to maintain competitiveness in the face of a stronger currency and of wage inflation exceeding gains in labour productivity. The constraints of the single currency and a 'one-size-fits-all' monetary policy meant that these external imbalances could not be accommodated through real external exchange rate adjustments, and this eventually led to the accumulation of increasingly large current account deficits.[37] Dwindling competitiveness combined with lower external borrowing costs encouraged the 'deficit countries' of

see Lastra, *International Financial and Monetary Law*, p. 295. By adopting the single currency, furthermore, Eurozone Member States have lost their currency devaluation powers.

31 Thomadakis, 'Growth, Debt and Sovereignty', 20.

32 Lastra, *International Financial and Monetary Law*, pp. 312–313.

33 Thomadakis, 'Growth, Debt and Sovereignty', 20.

34 *Ibid.*, 20; Lastra, *International Financial and Monetary Law*, p. 312; Paul De Grauwe and Yuemei Ji, 'Mispricing of Sovereign Risk and Multiple Equilibria in the Eurozone' (20 January 2012) *Centre for European Policy Working Paper* No. 61.

35 AMECO Database (2017), ec.europa.eu/economy_finance/ameco. General government 'primary fiscal/budget balance' measures the difference between government expenditures *excluding interest payments on debt* and revenues.

36 Thomadakis, 'Growth, Debt and Sovereignty', 20.

37 Yianni and Aggarwal, 'Eurozone Financial Rescue and Stabilization Measures', paras. 26.08–26.09.

the Euro Area to borrow heavily and to rely on consumption-led economic growth.[38]

Furthermore, the adoption of the euro led to a drastic increase in private debt, from 74 per cent of GDP in 2001 to 129.1 per cent of GDP in 2009. Important European private banks, especially French and German,[39] participated actively in this sharp increase, also through direct participation in Greek banks, often underestimating the credit risks, in Greece as well as in other Eurozone countries such as Ireland, Italy and Spain.[40]

After 2001, thus, economic growth in Greece was dependent on the continued ability of the country to obtain external finance. With the credit crunch that followed the 2007 global financial crisis, the illusion came to an end. At this point, the conservative government of Karamanlis enacted a policy of large fiscal expansion (2007–2009), probably in an attempt to stimulate demand and prevent the growth rate of the economy from declining any further.[41] This choice, however, proved completely misguided and provoked a critical deterioration of the country's fiscal position. The year 2008 was marked, for the first time after almost two decades of positive rates, by negative GDP growth. Primary fiscal deficit reached 5.4 per cent of GDP in 2008 and 10.1 per cent in 2009. Between 2007 and 2009, the debt-to-GDP ratio shot from 103.1 per cent to 113 per cent, before being revised to 126.7 per cent of GDP with Papaconstantinou's announcement in November 2009.[42]

As has been correctly remarked, however, Greece was the rule rather than the exception. In fact, every one of the member countries of the Eurozone experienced a major fiscal deterioration between 2007 and 2009 as a consequence of Europe's economic downturn and the added fiscal costs of various bank bailouts. While Greece's fiscal deficit widened by 9.3 percentage points of GDP during the two years, the fiscal position of the Eurozone as a whole widened by 5.7 percentage points (the UK's own 2009 budget deficit was equivalent to 11.3 per cent of GDP).[43] Furthermore, as mentioned in Chapter 2, in the aftermath of the 2007 crisis, a substantial increase in sovereign debt took place all over the world. According to the IMF, between 2008 and 2014, general government debt increased globally from 65 per cent to

38 Thomadakis, 'Growth, Debt and Sovereignty', 22; Truth Committee on Public Debt, 'Preliminary Report', 14.

39 Including BNP, Société Générale and Crédit Agricole for France (through its participation in the Greek bank Emporiki) and Commerzbank, Baden Bank, Postbank and DZ Bank for Germany, Truth Committee on Public Debt, 'Preliminary Report', 16, note 17.

40 *Ibid.*, 14; Lastra, *International Financial and Monetary Law*, p. 313.

41 Thomadakis, 'Growth, Debt and Sovereignty', 27.

42 AMECO Database (2017).

43 Porzecanski, 'Behind the 2012 Greek Default and Restructuring', p. 3.

79.8 per cent of GDP, from 78.8 per cent to 105.3 per cent of GDP in advanced economies and from 68.6 per cent to 94 per cent of GDP in the Euro Area.[44]

Nonetheless, the idea of a fiscal crisis has been contested, in particular, by the Greek Truth Committee on Public Debt.[45] With regard to the abrupt increase of the Greek deficit and debt levels between 2007 and 2009, the Committee has argued that in 2009, the newly elected socialist government of Papandreou intentionally 'falsified' statistical data to 'dramatize' the fiscal situation in Greece and, with the collaboration of the EU institutions, helped to present elements of what in reality was a *banking crisis*, as a *sovereign debt crisis*, in order to convince the public opinion in the country and in Europe to support a Greek bailout.[46] In this sense the Committee has highlighted, among several alleged cases of falsification, the irregular statistical treatment of hospital and public corporations' liabilities, and of certain Credit Default Swaps (CDS) with Goldman Sachs. The latter have been the object of heated criticism, as the US investment bank was accused of helping the Greek government to 'hide' part of its debt from the budget, by arranging additional credit to Greece through the use of CDS with fictional ('off-market') exchange rates. This was, nonetheless, done in accordance with Eurostat reporting rules.[47]

While these kinds of transactions are undoubtedly revelatory of the 'collusive' and opaque nature of the relationship between governments and private economic actors,[48] of the potentially illicit use of derivatives by the former,

44 Truth Committee on Public Debt, 'Preliminary Report', 20; IMF, 'Fiscal Monitor: Now is the time: Fiscal Policies for Sustainable Growth' (April 2015).

45 Established on 4 April 2015 by the former President of the Hellenic Parliament, Zoe Konstantopoulou (Coalition of the Radical Left, SYRIZA). Before being suppressed on 12 November 2015 by the new Parliament brought about by the snap election of September 2015, the Truth Committee released a further report on the 'Illegitimacy, Illegality, Odiousness and Unsustainability of the August 2015 MoU and Loan Agreement' (August 2015), cadtm.org/Illegitimacy-Illegality-Odiousness.

46 Truth Committee on Public Debt, 'Preliminary Report', 15 and 20.

47 For a clear explanation of the deal and the role of the debt managers of certain Eurozone countries in the lax drafting of the ESA95 rules, see Nicola Dunbar, 'Revealed: Goldman Sachs' Mega Deal for Greece', Risk.net, July 2003, www.risk.net/derivatives/structured-products/1498135/revealed-goldman-sachs-mega-deal-greece. On the issue, see also Tracy Alloway, 'Goldman's Trojan Currency Swap', Financial Times, 9 February 2010; Andrew Clark, Heather Stewart and Elena Moya, 'Goldman Sachs Faces FED Inquiry Over Greek Crisis', The Guardian, 26 February 2010; Jim Armitage and Ben Chu, 'Greek Debt Crisis: Goldman Sachs could be Sued for Helping Hide Debts When It Joined the Euro', The Independent, 10 July 2015; William D. Cohan, 'Plenty Deserve Blame for Greece's Woes, but Maybe Not Goldman Sachs', The New York Times, 13 July 2015.

48 It is widely acknowledged that other Eurozone countries, e.g. Italy, have used similar financial instruments, Dunbar, 'Revealed: Goldman Sachs' Mega Deal for Greece'.

and of intentional loopholes left available in fiscal reporting, and should correctly be the object of concern in their own right, they cannot be considered, in the Greek case, as having had a decisive effect on the country's fiscal situation. It has been speculated that, most likely, the cash flows were either used to help lower the debt/GDP ratio from 107 per cent in 2001 to 104.9 per cent in 2002, or interest payments from 7.4 per cent in 2001 to 6.4 per cent in 2002.[49] In any case, the fiscal imbalances of the country remained severe, notwithstanding the disputable transactions with Goldman Sachs.

Furthermore, the links between governments and financial systems are so intricate that they have become 'communicating vessels: strength or weakness in one flows to the other, and back [...]'.[50] As mentioned in the chapter's introduction, there are always two sides of the 'debt coin'. Certainly, behind the over-indebtedness of Greece, as behind that of most countries who suffered from a major debt crisis since the 1980s, there were unconscionable creditors, and the trigger of the economic crisis in Europe, it must not be forgotten, was the financial havoc caused by the 2007 sub-prime crisis in the United States. The law should certainly work to prevent and punish the misconduct and the irresponsibility of those involved. Nonetheless, to attribute the 2009 predicament of Greece to a banking crisis allegedly disguised as a sovereign debt crisis may risk overlooking the pre-existing economic difficulties of the country, and distract from the other, more fundamental questions that remain to be addressed: Why has Greece's economic 'survival' – as that of an increasing number of states, as argued in Chapter 2 – been so dependent on debt/external funding, including in the post-2001 economic and institutional context? Have the structural (economic and institutional) causes of such dependence been addressed by any of the political/institutional actors involved?

4.3 AFTER THE CRISIS: FINANCIAL ASSISTANCE FROM THE EU AND THE IMF (2010–2018)

Since 2010, Greece has received financial assistance from other Euro Area Member States and the IMF under three different programmes, launched respectively in 2010, 2012 and 2015.[51]

49 *Ibid.*

50 Anne Gelpern, 'Sovereign Debt and Banking Crises: An "Arial View"' in Lastra and Buchheit, *Sovereign Debt Management*, Chapter 15.

51 For full details and documentation on the three programmes, see European Commission, 'Financial Assistance to Greece'. A useful 'tracker' of Greece's repayments is available on the

It must be noted that, at the onset of the Eurozone crisis, the EU did not have a mechanism in place to assist Member States in financial difficulties. Besides a medium-term balance of payment (MTBoPA) facility available on the basis of article 143 TFEU under Council Regulation (EC) No. 332/2002[52] only to non-Eurozone Member States,[53] the only other provision in this sense was article 122 TFEU, which allows the Council, on a proposal from the Commission, to grant, under certain conditions, financial assistance to a Member State in difficulties or seriously threatened with severe difficulties that are caused by natural disasters or exceptional occurrences beyond the Member State's control.

Instead, articles 123 to 125 TFEU explicitly prohibit the monetisation of government debt, privileged access to financial institutions and the mutual guarantee of debts. In particular article 125 TFEU, or the so-called no bail-out rule, provides that neither the Union nor a Member State shall be 'liable for or assume the commitments of central governments, regional, local or other public authorities, other bodies governed by public law, or public undertakings of any Member State, without prejudice to mutual financial guarantees for the joint execution of a specific project'.[54] Therefore, different mechanisms to assist Greece and the other Euro Area Member States in financial difficulty were progressively put in place, remarkably outside the EU legal framework, by means of new intergovernmental agreements (as has been done as well in response to the currently ongoing COVID-19 crisis).

4.3.1 *The First Economic Adjustment Programme (8 May 2010)*

Under a *First Economic Adjustment Programme* (8 May 2010) – whose granting was controversially based on article 122(2) TFEU, since the situation of Greece was considered to be an 'exceptional occurrence beyond the country's control' – Greece was initially accorded assistance for €110 billion, to be disbursed

Financial Times' website, see 'Greek Debt Tracker', https://ig.ft.com/sites/2015/greek-debt-monitor/. *The Wall Street Journal* provides also an informative 'Greece's Debt Due' webpage, with data on Greek outstanding repayments by holder, until 2059, https://graphics.wsj.com/greece-debt-timeline/.

52 Council Regulation (EC) No. 332/2002 of 18 February 2002 establishing a facility providing medium-term financial assistance for Member States' balances of payments [2002] OJ L053.

53 Financial assistance under the MTBoPA (whose funds are raised by the Commission on behalf of the EU in international financial markets) was provided, at the beginning of the crisis, to Hungary, Latvia and Romania, see Lastra, *International Financial and Monetary Law*, p. 296, paras. 8.41–8.42. See also European Commission, 'Balance of Payments (BoP) Assistance'.

54 Lastra, *International Financial and Monetary Law*, p. 296; Rosa M. Lastra and Jean-Victor Louis, 'European Economic and Monetary Union: History, Trends and Prospects' (2013) 32 *Yearbook of European Law* 1, 43–44.

between May 2010 and June 2013. Out of the total, €80 billion was to be provided by the Euro Area Member States through bilateral, non-concessional loans on the basis of an Intercreditor Agreement[55] and a Loan Facility Agreement between the lenders (with the exception of Germany, who acted in this case through its bank KfW) and Greece.[56] The bilateral loans were centrally pooled by the European Commission, which, according to the Intercreditor Agreement, would represent the states parties in organising and administering the loans pursuant to the terms of the Loan Facility Agreement,[57] and would negotiate and sign on their behalf (subject to prior approval by all of them) the Loan Facility Agreement and the Memorandum of Understanding (MoU) with Greece (on which, see further in subsequent sections).[58] It must be noted that these loans were initiated with an 'onerous' interest rate.[59] Allegedly, this policy choice was meant to act as an incentive for Greece to return to market-based financing as soon as possible. However, as a result, the Truth Committee on Public Debt has reported that, by March 2012, Greece had transferred to the Euro Area Member States €2.614 billion of interest payments[60] and, since some of the creditor countries' borrowing costs were lower than the lending rate (e.g. Italy, among other

55 Intercreditor Agreement (hereinafter, IA) between Kingdom of Belgium, Federal Republic of Germany, Ireland, Kingdom of Spain, French Republic, Italian Republic, Republic of Cyprus, Grand Duchy of Luxembourg, Republic of Malta, Kingdom of the Netherlands, Republic of Austria, Portuguese Republic, Republic of Slovenia, Slovak Republic and Republic of Finland, 8 May 2010, 'Euro Area Loan Facility Act 2010' [Ireland], Schedule 1.

56 Loan Facility Agreement (hereinafter, LFA) between the following Member States whose currency is the euro: Kingdom of Belgium, Ireland, Kingdom of Spain, French Republic, Italian Republic, Republic of Cyprus, Grand Duchy of Luxembourg, Republic of Malta, Kingdom of the Netherlands, Republic of Austria, Portuguese Republic, Republic of Slovenia, Slovak Republic and Republic of Finland and KfW, acting in the public interest, subject to the instructions of an with the benefit of the guarantee of the Federal Republic of Germany, as Lenders and The Hellenic Republic as Borrower, the Bank of Greece as Agent to the Borrower, 8 May 2010, 'Euro Area Loan Facility Act 2010' [Ireland], Schedule 2. The initial amount was subsequently reduced by €2.7 billion, as Slovakia decided not to participate in the Loan Facility Agreement, and Ireland and Portugal stepped down from the facility as they requested financial assistance themselves, see European Commission, 'Financial Assistance to Greece'.

57 IA, Art. 1(1).

58 IA, Art. 2(1).

59 This was set at the variable rate of three-month Euribor plus 300 basis points. Consequently, in August 2011, the interest rate on the bilateral loans reached over 4.6 per cent. In 2011, thus, the spread was retroactively cut to 150 basis points and on 27 November 2012 the spread was cut to 50 basis points, see Zsolt Darvas and Pia Hüttl, 'How to Reduce the Greek Debt Burden?', Bruegel, 9 January 2015.

60 Truth Committee on Public Debt, 'Preliminary Report', 23. The Truth Committee extrapolated this figure by summing up all the interest payments (in EUR billion) charged to Greece by the euro area Member States between June 2010 and March 2012, as reported in European

countries, has financed its loans to Greece by issuing medium- and long-term bonds)[61] some lenders actually profited out of the loans.

The remaining €30 billion planned as part of the assistance, was to be provided by the IMF, under a three-year stand-by arrangement (SBA).[62] It must be noted that, in order to participate in the assistance under the terms dictated by the EU, the IMF had to bend its core rule of providing financial support only to remedy temporary problems of liquidity and not of prolonged and unsustainable indebtedness (i.e. insolvency), by amending its Policy for Exceptional Access Lending's requirement of 'high probability of public debt being sustainable in the medium term' and creating a so-called 'systemic exemption', to allow for large-scale financing without a prior debt reduction operation to go ahead where 'there is a high risk of international systemic spillovers' (and Greece, as part of the Eurozone, was deemed to meet this definition).[63] Secondly, the IMF had to accept the EU's opposition to an ex ante debt restructuring, contrary to previous IMF practice, despite the vast majority of IMF officials and several commentators in 2010 considered a restructuring of the Greek debt as necessary and inevitable.[64] In a later 2013 report on the evaluation of the assistance provided to Greece in 2010, the Fund admitted that

> [i]n the event, the SBA-supported program served as a holding operation. [...] *An upfront debt restructuring would have been better for Greece* although this was not acceptable to the Euro partners. A *delayed debt restructuring also provided a window for private creditors to reduce exposures and shift debt into official hands*. As seen earlier, this shift occurred on a significant scale and limited the bail-in of creditors when [Private Sector Involvement] eventually

Commission, 'The Second Economic Adjustment Programme for Greece' (March 2012) *Occasional Papers* No. 94, 45.

61 Law No. 99 of 22 June 2010, 'Conversione in legge del decreto-legge 10 maggio 2010, n. 67, recante disposizioni urgenti per la salvaguardia della stabilità finanziaria dell'area euro. Ordine di esecuzione dell'accordo denominato "Intercreditor Agreement" e dell'accordo denominato "Loan Facility Agreement" stipulati in data 8 maggio 2010', GU No. 150 of 30 June 2010.

62 LFA, Preamble, para. (3).

63 IMF, Decision No. 14064-(08/18) of 22 February 2008, as amended by Decision Nos. 14184-(08/93) of 29 October 2008, 14284-(09/29) of 24 March 2009, BUFF/10/56 of 9 May 2010, and 14716-(10/83) of 30 August 2010, 'Access Policy and Limits in the Credit Tranches and under the Extended Fund Facility and on Overall Access to the Fund's General Resources, and Exceptional Access Policy – Review and Modification', in IMF, *Selected Decisions and Selected Documents of the International Monetary Fund*, 35th Issue, 31 December 2010, 426–427; IMF, 'Sovereign Debt Restructuring – Recent Developments and Implications for the Fund's Legal and Policy Framework' (26 April 2013), 20, para. 22, www.imf.org/external/np/pp/eng/2013/042613.pdf.

64 Leslsy Wroughton, Howard Schneider and Dina Kyriakidou, 'How the IMF's Greek Misadventure is Changing the Fund', Ekathimerini.com, 28 August 2015.

took place [in 2012, see further below], leaving taxpayers and the official sector on the hook.[65]

Furthermore, in 2015 the IMF removed the 'systemic exemption' from its Policy for Exceptional Access Lending, arguing i.a. that, besides aggravating moral hazard in the international financial system, the exemption 'reduce[d] safeguards for Fund resources since, if a debt restructuring is eventually needed, a smaller pool of private sector claims would be available to absorb losses'.[66]

In fact, it has been argued – and the just-quoted IMF statement seems to confirm – that the high exposure of foreign banks to Greece was the key reason behind the unwillingness to apply an early haircut on bonds, and that the first assistance package was essentially aimed at rescuing Greece's private creditors, that is, European banks, rather than the country itself.[67] During the implementation of the programme, in fact, there was a dramatic transformation in the profile and ownership of the Greek debt. European and Greek banks massively sold off Greek bonds, so that public debt privately owned was eventually transferred into public hands, to the other Eurozone Member States and the Member States of the IMF (while, in the meantime, private debt was being 'socialised' with taxpayers' money through the bailouts of banks across Europe). Euro Area banks' exposure to Greece, which had peaked at about €128 billion in 2008, progressively dropped to €12 billion in September 2013,[68] while the share of 'official' loans to the country increased from 5.2 per cent to 73.06 per cent in 2014.[69]

4.3.2 *The Second Economic Adjustment Programme (14 March 2012) and the Greek Debt Restructuring (2012)*

On 14 March 2012, Greece was granted further assistance under a *Second Economic Adjustment Programme*, covering the period 2012–2014 (assistance

65 IMF, 'Greece: Ex Post Evaluation of Exceptional Access under the 2010 Stand-By Arrangement' (June 2013) *IMF Country Report No. 13/156*, 28, para. 57, www.imf.org/external/pubs/ft/scr/2013/cr13156.pdf (emphasis added); see also Lastra and Buchheit, *Sovereign Debt Management*, paras. 5.02 and 5.39.

66 IMF, 'The Fund's Lending Framework and Sovereign Debt-Further Considerations', Policy Paper (9 April 2015), 3 and 18–20.

67 Truth Committee on Public Debt, 'Preliminary Report', 19; Ronald Janssen, 'Greece and the IMF: Who Exactly is Being Saved?' (Center for Economic and Policy Research, July 2010, 6; Varoufakis, *Adults in the Room*.

68 By March 2012, German banks' exposure to Greek public debt was down to less than €795 million; French banks had totally eliminated Greek debt from their books by December 2012; and UK banks' exposure, which was €13bn in March 2008, dropped to €4.3bn by December 2012, *ibid.*; Alberto Nardelli and Silvia Merler, 'The Greek Debt: What Creditors May Stand to Lose', The Guardian, 19 June 2015.

69 Truth Committee on Public Debt, 'Preliminary Report', 20.

was later extended to 30 June 2015) for a total amount of €164.5 billion. These comprised the unreleased amounts of the first programme, plus an additional €130 billion, and mandated an initial allocation of €48 billion for the recapitalisation of the Greek banks who suffered losses from the debt restructuring (on which see further).[70] Out of the total, €144.7 billion was provided by Euro Area Member States, this time via the European Financial Stability Facility (EFSF), a société anonyme (limited liability company) incorporated in Luxemburg and whose sole shareholders are the Euro Area Member States, established in June 2010 by an intergovernmental agreement.[71] The IMF, on its part, contributed €19.8 billion under a four-year Extended Fund Facility approved in March 2012.[72]

4.3.2.1 The Greek Debt Restructuring of 2012

As mentioned earlier, the second 'rescue plan' was preceded by a restructuring of the Greek debt owned by private sector investors, known as Private Sector Involvement (PSI), which represented the largest restructuring in world history and the first major one in Europe since the defaults preceding the Second World War.[73] Private sector holders of €205.5 billion of Greek debt were 'invited'[74] to forgive 53.3 per cent of what they were owed under 135 series of bonds, and to exchange 31.5 per cent of their remaining principal for new, low-coupon Greek bonds with maturities of eleven to thirty years and the rest (15 per cent) for two-year notes issued by the EFSF.[75] Loans from the European Union and the IMF (€74 billion), who were providing new funding to Greece, were reasonably excluded from the deal. More controversially, however, the ECB had also set its holdings apart from and above all other bonds by concluding an agreement with Greece, on 15 February 2012, for the exchange of its Greek debt instruments (approximately €50 billion) and those held by national central banks for new securities whose nominal value, interest rate and interest payment and repayment

70 *Ibid.*

71 'EFSF Framework Agreement' of 7 June 2010.

72 Yianni and Aggarwal, 'Eurozone Financial Rescue and Stabilization Measures', p. 426, footnote 27.

73 Jeromin Zettelmeyer, Christoph Trebesh and Mitu Gulati, 'The Greek Debt Restructuring: An Autopsy' (2013) 28 *Economic Policy* 75, 513–563; Alexander Metallinos, 'The Greek Sovereign Debt Restructuring' in Bruno, *Sovereign Debt and Debt Restructuring*; Porzecanski, 'Behind the 2012 Greek Default and Restructuring'.

74 For the original text of the 'Invitation Memorandum', see 'Invitation of the Hellenic Republic', 24 February 2012, http://ftalphaville.ft.com/files/2012/02/Reg_S_Invitation_Memorandum.pdf.

75 Porzecanski, 'Behind the 2012 Greek Default and Restructuring', pp. 40–41.

dates were identical to the original securities, but which bore different serial numbers and dates.[76] Furthermore, the European Investment Bank was also exempted from any haircut, prompting complaints from private investors and criticism by various commentators.[77]

Although the PSI was labelled as a 'voluntary transaction' and included some incentives,[78] it has been correctly observed that it was not genuinely voluntary in various respects. In particular, with a so-called Bondholders Act[79] the Greek Parliament retroactively introduced collective action clauses (CACs) into the €177 billion of targeted bonds governed by Greek law,[80] enabling bondholders to conclude a collective agreement with the state, deciding by an enhanced majority. Therefore, once the consent of €152 billion of bonds (representing almost 86 per cent of holders) was received, the terms of the remaining €25 billion were amended as if they too had consented.[81] As a result, bonds with outstanding principal value of €199 billion were successfully restructured (i.e. 96.6 per cent of total €205.5 billion of eligible bonds), and the total amount of debt prior to the exchange (€356 billion as of end 2011) was reduced by €106 billion.

The PSI has been criticised on various fronts, including, prominently, because it imposed big losses on public entities and small bondholders.[82] These were not compensated in any way while, at the same time, as mentioned, the second economic adjustment programme earmarked almost €50 billion for bank recapitalisation, thus providing full compensation to the banks who had taken part in the PSI (Greece's four biggest banks reported a combined loss of €27.9 billion).[83]

Pension schemes in particular lost €14.5 billion out of total capital reserves of €21 billion. It is estimated that more than 15,000 families lost their life savings and, among these, at least seventeen suicides have been

76 *Ibid.*

77 *Ibid.*

78 Metallinos, 'The Greek Sovereign Debt Restructuring', pp. 22–23.

79 Law 4050/2012 of 23 February 2012 on Rules relating to the adjustment of securities, their issue or guarantee by the Greek state with the agreement of the bond holders. For an unofficial translation of the bill, see Andreas Koutras, 'A Better Translation of Bondholders Act 4050', andreaskoutras.blogspot.com.au/2012/03/better-tarnslation-of-bondholders-act.html.

80 In 2012, there were €29 billion of bonds held by private sector creditors that were issued under foreign law, €5.5 billion of which have remained, after the PSI, in the hands of holdout investors, see Porzecanski, 'Behind the 2012 Greek Default and Restructuring'.

81 Metallinos, 'The Greek Sovereign Debt Restructuring', p. 24; Porzecanski, 'Behind the 2012 Greek Default and Restructuring', p. 41.

82 See also the IMF statement quoted above, Section 4.3.1.

83 Porzecanski, 'Behind the 2012 Greek Default and Restructuring'; Metallinos, 'The Greek Sovereign Debt Restructuring'; Truth Committee on Public Debt, 'Preliminary Report', 20.

recorded.[84] In his 2014 report on his first mission to Greece, the former Independent Expert on Foreign Debt and Human Rights Cephas Lumina expressed his concern at allegations that 'when purchasing their bonds, some Greek investors were misled by bank personnel who failed to adhere to the Markets in Financial Instruments Directive (MiFID Directive 2004/39/EC)', and that 'bondholders relied on representations contained in official European Union and European Central Bank documentation, as well as statements made by public institutions, namely the Bank of Greece and the Public Debt Management Agency, on the State's economic health'.[85] He emphasised the 'serious financial hardship' experienced by bondholders who had invested most of their savings in what they understood to be relatively safe investments, to fund their retirement, own healthcare needs or care of disabled family members, while severe cuts to pensions and other social benefits were also being implemented.

The appeals filed by small investors before national and supranational courts all essentially resolved with the courts 'avoiding' engagement with the restructuring decision of the state, paying extreme deference to the authorities' margin of appreciation, and shifting most of the consequences of the 'risk' on small investors.[86]

In 2014, in the case of *Mamatas and others* v. *Greece*,[87] 6,320 Greek private bondholders petitioned the European Court of Human Rights (ECtHR) alleging that their forcible participation in the 2012 restructuring had amounted to a de facto expropriation of their property, and that they had suffered discrimination as compared with other creditors, particularly institutional creditors, holding bonds for a total value of several billion euros.

84 *Ibid.* See also 'Greek Debt Haircut Led 15 Bondholders to Kill Themselves', The National Herald, 4 December 2014. Suicide cases related to bank rescues have been reported also in other countries, e.g. Italy, see Jim Brunsden and Patrick Jenkins, 'Bank Rescues: Putting Bondholders on the Hook', Financial Times, 4 January 2016.

85 HRC, 'IE 2014 Report on first mission to Greece', paras. 26–28.

86 Although this chapter only focuses on the case law of international human rights monitoring bodies, it must be noted that several legal actions have been brought also before national and supranational courts, see e.g. European General Court, Judgment of 7 October 2015, *Alessandro Accorinti and others* v. *ECB*, Case T-39/13. In this case, the court essentially held that the loss suffered in 2012 by the private, mostly Italian, holders of Greek debt instruments in connection with the restructuring of the public debt of the Greek state is not attributable to the ECB, but to the economic risks ordinarily inherent in financial sector activities. The applicants 'had to be aware of those hazards and risks of a considerable loss in the value of the bonds which they purchased. That applies a fortiori because, even before the beginning of its financial crisis in 2009, the issuing Greek State was already faced with high indebtedness and a high deficit', *ibid.*, para. 121.

87 ECtHR, *Mamatas and others* v. *Greece*, App nos. 63066/14, 64297/14 and 66106/14 (ECHR, 21 July 2016).

Although admitting that the applicants' forcible participation amounted to an interference with their right to respect for their property for the purposes of article 1 of Protocol No. 1 to the Convention, the court held that such interference, prescribed by law, pursued the legitimate public-interest aim of preserving economic stability and restructuring the debt in the general interests of the community, at a time of serious economic crisis. The court affirmed, among other things, that the applicants had not suffered any special or excessive burden and the CACs and the restructuring of the public debt were an appropriate and necessary means of reducing the public debt and saving the state from bankruptcy, emphasising that investing in bonds was never risk-free and that the applicants should have been aware of the vagaries of the financial market and the risk of a possible drop in the value of their bonds, considering the Greek deficit and the country's large debt, even before the 2009 crisis. Finally, the court excluded that the bond exchange procedure had been discriminatory under article 14 ECHR, particularly, in the court's opinion, because of the risk of jeopardising the whole operation, with disastrous consequences for the economy, and the need to act rapidly in order to restructure the debt. Overall, the court seemed primarily concerned with safeguarding the margin of appreciation of the Greek authorities in adopting emergency measures to cope with the economic crisis.

As with the other crisis-related developments discussed in previous chapters, the legal reasoning of the ECtHR in the case of *Mamatas and others* v. *Greece* provides elements – particularly the pre-eminence given to notions of formal rather than substantive equality (in this case among creditors), personal responsibility, and the unconditional prioritisation of economic objectives over the state's socio-economic rights obligations – that may be interpreted as manifesting the incorporation of a neoliberal logic in the court's assessment of the facts and conduct of those involved.

With regard to the notion of formal equality, no mechanism currently exists to differentiate among bondholders, despite the fact that they can represent a very diverse universe, such as small savers, institutional investors, commercial banks, pension funds, hedge funds and vulture funds.[88] The principle that is generally adopted in debt restructurings, and which the ECtHR reiterated in the case of *Mamatas and others* v. *Greece*, is that of the equal treatment of bondholders, except for creditors with preferential status. The latter usually refers to the IMF, the World Bank, regional development banks and, in the Greek case, the ECB.

88 Annamaria Viterbo, 'La ristrutturazione del debito sovrano greco allo scrutinio della Corte europea dei diritti umani: nessuna tutela per i piccoli investitori' (2017) 11 *Diritti Umani e Diritto Internazionale* 1, 295.

In interpreting the principle of equality, the court endorsed the strict notion of formal equality already promoted by the Greek Council of State in its earlier decision on the case,[89] which 'does not impose a [positive] obligation upon the state to reserve a favourable treatment to some of its creditors, [who are] natural persons, in reason of their personal circumstances (life expectancy and economic situation)', but 'requires an action on an "equal footing"'.[90]

The court, then, provided a list of 'objective and reasonable' motivations to justify such interpretation,[91] including the difficulty of locating the persons concerned (given the volatility of the bond market and the fact that many bondholders had purchased their securities on the secondary market) and of laying down detailed criteria to differentiate between the bondholders. Besides, the court took into account the Greek government's arguments concerning the risk of jeopardising the whole operation and its interest in maintaining the operation's dynamics and acting quickly.

As has been observed, however, it could have been technically possible and legitimate under the European Convention on Human Rights to allow a differential treatment of small bondholders who had acquired Greek bonds with no speculative intentions when the Greek default was not yet predictable and imminent by investing a large part of their personal savings. The Greek government had actually made a proposal along these lines, which was to offer small bondholders who had invested up to a certain amount, for example, €100,000, a 'tax refund' equivalent to the haircut. The international financial institutions involved in assistance to the country nonetheless opposed this solution (and their reasons were, afterwards, conveniently appropriated by the government itself, to support its position before the ECtHR).[92]

The ECtHR further added that

> [i]f dissident bondholders [...] had feared that the value of their bonds would decrease as soon as the collective action clauses were implemented, they could have exercised their rights as bondholders and sold their bonds on the market [...]. Investing in bonds is never risk-free; [...] the private investors in question [...] were supposed to be aware of the highly instable economic

[89] Greek Council of State, Judgement No. 1116/2014 of 21 March 2014.

[90] ECtHR, *Mamatas and others* v. *Greece*, para. 133: 'le principe constitutionnel de l'égalité n'imposait pas à l'État de réserver un traitement favorable à certains de ses créanciers, personnes physiques, en fonction de leur situation personnelle (espérance de vie et situation économique), qui percevaient leur propre comportement comme étant celui d'un épargnant et non celui d'un investisseur. En revanche, ce principe imposait une action "sur une base égalitaire" de sorte que, en cas d'impossibilité de satisfaire l'ensemble des créanciers, chaque créancier puisse être satisfait au prorata de sa créance'.

[91] *Ibid.*, para. 135.

[92] Viterbo, 'La ristrutturazione del debito sovrano greco', 299.

> situation causing fluctuations in the value of the Greek debt instruments which they had purchased, as well as highly volatile markets [. . .] they ought to have known of the said vagaries and risks as regards possibly large drops in the value of the bonds purchased.[93]

Besides the fact that the court seemed to equate the unilateral amendment of bonds' contractual terms, decided by the Greek state for the purposes of restructuring, to the 'vagaries of the market', it also appeared to embrace a typically neoliberal idea of personal responsibility whereby individual conduct is assessed with no regard for structural and contextual circumstances, in this specific case, inter alia, the fact that the liquidity of the applicants' bonds at the time of the restructuring was utterly reduced.[94]

Finally, the absolute pre-eminence attributed by the ECtHR to the aim of preserving the economic and financial stability of the state, transformed such an objective into the actual criterion to evaluate whether the measures adopted by Greece and interfering with the rights of the applicants were proportionate under the ECHR.

The 2012 restructuring, however, failed to reduce Greece's debt burden, as the country was concurrently taking out a new €130 billion loan under its second adjustment programme.

With regard to the use of loans, although these were portrayed as if they have been used to assist Greece in covering for its primary fiscal balance, only a small share has actually contributed to regular government expenditure. In fact, 86 per cent of the bilateral loans (2010), between May 2010 and September 2011, was used for debt repayment, and a large part of the remainder was used for the setting up of the Hellenic Financial Stability Fund. The €144.7-billion EFSF loans (2012) – the majority of which was disbursed in kind (i.e. EFSF securities) and not in euros – were used to subsidise the PSI (€34.6 billion notes), in the 'Debt buy back' (€11.3 billion notes) or were borrowed for the recapitalisation of Greek banks (€37.3 billion).[95] A 2016 study published by the European School of Management and Technology in Berlin confirms that only a very small fraction of the assistance provided to Greece under the first and second adjustment programmes, that is, 9.7 billion or less than 5 per cent, ended up in the public budget of Greece. 64 per cent of the loans was just used to pay back the existing debt and interest, 37.3 billion or 17 per cent was used to recapitalise Greek banks, while 29.7 billion or

93 ECtHR, *Mamatas and others* v. *Greece*, paras. 117–118.

94 Viterbo, 'La ristrutturazione del debito sovrano greco', 298.

95 Truth Committee on Public Debt, 'Preliminary Report', 23.

14 per cent of the amount was used to provide incentives for investors to engage in the PSI.[96]

4.3.3 *The Third Stability Support Programme (14 August 2015)*

In January 2015, the Coalition for the Radical Left, Syriza, which had consistently opposed the implementation of austerity measures, won snap elections. This led, during the first half of 2015, to an uneasy relationship between Greece and its Eurozone partners, as they insisted that the country fully implement adjustment measures, while the new government stressed the need for debt relief. An agreement could not be reached, while the financial situation in Greece became increasingly dramatic. At the beginning of June 2015, a $300 million debt repayment to the IMF was postponed, raising fears of a possible default. When the alternative measures proposed by Syriza in late June were declined by the lenders,[97] the government announced that it would hold a referendum asking the Greek people for a yes or no vote on the latest bailout terms put forward by Greece's international creditors.[98] On 5 July, more than 61 per cent of eligible Greeks voted 'Oxi/No' to these terms, despite an ongoing European 'campaign of bullying'[99] against Greece ('financial terrorism' in the heated words of Yanis Varoufakis, then Greek Minister of Finance).[100]

After the announcement of a referendum, in fact, the Eurogroup decided not to grant the one-month extension of the Master Financial Assistance Facility (MFAFA) requested by Greece (according to the Greek government, in order to allow for the referendum to take place undisturbed and for later

96 HRC, Independent Expert Foreign Debt and Human Rights, 'End-of-Mission Statement. Visit to the European Union institutions' (8 December 2015), 3, quoting Jörg Rocholl and Axel Stahmer, 'Where Did the Greek Bailout Money Go?' (2016) *ESMT White Paper No. WP–16–02*.

97 In its latest proposal of 22 June for a Staff Level Agreement, although making some 'austerian' concessions 'in a bid to placate the institutions and thus come closer to an agreement', Greece had excluded further cuts in pensions and social expenditure, while advancing the possibility of a 12 per cent one-off levy on company profits over €0.5m, a rise in corporation tax from 26 per cent to 29 per cent, and a luxury tax on yachts, see Yanis Varoufakis, 'As It Happened – Yanis Varoufakis Intervention During the 27th June Eurogroup Meeting', 28 June 2015, www.yanisvaroufakis.eu/2015/06/28/as-it-happened-yanis-varoufakis-intervention-during-the-27th-june-2015-eurogroup-meeting/; 'Can Tsipras' New Proposals Revive a Deal?', The Guardian, 24 June 2015.

98 The question asked in the referendum was: 'Do you accept the institutions' proposal as it was presented to us [i.e. the Greek government] on 25th June in the Eurogroup?'.

99 Paul Krugman, 'Ending Greece's Bleeding', The New York Times, 6 July 2015.

100 Yanis Varoufakis, 'Minister No. More!', 6 July 2015, yanisvaroufakis.eu/2015/07/06/minister-no-more/#more-8433.

debt negotiations to fully take its outcome into account), leading the country to default on its €1.6 billion repayment to the IMF on the 30 June. On 27 June, Greece was also arbitrarily excluded from the Eurogroup meeting, where the remaining eighteen members discussed the forthcoming expiration of its current EFSF financial arrangement and issued a statement breaking, for the first time in history, the Eurogroup conventional unanimity rule.[101] On 28 June, the ECB '[took] note of [the] decision on [the] Greek referendum'[102] and decided 'to maintain the ceiling to the provision of emergency liquidity assistance (ELA) to Greek banks',[103] in other words, not to provide further support, although it was clear that funds were leaving the country and bank reserves running low (more than €7 billion-worth of deposits left Greek banks in less than a week, as a 'mini bank run' took place).[104] This forced, on 29 June, the Greek authorities to impose a bank closure and capital controls, capping money withdrawals at €60 per day, in order to avoid financial panic. The everyday-life scenes that followed these announcements were sadly familiar: queues at ATMs, car lines at petrol stations, supermarkets reporting unusual volumes of sales as people were making stocks of basic goods in fear of the worst. As the former Independent Expert on Foreign Debt and Human Rights Juan Pablo Bohoslavsky has noted, some observers perceived the ECB decision to reduce emergency credit to Greek banks shortly before the referendum 'as an attempt to influence the outcome of the democratic decision-making process in Greece'[105] (to say the least).

After the provision, in July 2015, of short-term bridge loans through the European Financial Stabilisation Mechanism (EFSM),[106] a *Third Stability Support Programme* was finally agreed (14 August 2015), providing Greece

101 Eurogroup, Ministerial Statement of 27th June 2015, No. 534/15, 27 June 2015, www.consilium.europa.eu/press-releases-pdf/2015/6/40802199989_en.pdf. Varoufakis, reported that, when he asked the Secretariat for legal advice on whether the President of the Eurogroup can convene a meeting without inviting the Finance Minister of a Eurozone Member State and issue a statement without the conventional unanimity, he received the following official response: 'The Eurogroup is an informal group. Thus, it is not bound by Treaties or written regulations. While unanimity is conventionally adhered to, the Eurogroup President is not bound to explicit rules', see Varoufakis, 'As It Happened'.

102 European Central Bank, 'ELA to Greek Banks Maintained at Its Current Level', Press release, 28 June 2015, www.ecb.europa.eu/press/pr/date/2015/html/pr150628.en.html.

103 *Ibid.*

104 Helena Smith, 'Greek Crisis: Episodes of Despair and Drama as Moment of Truth Nears', The Guardian, 21 June 2015; Claire Jones, Kerin Hope and Henry Foy, 'Greek Banks Given One-Day Reprieve as Depositors Pull Out €1.6bn', Financial Times, 22 June 2015.

105 HRC, 'IE End of Mission Statement', 2.

106 Council Regulation (EU) 407/2010 of 11 May 2010 establishing a European Financial Stabilisation Mechanism [2010] OJ L118, later amended by Council Regulation (EU) 2015/1360 of 4 August 2015 amending Regulation (EU) No. 407/2010 establishing a European

with up to €86 billion in financial assistance over the period 2015–2018, this time through the European Stability Mechanism (ESM), that is, the treaty-based permanent international financial institution established in 2012 by the Euro Area Member States to ensure financial stability in the EMU.[107] The ESM stability support programme for Greece concluded on 20 August 2018.

Nonetheless, the unsustainability of the Greek debt has been increasingly acknowledged. Among others, the former Independent Expert on Foreign Debt and Human Rights reaffirmed his conviction that the Greek debt is 'financially and socially unsustainable',[108] and that a solution to the country's economic deadlock necessarily requires debt relief. Three consecutive adjustment programmes have so far largely failed to reduce the level of the Greek public debt.[109] As mentioned in this chapter's introduction, in 2019, Greece's debt stands at 180.5 per cent of GDP, well above its 2009 level (126.7 per cent of GDP), when the Greek crisis began unfolding.

4.4 SOCIO-ECONOMIC RIGHTS IN GREECE SINCE THE CRISIS

As a precondition for securing financial assistance from the Euro Area Member States and the IMF, Greece has been implementing a series of fiscal and economic reform measures ('conditionalities') which have touched upon key areas of welfare provision. As this section will describe, these measures had significant regressive impacts on the enjoyment of human rights in Greece, particularly certain socio-economic rights. They also increased inequality in income and wealth,[110] and pushed the Greek economy into a deeper

financial stabilisation mechanism [2015] OJ L210. Under the EFSM, the European Commission was entitled to borrow from financial markets up to €60 billion through the issuance of bonds on behalf of the EU (under an EU budget 'guarantee') and to provide financial assistance (in the form of loans or credit lines) to any EU country experiencing or threatened by severe financial difficulties, conditional on the implementation of reforms. In addition to the short-term bridge loans provided to Greece in 2015, the EFSM has been used to provide assistance to Ireland and Portugal between 2011 and 2014, see European Commission, 'European Financial Stabilisation Mechanism (EFSM)', ec.europa.eu.

107 Treaty establishing the European Stability Mechanism (signed 1 February 2012, entered into force 27 September 2012) D/12/3, www.esm.europa.eu/sites/default/files/20150203_-_esm_treaty_-_en_1.pdf (the ESM became fully operational on 8 October 2012).

108 HRC, 'IE 2016 Report on mission to the EU', para. 41.

109 *Ibid.*, para. 42. Greece's debt to GDP ratio will further increase to about 250 per cent by 2060, if no front-loaded debt relief is provided, HRC, 'IE End of Mission Statement', 3, quoting IMF, 'Greece, Preliminary Debt Sustainability Analysis – Updated Estimates and Further Considerations' (May 2016) *IMF Country Report* 13/130, www.imf.org/external/pubs/ft/scr/2016/cr16130.pdf.

110 HRC, 'IE 2016 Report on mission to the EU', para. 77.

recession.[111] After a brief preliminary introduction on the principle of conditionality and some remarks on its post-crisis incorporation under EU law, this section will review the main 'fiscal consolidation' measures implemented in Greece since 2010 and their impacts on the rights to work/labour rights, health, education, adequate housing and social security (especially pensions).

4.4.1 *Conditionality, Its Incorporation under EU Law and the Increased Neoliberalisation of EU Economic Governance*

As is well known, conditionality is a well-established practice of international financial institutions, notably the IMF,[112] and, since 2010, it has become a key principle of EU economic governance.[113] In *Pringle*, the Court of Justice of the European Union established that 'strict conditionality' is a necessary requirement for financial assistance to be compatible with article 125 TFEU[114] and, in 2011, the conditionality principle was enshrined in EU primary law, with the amendment to article 136 TFEU. The added paragraph 3 – besides allowing Euro Area Member States to establish the ESM – mandates making the granting of any required financial assistance under the mechanism subject to 'strict conditionality'.[115]

In essence, conditionality makes the provision of funds contingent upon the acceptance by a state of specific obligations. These obligations (generally entailing reforms that are essentially inspired by neoliberal economic policies, such as deregulation, austerity measures and privatisations)[116] are fully detailed in a MoU, signed by the requesting state and the financing institution(s), that is, in the Greek case, the European Commission on behalf of either Euro Area

[111] *Ibid.*, para. 14.

[112] Axel Dreher, 'IMF Conditionality: Theory and Evidence' (2009) 141 *Public Choice* 141, 233–267; Cesare Pinelli, 'Conditionality' in Anne Peters and Rüdiger Wolfrum (eds.), *Max Planck Encyclopedia of Public International Law* (November 2013).

[113] See i.a. Annamaria Viterbo and Francesco Costamagna, 'L'impatto sociale della politica di condizionalità nel contesto della crisi nell'area euro: profili giuridici' in Nicola Napoletano and Andrea Saccucci (eds.), *Gestione internazionale delle emergenze globali. Regole e valori* (Napoli: Editoriale Scientifica, 2013), pp. 167–194.

[114] Court of Justice, Judgement of 27 November 2012, *Thomas Pringle* v. *Government of Ireland*, Case C-370/12, paras. 135–143.

[115] Council Decision 2011/199/EU of 25 March 2011 amending Article 136 of the Treaty on the Functioning of the European Union with regard to a stability mechanism for Member States whose currency is the euro [2011] OJ L91.

[116] John Williamson, 'What Washington Means by Policy Reform' in John Williamson (ed.), *Latin American Readjustment: How Much Has Happened?* (Washington: Institute for International Economics, 1990) 7–20. On the typology of conditionalities generally attached to EU/IMF lending and financial assistance, see further Section 4.4.2.

Member States (first and second adjustment programmes) or the ESM (third stability support programme).[117] Memoranda – in the case of the first Greek adjustment programme, in effect, three distinct MoUs, that is, a Memorandum of Economic and Financial Policies (MEFP), a Memorandum of Understanding on Specific Economic Policy Conditionality and a Technical Memorandum of Understanding – are then generally annexed to the assistance facility agreement between the state and the financing institution(s). Where the IMF is also providing assistance, the same conditionalities, again in the form of a MoU, are attached to a Letter of Intent directed by the recipient state to the IMF Managing Director.

The legal nature – both under international and EU law – and binding force of MoUs are notoriously controversial, as demonstrated also by the divergent conclusions reached by the Greek Council of State (i.e. MoUs are policy documents)[118] and the Portuguese Constitutional Court (i.e. MoUs are legally binding instruments)[119] in respect of the Memoranda agreed by Greece and Portugal, respectively, in the context of their adjustment programmes.[120]

Furthermore, the negotiation of the obligations contained in the MoUs, whose procedure is now regulated under Regulation (EU) No. 472/2013,[121] has been the object of strong criticism, inasmuch as it is characterised by a certain opacity in terms of the role, relative bargaining power and legitimacy of the actors involved.[122] In fact, the wording of Regulation 472/2013/EU follows the IMF approach of presenting the Member State that requests financial

117 See also Article 13(4) ESM Treaty.

118 Greek Council of State, Judgement No. 668/2012 of 20 February 2012, para. 28.

119 See *inter alia* Portuguese Constitutional Court, Decision No. 187/2013 of 5 April 2013, para. 29, www.tribunalconstitucional.pt/tc/acordaos/20130187.html.

120 For some insights and further references on the many constitutional issues raised by MoUs, see i.a. European University Institute, 'Constitutional Change through Euro Crisis Law: A Multi-level Legal Analysis of Economic and Monetary Union', 2015, eurocrisislaw.eui.eu; Xenofon Contiades (ed.), *Constitutions in the Global Financial Crisis: A Comparative Analysis* (Abingdon: Routledge, 2016); Tuori and Tuori, *The Eurozone Crisis*.

121 Regulation (EU) 472/2013 of the European Parliament and of the Council of 21 May 2013 on the strengthening of economic and budgetary surveillance of Member States in the Euro Area experiencing or threatened with serious difficulties with respect to their financial stability [2013] OJ L140. For the procedure in the context of financial assistance provided by the IMF, see i.a. Lastra, *International Financial and Monetary Law*, Section 13.137 ff., and UN General Assembly, 'Responsibility for complicity of international financial institutions in human rights violations in the context of retrogressive economic reforms', Report of the Independent Expert on the effects of foreign debt and other related international financial obligations of states on the full enjoyment of all human rights, particularly economic, social and cultural rights, UN Doc. A/74/178 (16 July 2019), 5 ff.

122 See e.g. Francesco Costamagna, 'Saving Europe "Under Strict Conditionality": A Threat for EU Social Dimension?' (2012) *LPF Working Paper No. 7*.

assistance as the primary responsible for conditionality, and the involvement of its counterparts (i.e. the European Commission, the ECB and the IMF) merely in terms of 'consultation', 'negotiation' or sometimes 'agreement'.

The ESM Treaty as well as the EFSF Framework Agreement and the Greek Loan Facility before it adopt the same contractual approach. 'Domestic ownership' of conditionality is at all points encouraged, and MoUs 'are so drafted as to imply that their content expresses a commitment of the recipient government that is simply accepted as sufficient by the lenders, rather than a set of measures some of which are imposed by the latter'.[123]

Nonetheless, several studies have highlighted that bargaining power may significantly tilt in favour of lenders.[124] Evidence of this was also put forward by some of the responses provided to the questionnaire sent by the European Parliament to the Member States under financial assistance, in the context of the Parliament's 2013 enquiry on the role and operations of the 'Troika'.[125] The Greek Truth Committee on Public Debt has also been very vocal on the matter of possible 'coercion'.[126]

The procedural and substantive ambiguity of conditionality, however, makes it difficult to identify who actually defines the content of these obligations, based on what legitimacy, and to what ends. It also entails that any attribution of responsibility under international law in relation to conditionality can prove intricate, because of the complex nature of the decision-making processes, the multiplicity of actors involved, and the peculiarities of the legal instruments adopted.[127]

Finally, intrusiveness is another variable but widely recognised characteristic of conditionality. In some cases, as for instance in the case of Greece's second economic adjustment programme, conditionalities were extremely detailed and specific, and de facto left no discretion to national authorities with regard to fiscal and economic policymaking.[128]

[123] Michael Ioannidis, 'EU Financial Assistance Conditionality after "Two Pack"' (2014) 74 *Zeitschrift für ausländisches öffentliches Recht und Völkerrecht* 1–44, papers.ssrn.com/sol3/papers.cfm?abstract_id=2398914.

[124] *Ibid.*, 34–35. See also UN General Assembly, 'Responsibility for complicity of international financial institutions in human rights violations', 5 ff.

[125] European Parliament, 'Report on the enquiry on the role and operations of the Troika (ECB, Commission and IMF) with regard to the Euro Area programme countries', 2013/2277(INI) (28 February 2014).

[126] Truth Committee on Public Debt, 'Preliminary Report' and report on the 'Illegitimacy, Illegality, Odiousness and Unsustainability of the August 2015 MoU and Loan Agreement'.

[127] For a significant attempt, however, see De Schutter and Salomon, 'Economic Policy Conditionality'.

[128] On the point of intrusiveness, see i.a. André Sapir, Guntram B. Wolff, Carlos de Sousa and Alessio Terzi, 'The Troika and Financial Assistance in the Euro Area: Successes and Failures'

4.4.1.1 The Incorporation of the Principle of Conditionality under EU Law as a Further Element of the Increased Neoliberalisation of EU Economic Governance

Besides the above-mentioned typically neoliberal content of conditionalities, the incorporation of conditionality in the EU legal framework can be interpreted as a further manifestation of the latter's neoliberalisation in a different sense. In fact, it represents the sanctioning by law of a practice, as said, most certainly characterised by asymmetrical bargaining power between debtor states and international creditors, and which consequently submits economic and, indirectly, social policymaking to a contractual, market-modelled logic. This makes the content of policies having direct effects on the realisation of socio-economic rights negotiable (in exchange for assistance) and gives pre-eminence, in that negotiation, to market objectives over human rights, thus reinforcing the subordination of social policymaking to the economic objectives of the EMU, as mentioned in Chapter 2.

The embedding into EU law of a possibly coercive practice such as conditionality further signals a possible estrangement of the post-crisis EU legal framework from well-established international principles, such as sovereign equality, non-intervention and self-determination,[129] and from the principle of international cooperation (Chapter 2). These represent, instead, an important legal protection for economically more vulnerable states against the possible interference of their powerful counterparts.[130]

4.4.2 *The Impacts of Conditionality on Socio-Economic Rights in Greece*

The conditionalities implemented by Greece include wide-ranging fiscal and economic measures that largely replicate the measures attached to IMF structural adjustment programmes in the 1980s and 1990s,[131] and are mainly of three kinds: (1) budgetary measures, generally directed to reduce public, mainly *social* expenditure, and to increase revenues by means of tax hikes; (2) structural reforms of the labour market, public administration, pension and

(European Union, 2014) *Study on the Request of the Economic and Monetary Affairs Committee of the European Parliament* 16.

129 Ilias Bantekas, 'Sovereign Debt and Self-Determination' in Bantekas and Lumina, *Sovereign Debt and Human Rights*, pp. 267–283.

130 Salomon, 'Winners and Others', p. 273.

131 On the 'typology of austerity' characterising EU/IMF conditionality, see also CoE Commissioner for Human Rights, 'Safeguarding human rights'; Costamagna, 'Saving Europe "Under Strict Conditionality"', 9.

TABLE 4.1 *Percentage change in general government social expenditure, 2008–2014*

	Greece	*EU-28*
Social exclusion and poverty	–66.5	+20.4
Healthcare	–54.9	+4
Unemployment	–44	+5.4
Benefits for sick and disabled persons	–31.6	+6.2
Education	–22.3	–4.8

Source: HRC, IE 2016 Report on his mission to the EU

social security, healthcare and education systems (i.e. key areas of welfare intervention) and (3) privatisation of public assets.[132]

In terms of overall expenditure trends, as noted by the Independent Expert on Foreign Debt and Human Rights on the occasion of his mission to the institutions of the European Union, between 2008 and 2014, social expenditure in Greece was in 'free fall', with extreme cuts in expenditure on social exclusion and poverty (–66.5 per cent compared with an average +20.4 per cent change in the EU-28), health care (–54.9 per cent compared with +4 per cent in the EU-28), unemployment (–44 per cent compared with +5.4 per cent in the EU-28), benefits for sick persons and persons with disabilities (–31.6 per cent compared with +6.2 per cent in the EU-28) and education (–22.3 per cent compared with –4.8 per cent in the EU-28)[133] (see Table 4.1).

In absolute terms, in 2015 Greece was spending less than EU-28 countries on housing (0.2 per cent versus 0.6 per cent of GDP), health care (4.5 per cent versus 7.2 per cent of GDP), recreation, culture and religion (0.7 per cent versus 1 per cent of GDP) and education (4.3 per cent versus 4.9 per cent of GDP). Expenditure for social protection in 2015 was slightly above the average of the Euro Area with 19 Member States (EA-19) (20.5 per cent of GDP in Greece versus 20.1 per cent of GDP in EA-19), although Greece is spending less than EA-19 countries for sickness and disability, family and children, unemployment, housing and social exclusion, and above EA-19 average only for old age (15.7 per cent versus 10.8 per cent of GDP in 2015). It must be noted, however, that Greece is still spending above EA-19 average on defence (2.7 per cent of GDP in 2015

132 CoE Commissioner for Human Rights, 'Safeguarding human rights', 16.

133 HRC, 'IE 2016 Report on mission to the EU', para. 45 and table at 13.

versus 1.2 per cent of GDP for EA-19) and for general public services (9.9 per cent versus 6.6 per cent of GDP), which includes debt transactions.[134]

The following subsections will briefly present the specific conditionalities implemented by Greece in the course of the past seven years, and their impacts on the rights to work/labour rights, health, education, adequate housing and social security.

4.4.2.1 Measures Impacting on the Right to Work/Labour Rights

The right to work and labour rights[135] more generally have been the most affected by conditionality.[136] The measures implemented in Greece since 2010 involved both the public and the private sector.

Reforms in the public sector have been aimed at reducing both the number and the cost of public sector employees, i.a. by reducing the Easter, summer and Christmas bonuses and allowances paid to civil servants, by reforming the public sector employee compensation by adjusting the payroll for special regimes, including judges, diplomats, doctors, professors, police and armed forces, and by implementing the rule of only one recruitment for each five retirements. Public sector employment decreased from 942,625 to 675,530 between 2009 and 2013.[137] Between January 2010 and January 2013, public sector pay declined by over 25 per cent on average.

In 2012, in the case of *Koufaki and ADEDY* v. *Greece*, the cuts in wages and pensions of public servants resulting from the Laws Nos. 3833/2010, 3845/2010 and 3847/2010 (the latter two implementing the first Greek Economic Adjustment Programme) were challenged before the European Court of

[134] See 'General Government Expenditure by Function (COFOG)' data on Eurostat database, appsso.eurostat.ec.europa.eu/nui/show.do?dataset=gov_10a_exp&lang=en; HRC, 'IE 2016 Report on second mission to Greece', para. 36.

[135] ICESCR, Article 6; Charter of Fundamental Rights of the EU, Articles 15 and 27–31; European Social Charter (revised), Articles 1–10; several ILO conventions; Greek Constitution, Article 22(1). Greece has ratified the following fundamental ILO Conventions: Forced Labour Convention, 1930 (No. 29); Abolition of Forced Labour Convention, 1957 (No. 105); Freedom of Association and Protection of the Right to Organise Convention, 1948 (No. 87); Right to Organise and Collective Bargaining Convention, 1949 (No. 98); Equal Remuneration Convention, 1951 (No. 100); Discrimination (Employment and Occupation Convention, 1958 (No. 111); Minimum Age Convention, 1973 (No. 138); Worst Forms of Child Labour Convention, 1999 (No. 182). On the contrary, the country is not party yet, among others, to the ILO Domestic Workers Convention, 2011 (No. 189).

[136] Styliani Kaltsouni and Athina Kosma, 'The Impact of the Crisis on Fundamental Rights Across Member States of the EU: Country Report on Greece' (2015) *Study for the LIBE Committee of the European Parliament*, 60 (hereinafter 'LIBE report'); Truth Committee on Public Debt, 'Preliminary Report', 38.

[137] 'LIBE report', 63–64 and 75–81.

Human Rights (ECtHR). The appellants claimed that such measures were incompatible with article 1 of Protocol No. 1 to the European Convention on Human Rights, protecting the right to the peaceful enjoyment of possessions.[138] The court admitted that the measures in question constituted an 'interference' (not a 'deprivation of possessions', as claimed by the applicants) with such right. Nonetheless, this interference was justified under the Covenant, according to the court, 'by the existence of an exceptional crisis without precedent in recent Greek history'.[139] Besides being 'lawful', since it was provided for by the above-mentioned laws, the court held that the reduction in the salaries, allowances, bonuses and retirement pensions of persons working in the public service imposed by the Greek government pursued a 'legitimate aim in the public interest'. According to the court, it

> formed part of a wider programme of public finance adjustment and structural reform of the Greek economy which, taken as a whole, was designed to meet the country's pressing financing needs and to improve its future economic and financial prospects. Those aims were in the general interest and also coincided with those of the Euro Area Member States, in view of the requirement under European Union legislation to ensure budgetary discipline and preserve the stability of the Euro Area. By their very nature, the measures in question therefore contributed to an immediate reduction in public spending.[140]

The court seems to implicitly assume that the 'public interest' necessarily coincides with a *competitive state* (able to satisfy its financing needs under market rules, perform fiscally and contribute to the financial stability of the EA). Furthermore, it paid particular deference to the margin of appreciation of the national authorities in regulating their social policy, affirming that '[a]s the decision to enact laws to balance State expenditure and revenue will commonly involve consideration of political, economic and social issues, [. . .] the national authorities are in principle better placed than the international judge to choose the most appropriate means of achieving this and will respect their judgment unless it is manifestly without reasonable foundation'.[141] According to the court, '[t]his margin is even wider when the issues involve an assessment of the priorities as to the allocation of limited State resources'.[142] Crucially, the court gave 'special weight' also to the

138 *Koufaki and ADEDY* v. *Greece*, App Nos. 57665/12 and 57657/12 (ECHR, 7 May 2013).
139 *Ibid.*, para. 37.
140 *Ibid.*, para. 38.
141 *Ibid.*, para. 31.
142 *Ibid.*

judgement of national authorities as to what is to be considered *in the public interest*, 'unless that judgement is manifestly without reasonable foundation', concluding that it has 'no reason to doubt that, in deciding to cut public servants' wages and pensions, the legislature was acting in the public interest'.[143] Finally, the court held that the measures adopted where 'reasonably proportionate' to the aim they sought to realise, and that a 'fair balance' had been struck between the demands of the general interest of the community and the requirements of the protection of the fundamental rights of the applicants. In fact, the court judged that 'the extent of the reduction in the first applicant's salary [Ms Koufaki, from €2,435.83 to €1,885.79] was not such as to place her at risk of having insufficient means to live on and thus to constitute a breach of article 1 of Protocol No. 1', so that, in view also 'of the particular context of crisis in which the interference in question occurred, the latter could not be said to have imposed an excessive burden on the applicant'.[144] As to the proportionality of the cuts implemented in respect of public servants more generally, represented before the ECtHR by the Confederation of Public-Sector Trade Unions (ADEDY), the court simply recalled the fact that they were also accompanied by a compensation mechanism in the form of a flat-rate bonus, introduced with the aim of protecting those in the lowest income segments.[145] Consequently, the court declared the case inadmissible as manifestly ill-founded.

Private sector reforms, involving far-reaching amendments to both collective and individual labour laws were essentially directed towards the promotion of non-standard employment (i.e. fixed-term employment and agency work, or employment under contracts with less pay and job security, or with extended probation periods), the reduction of job security (i.a. by shortening notice periods and eliminating or weakening the right to be reinstated after unfair dismissal or mass layoffs), the decentralisation and weakening of collective bargaining (i.a. by eliminating or suspending national collective agreements) and the weakening of trade unions (e.g. through facilitating the conditions for non-union employee representatives to conclude collective agreements).[146]

[143] *Ibid.*, paras. 39–41.

[144] *Ibid.*, para. 46.

[145] *Ibid.*, para. 47.

[146] HRC, Report of the Independent Expert on the effects of foreign debt and other related international financial obligations of states on the full enjoyment of all human rights, particularly economic, social and cultural rights, A/HRC/34/57 (27 December 2016), 7 (hereinafter, 'Labour rights report'); 'LIBE report', 65–74; Greek National Commission for Human Rights, 'NCHR Recommendation: On the imperative need to reverse the sharp decline in civil liberties and social rights' (8 December 2011), www.nchr.gr/images/Englis

In 2012, the European Committee of Social Rights held that the provision contained in the Greek Act 3899/2010, allowing the dismissal of a person without notice or severance pay during the probation period (i.e. the first twelve months of employment) in a permanent contract, constituted a violation of the right to a reasonable period of notice for termination of employment protected under article 4(4) of the 1961 European Social Charter as part of the right to a fair remuneration.[147] On that occasion, the Committee reiterated its position that

> the economic crisis should not have as a consequence the reduction of the protection of the rights recognised by the Charter. [...] [W]hile it may be reasonable for the crisis to prompt changes in current legislation and practices [...] to restrict certain items of public spending or relieve constraints on businesses, these changes should not excessively destabilise the situation of those who enjoy the rights enshrined in the Charter. The Committee considers that a greater employment flexibility in order to combat unemployment and encourage employers to take on staff, should not result in depriving broad categories of employees, particularly those who have not had a stable job for long, of their fundamental rights in the field of labour law, protecting them from arbitrary decisions by their employers or from economic fluctuations. [...][148]

Conditionalities also included wage cuts and cuts to minimum wage levels, especially for the young, in some cases below the poverty threshold. In 2012, the European Committee of Social Rights held, inter alia, that the 32 per cent reduction of the monthly minimum wage for employees under the age of 25, provided by Law 3863/2010 and resulting in a minimum wage of approximately €496 per month, was below the poverty level (i.e. €580 per month) and, thus, constituted a violation of the right to a fair remuneration protected by article 4(1) of the 1961 European Social Charter.[149]

h_Site/CRISIS/nchr_crisis.pdf; Christoph Hermann, 'Structural Adjustment and Neoliberal Convergence in Labour Markets and Welfare: The Impact of the Crisis and Austerity Measures on European Economic and Social Models' (2014) 18 *Competition and Change* 2, 119 and 121.

147 *General Federation of employees of the national electric power corporation* (GENOP-DEI) / *Confederation of Greek Civil Servants' Trade Unions* (ADEDY) v. *Greece*, Complaint No. 65/2011 (ECSR, 23 May 2012), paras. 25–28.

148 *Ibid.*, paras. 16–18.

149 *General Federation of employees of the national electric power corporation* (GENOP-DEI) / *Confederation of Greek Civil Servants' Trade Unions* (ADEDY) v. *Greece*, Complaint No. 66/2011 (ECSR, 23 May 2012), paras. 57–65; ILO, *Conclusions of the Report on the High-Level Mission to Greece (Athens, 19–23 September 2011)* (22 November 2011), para. 309. See also European Committee of Social Rights, *Conclusions* XX-3 – *Greece* – *Article* 4-1, XX-3/def/GRC/4/1/EN (15 December 2014).

Furthermore, as required by the second adjustment programme, Law 4093/2012 abolished the annual practice of setting minimum wages through collective bargaining, attributing, for the first time, minimum wage setting to the government.[150]

The Independent Expert on Foreign Debt and Human Rights has acknowledged that the overall trend has been 'to scale down labour rights', in accordance with the 'dominant tendency in the approach of international financial institutions to labour reform, notably the IMF', whose 'prevalent stance [...] has been a deregulatory one'.[151] Conditionality-related reforms have brought about, according to the Independent Expert, 'significant changes – sometimes even a transformation – in domestic labour law'.[152] As a result, the level of protection of labour law and trade unions has been 'substantially reduced'.[153]

Unemployment in Greece has risen substantially since the crisis, from 7.3 per cent in June 2008 to 23.6 per cent in 2016, or 1,131,000 unemployed persons out of an active population of 4,732,000, compared with an 8.5 per cent average rate in the EU-28 in the same year. Youth unemployment peaked at 64.9 per cent in May 2013, and in 2016 was still at 47.3 per cent. Women and migrants have also been disproportionally affected by the loss of jobs. The female unemployment rate in 2016 was at 28.1 per cent of active population, compared with 19.9 per cent for men. Employment in the informal sector has increased as well, from 25 per cent in 2010 to 36.2 per cent in 2012.[154]

More worryingly, in 2016, 72 per cent of all the unemployed in Greece have been without a job for more than twelve months, and 51.9 per cent for more than twenty-four months. Since spending on unemployment-related social security also went down, this means that the majority of those without a job have either never received unemployment benefits or have lost their entitlement to receive them owing to long-term unemployment.

Between 2008 and 2013, the average annual income of the Greek household fell by 31.8 per cent (from €44,581 to €30,400).[155]

150 'LIBE report', 74 and 82; Truth Committee on Public Debt, 'Preliminary Report', 38.
151 'Labour rights report', para. 14; see also Hermann, 'Structural Adjustment and Neoliberal Convergence', 111 ff.
152 'Labour rights report', para. 19.
153 *Ibid.*
154 Report of the Independent Expert on the effects of foreign debt and other related international financial obligations of states on the full enjoyment of all human rights, particularly economic, social and cultural rights on his mission to institutions of the European Union, UN Doc. A/HRC/34/57/Add.1 (2016).
155 'LIBE report', 13.

Anchored poverty, that is, poverty relative to its pre-crisis income level, almost tripled between 2007 and 2013, and one third of the population was in poverty in 2013.[156] In 2015, 34.9 per cent of the total population (28.4 per cent in 2007) and one out of every two people aged 18–24, that is, 51.5 per cent, compared with 33.9 per cent in 2007, was at risk of poverty or social exclusion. The rate of children exposed to such risk has also dramatically increased by 9.1 percentage points between 2008 and 2015 (compared with an increase of 0.5 per cent in the EU over the same period).[157]

For those still in the job market, job insecurity and (involuntary) part-time employment, especially for women,[158] have increased significantly. Full-time contracts have been progressively converted to part-time or rotating employment contracts. While in 2001, only 4 per cent of the total workforce were part-time workers, in 2016, this rose to 9.7 per cent (the EA-19 average in 2016 was 21.2 per cent).[159] It is significant that, in 2015, 22.4 per cent of the employed in Greece were nonetheless at risk of poverty or social exclusion (18.5 per cent in 2007).[160]

A 2014 study has provided systematic evidence of a causal link between fiscal austerity, higher unemployment rates, negative economic growth, reduced fertility and suicide rates in Greece, particularly for males between 45 and 89 years of age.[161]

4.4.2.2 Measures Impacting on the Right to Health[162]

Reforms implemented in the healthcare sector include both cost-containment measures and structural reforms, for example, the creation in 2011 of a single

156 OECD, 'Economic Surveys: Greece' (March 2016), 14.

157 HRC, 'IE 2016 Report on mission to the EU', para. 59.

158 Human Rights Council, Working Group on the Universal Periodic Review, 'Summary prepared by the Office of the United Nations High Commissioner for Human Rights in accordance with paragraph 15 (c) of the annex to Human Rights Council resolution 5/1 and paragraph 5 of the annex to Council resolution 16/21 – Greece', Un Doc. A/HRC/WG.6/25/GRC/3 (22 February 2016), para. 26.

159 'LIBE report', 82–86; Truth Committee on Public Debt, 'Preliminary Report', 38; HRC, 'IE 2016 Report on mission to the EU', paras. 45, 51–53 and 59. All data reported in these documents have been updated with the most recent data available from the Eurostat database.

160 Eurostat data, 'People at Risk of Poverty or Social Exclusion by Most Frequent Activity Status (Population Aged 18 and Over)'.

161 Nikolaos Antonakakis and Alan Collins, 'The Impact of Fiscal Austerity on Suicide: On the Empirics of a Modern Greek Tragedy' (2014) 112 *Social Science & Medicine* 39–50; 'The Impact of Fiscal Austerity on Suicide Mortality: Evidence Across the "Eurozone Periphery"' (2015) 145 *Social Science & Medicine* 63–78.

162 UDHR, Article 25; ICESCR, Article 12; CEDAW, Article 12; CERD, Article 5; CRPD, Article 25; CRC, Article 24; European Social Charter (revised), Article 11; Charter of Fundamental Rights of the EU, Article 35; Greek Constitution, Articles 21(2) and (3).

healthcare insurance fund and provider, the EOPYY, which in 2014 was transformed into a unique buyer of medicines and healthcare services for all those insured.[163]

The First Economic Adjustment Programme required that public health expenditure be limited at or below 6 per cent of GDP (a target that Greece reached in 2012) while, in theory, maintaining universal access and improving the quality of care delivery. The Second Economic Adjustment Programme demanded reducing further hospital operating costs by 8 per cent in 2012, and bringing average public spending on outpatient pharmaceuticals to about 1 per cent of GDP (EU average).[164] These requirements caused, among other effects, a reduction of healthcare staff and available public hospital beds – contributing further to pre-existing shortages – and the increase in co-payments/user-fees for outpatient treatment or medication. 137 public hospitals were merged into 83, and 330 out of 1,950 clinics in public hospitals were merged and distributed among hospitals. Functional beds were reduced from approximately 36,000 to 32,000. Clinics for chronic illnesses, rehabilitation centres and specialised clinics for children and people with disabilities were also reformed, and mental health institutions were shut down or subject to staff cuts.[165]

Greece's health expenditure decreased, from 6 per cent of GDP in 2007 (i.e. almost €14 billion) to 4.5 per cent of GDP in 2015 (approximately €8 billion, i.e. –75 per cent). The EU-28 average expenditure over the same period, conversely, increased from 6.5 per cent to 7.2 per cent of GDP.[166] The decrease in pharmaceutical spending in Greece was much higher than the OECD average, leading at times to internal shortages, also within hospitals.[167]

As has been noted, reforms were 'adopted within a very short time-frame and under extreme pressure to secure the disbursal of the next tranche' and 'focused primarily on the structural, financial and managerial aspects of the NHS, and not so much on patients' needs'.[168] One of the most serious consequences of conditionality is that a large number of individuals are reported to have dropped out of the public health insurance scheme. An increasing number of long-term unemployed and self-employed professionals, for instance, who are unable to pay their social security contributions, are not

163 'LIBE report', 46.
164 *Ibid.*, 44–45; Truth Committee on Public Debt, 'Preliminary Report', 38.
165 'LIBE report', 48.
166 Eurostat data.
167 'LIBE report', 52–53 and 56.
168 *Ibid.*, 54.

covered by public health insurance. According to the OECD, in 2013, around 10 per cent of the population was not eligible for health insurance;[169] in 2015, 25 per cent of the population was without health insurance.[170] The Independent Expert on Foreign Debt and Human Rights reported that in 2014, 17.3 per cent of all persons belonging to the lowest income quintile have not been able to undergo necessary medical treatment, either because of waiting lists, costs or because of the physical distance of the services. Many have been forced to resort to 'alternative care' options. So-called open polyclinics and social pharmacies, operated by local and international NGOs and staffed by volunteer medical personnel, have been set up to service patients who are not able to get adequate treatment in public healthcare facilities.[171]

Appalling evidence of increased incidence of infant mortality, mental health disorders, alcohol abuse and outbreaks of infectious diseases (particularly HIV, and the re-emergence of malaria and tuberculosis) has also been reported by various sources.[172] In a 2016 report, the Bank of Greece noted an increase in infant mortality by nearly 50 per cent (mainly due to an increase in the number of deaths of infants of less than one year of age, and the decline of births by 22.1 per cent), and an increase in the number of individuals with mental health problems, especially depression, from 3.3 per cent in 2008 to 12.3 per cent in 2013. The same study also reported an increase in the number of people affected by chronic diseases by approximately 4 per cent.[173]

A major law concerning healthcare was adopted on 20 February 2016 (Law No. 4368/2016), which opened access to the public health system to uninsured

169 OECD Economic Surveys, 'Greece' (November 2013), 31, www.oecd.org/eco/surveys/GRC_Overview_Eng_2013.pdf.

170 Truth Committee on Public Debt, 'Preliminary Report', 38; World Health Organization, 'Barriers and facilitating factors in access to health care services in Greece', 2015.

171 HRC, 'IE 2016 Report on mission to the EU', paras. 54–55.

172 Truth Committee on Public Debt, 'Preliminary Report', 39; 'LIBE report', 59; Antonakakis and Collins, 'The Impact of Fiscal Austerity on Suicide', 64 (also for further references on the issue); David Stuckler and Sanjay Basu, *The Body Economic: Why Austerity Kills* (New York: Basic Books, 2013); Charlie Cooper, 'Tough Austerity Measures in Greece Leave Nearly a Million People with No Access to Healthcare, Leading to Soaring Infant Mortality, HIV Infection and Suicide', The Independent, 21 February 2014; Human Rights Council, Working Group on the Universal Periodic Review, 'Summary prepared by the Office of the United Nations High Commissioner for Human Rights in accordance with paragraph 15 (c) of the annex to Human Rights Council resolution 5/1', para. 15.

173 Bank of Greece, 'Monetary Policy Report 2015–2016', 2016 (in Greek only). For a summary of the report's chapter on 'Reforms in health, economic crisis and impact on the health of population', see Alex Christoforou, 'EU Austerity Killing Greece. Report Shows Suicide, Infant Death, and Mental Illness on the Rise', Global Research, 18 June 2016.

and more vulnerable people, including pregnant women, children and chronically or seriously ill individuals. The new law also introduced exceptions to the legislation prohibiting care beyond emergency treatment for adult undocumented migrants (Law No. 4251/2014), allowing the most vulnerable categories of people to access health care, including children up to 18 years old, pregnant women, chronically ill people, beneficiaries of a form of international protection, holders of a residence permit for humanitarian reasons, asylum seekers and their families, persons accommodated in mental healthcare units, victims of certain crimes, people with severe disabilities, seriously ill people and prison inmates.[174]

4.4.2.3 Measures Impacting on the Right to Education[175]

The Second Economic Adjustment Programme required changes in the Greek compulsory education system, aimed at its 'rationalisation'.[176] Conditionalities included reduced budgetary allocation from the state budget for the Ministry of Education (in 2011, –17 per cent for pre-primary, primary and secondary education), and the merging or shutting down of schools (between 2008 and 2012, 1,053 schools were closed and 1,933 school units merged into 877 units). Similarly, there has been a reduction in teachers' recruitment and remuneration (compared to 2009 levels, teachers' statutory salaries in 2014 had been reduced by 40 circa per cent, and were worth 77 per cent of what teachers of comparable training and experience earned in 2005),[177] and the placement of teachers in the labour reserve scheme, or their reallocation to other (e.g. administrative) positions, through mobility schemes.[178]

Among the adverse effects of the reforms, difficulties fully meeting the basic needs of students have been caused by the reduction of the budget available for schools' operational costs, for example, heating, stationery or

174 Médecins du Monde, International Network, 'Access to healthcare for people facing multiple vulnerabilities in health in 31 cities in 12 countries', 2016 Observatory Report, November 2016, 10, mdmgreece.gr/app/uploads/2016/11/PDF-BD-Observatory-report2016_EN.pdf.

175 UDHR, Article 26; ICESCR, Articles 13–14; CEDAW, Articles 10 and 14; CFC, Articles 28–29 and 40; CERD, Article 5; CRPD, Article 24; Charter of Fundamental Rights of the EU, Article 14; ECHR, Article 2; European Social Charter (revised), Articles 15, 17 and 30; Greek Constitution, Article 16(2).

176 'LIBE report', 32 and 38; European Commission, 'The Second Economic Adjustment Programme for Greece – March 2012' (March 2012) *European Economy – Occasional Papers* No. 94, 80.

177 A married teacher with two children earned, on average, €26,400 (gross) per year in 2009, and €21,280 (gross) per year in 2011 after the adoption of Law 4024/2011 introducing the new single payroll, see 'LIBE report', 38.

178 *Ibid.*, 36–38.

facilities maintenance. In some cases, private initiatives made up for the lack of funds, for example, in 2013 the Open Society Foundation of George Soros contributed to heating expenses of schools and other institutes in the municipalities of Thessaloniki and Athens.[179] The measures adopted resulted, furthermore, in a shortage of teachers, impairing, among other things, the provision of all-day programmes in some kindergartens and primary schools.[180] One of the ways the Ministry reportedly considered addressing this issue was to use *volunteer* teachers, that is, give them points they could use in future recruitment procedures instead of a salary.[181]

Particularly affected was the right to education of children with disabilities, as the allocation of resources did not take into account the obligations arising from the legal framework on special education.[182]

4.4.2.4 Measures Impacting on the Right to Housing

Several conditionalities impacted on the enjoyment of the right to adequate housing,[183] particularly by vulnerable groups such as homeless, migrants and the unemployed.

Under the Second Adjustment Programme (2012), Greece was requested, as a 'prior action' (i.e. as a measure to be implemented upfront, before programme approval), to enact legislation 'to close small earmarked funds engaged in non-priority social expenditures'.[184] These included funds destined to the Workers' Housing Organisation (OEK), the only major institution providing housing benefits in Greece, which was thus abolished with Law No. 4046/2012.[185] Consequently, rental subsidies to 120,000 households and housing benefits for the elder were eliminated.

179 'George Soros Donates Funds to Help Heat Schools in Greece', Greek Reporter, 15 December 2013.

180 'LIBE report', 39; Human Rights Council, Working Group on the Universal Periodic Review, 'Summary prepared by the Office of the United Nations High Commissioner for Human Rights in accordance with paragraph 15 (c) of the annex to Human Rights Council resolution 5/1', para. 6.

181 'LIBE report,' 39.

182 *Ibid.*, 40.

183 UDHR, Article 25(1); ICESCR, Article 11(1); CERD; CEDAW, Article 14; CRC, Article 27; CRPD, Article 28; European Social Charter (revised), Article, 16, 23, 30–31; Greek Constitution, Articles 4 and 21(4).

184 European Commission, Directorate-General for Economic and Financial Affairs, 'The Second Economic Adjustment Programme for Greece – March 2012' (March 2012), 148.

185 Truth Committee on Public Debt, 'Preliminary Report', 39; HRC, 'IE 2016 Report on mission to the EU', paras. 50–60; 'IE 2016 Report on second mission to Greece', paras. 31–42; 'IE 2014 Report on first mission to Greece', paras. 40–89.

Other reforms impacted on the right to adequate housing, for instance, by increasing the risks of foreclosures and evictions of poorer tenants. In a Communication of 2013 to the Greek government in 2013, the United Nations' Special Rapporteur on adequate housing noted that the crisis had led to a rising number of evictions. These had been allegedly facilitated and accelerated by an amendment to article 15 of Law No. 4055/2012, allowing for the eviction of rental tenants who failed to pay the rent within 15 days after the first notice, without prior judicial proceedings.[186] The Special Rapporteur noted, furthermore, that, since 2010, 'thousands of households have been living without electricity due to their inability to pay for the rising electricity prices',[187] and due to the Urgent Special Charge on Electrified Built Surfaces, introduced by Law No. 4021/2011, which is collected by the Public Power Corporation. The latter was authorised to cut and, according to unofficial estimates quoted by the Special Rapporteur, has cut the electricity supply to thousands of households due to outstanding debts.

It has been reported that, since 2009/2010, there has been an increase in homelessness, and that, in 2014, over 500,000 people in Greece lived in conditions of homelessness, insecure or inadequate housing.[188] Since the crisis, furthermore, a new generation of homeless ('neo-homeless') has emerged, consisting of individuals who, until recent years, had enjoyed satisfactory living standards and have, generally, a higher educational level compared to 'traditional' homeless, but who found themselves homeless due to financial difficulties and unemployment. Also migrants who are among the neo-homeless are individuals who previously enjoyed a good level of societal integration.[189] The access of homeless people to health services, housing and benefits has also deteriorated.

Some have noticed the rise and, more worryingly, consolidation, since the crisis, of an 'emergency model of social crisis governance', characterised by a preference for short-term solutions, the shift of social policy tasks to non-governmental organisations, reliance on charitable funding, and preference

186 HRC, Mandate of the Special Rapporteur on adequate housing as a component of the right to an adequate standard of living, and on the right to non-discrimination in this context, 'Communication to Greece', GRC 1/2013 (19 February 2013), in Communications report of Special Procedures, 'Communications sent, 1 December 2012 to 28 February 2013; Replies received, 1 February to 30 April 2013', UN Doc. A/HRC/23/51 (22 May 2013).

187 *Ibid.*

188 Truth Committee on Public Debt, 'Preliminary Report', 39; Vassilis Arapoglou and Kostas Gounis, 'Caring for the Homeless and the Poor in Greece: Implications for the Future of Social Protection and Social Inclusion', Executive Summary, Hellenic Observatory of the London School of Economics, 2014.

189 Olga Theodorikakou, Alexandra Alamanou and Kyriakos Katsadoros, '"Neo-Homelessness" and the Greek Crisis' (2013) 7 *European Journal of Homelessness* 2, 207.

for assistance in kind.[190] With regard to housing in particular, the authors of the study have observed that:

> a model of 'emergency' shelters and assistance in kind has been introduced by the policies of the Ministry of Labour, and is gradually consolidating. Night shelters, Day Centres, food banks, social pharmacies and social groceries have been established in this context. [...] It is premature to assess their impact, but the American experience suggests the ineffectiveness of emergency provisions. Our site visits and interviews informed us about a significant aspect in the operation of Day Centres. Namely, Day Centres not only attract street homeless individuals but an array of invisible poor in their search for healthcare services. Especially those Day Centres that are linked to day clinics open a door for health care and assistance. It has been a matter of great concern that a poor population with no health insurance or incapable of paying contributions for medication revolves around Day Centres and clinics.[191]

Several key local organisations have also confirmed that '"emergency" provisions are increasingly becoming a stable feature of social policies'[192] in the field of housing.

4.4.2.5 Measures Impacting on the Right to Social Security, Including Pensions[193]

Finally, the adjustment programmes implemented in Greece since 2010 mandated a number of reforms of the pension and social welfare systems, whose effects amplified the negative impacts of the economic crisis, especially on the most vulnerable, at a time in which social security should have rather provided a safety net.

On one side, welfare reforms included cuts and tightened eligibility conditions for unemployment benefits and benefits for families, children and persons with disabilities. Total expenditure on social protection benefits decreased from approximately €58.5 million in 2009 to €45.4 million in 2014 (although, as a percentage of GDP, it remained quite stable from 24.6 per cent

[190] Vassilis Arapoglou and Kostas Gounis, 'Poverty and Homelessness in Athens: Governance and the Rise of an Emergency Model of Social Crisis Management', GreeSE Paper No. 90, Hellenic Observatory Papers on Greece and Southeast Europe, March 2015.

[191] *Ibid.*, 24.

[192] *Ibid.*, 26.

[193] UDHR, Articles 22 and 25; ICESCR, Articles 9 and 10; CEDAW, Articles 11 and 13–14; CRC, Articles 18, 23 and 26–27; CERD, Articles 2 and 5; CRPD, Article 28; European Social Charter (revised), Articles 8(1), 12, 14, 16, 17 and 27(1); ECHR, Article 1 of Protocol No. 1; Charter of Fundamental Rights of the EU, Articles 17 and 34; Greek Constitution, Article 22(5).

to 25.5 per cent, due to the concurrent GDP contraction). Expenditure on disability benefits was also cut from €3.6 million in 2009 to €2.9 million in 2014.[194]

It has been noted that, against a background of mounting unemployment, benefit coverage remained very low. In the case of contributory unemployment insurance, that is, the ordinary unemployment benefit, which in 2012 was reduced from €454 to €360 per month, the coverage rate fell from 86 per cent in 2010 to 51 per cent in 2013. In the case of non-contributory unemployment assistance, that is, for long-term unemployment, the coverage rate increased only from 0.7 per cent in 2010–2011 to 2.8 per cent in 2012, while the benefit rate was kept identical, in nominal terms, to the 2003 rate, that is, €200 per month, and the maximum duration remained twelve months. In this respect, it has been correctly observed that '[w]hile not all those concerned are poor, it is difficult to see how anyone can argue that paying €200 per month for no longer than 12 months to such a low proportion of the long-term unemployed amounts to adequate income support'.[195]

Several other sources have likewise remarked that the post-reform guaranteed coverage and level of social security and benefits are inadequate to ensure a decent living for the recipients, and not in line with the right to social security, as recognised inter alia under article 9 ICESCR.[196] Expenditure for unemployment benefits decreased from €3.4 million in 2009 to €1.9 million in 2014 despite, over the same period, the unemployment rate increasing, as noted earlier also, from 9.6 per cent to 26.5 per cent. The Independent Expert on Foreign Debt and Human Rights has observed that, as of April 2016, only about 10 per cent of all registered unemployed persons [were] actually receiving unemployment benefits.[197]

Pension reforms, on their part, included structural and organisational changes (e.g. the consolidation of pension funds and the introduction of a distinction between basic and contributory pensions), measures affecting the entitlement to benefits (e.g. more stringent retirement conditions and increases of the official retirement age) and measures affecting the amount

194 Latest data available, Eurostat database, 'Tables by Functions, Aggregated Benefits and Grouped Schemes'.

195 Manos Matsaganis, 'The Greek Crisis: Social Impact and Policy Responses' (Friedrich Ebert Stiftung, November 2013), 21.

196 HRC, 'IE 2016 Report on second mission to Greece', para. 60; CESCR, Concluding observations on the second periodic report of Greece, UN Doc. E/C.12/GRC/CO/2 (27 October 2015), para. 23.

197 HRC, 'IE 2016 Report on second mission to Greece', para. 60.

of granted and future pensions and pension-related benefits (including cuts or freezing of existing and future pensions, and cuts or abolition of bonuses).[198] As noticed by the Greek Ombudsman, over the period 2010–2014, seventeen alterations of the social security legislation were made and around forty Circulars were issued.[199]

A number of provisions contained in over ten different legislative acts, adopted by the Greek government between 2010 and 2012, have been challenged before the European Committee of Social Rights.[200] They concerned reductions in primary and auxiliary pensions, bonuses, the pensioners' social solidarity contribution (which is levied from pensions of €1,400 or more), the suspension or reduction of pensions for pensioners with an occupation, and the reduction of private sector pensioners' social solidarity benefit. The Committee has affirmed that, whilst certain of these reductions do not in themselves amount to a violation of the Charter (e.g. the restrictions introduced in respect of holiday bonuses or of pension rights, in cases where the level of pension benefits is sufficiently high, or in cases where people are of such a low age that it is legitimate for the state to conclude that it is in the public interest for such persons to be encouraged to remain part of the workforce), their *cumulative effect* 'is bound to bring about a significant degradation of the standard of living and the living conditions of many of the pensioners concerned'.[201] Consequently, the Committee has concluded that such measures constitute a violation of article 12(3) of the 1961 European Social Charter, protecting the right to social security.[202]

As a consequence of these reforms, the ILO has reported, among others, that 'the rates of relative poverty and the material deprivation for people over 65 have worsened more than for the population on average'.[203]

[198] 'LIBE Report', 91.

[199] *Ibid.*, 103.

[200] *Federation of employed pensioners of Greece (IKA-ETAM)* v. *Greece*, Complaint No. 76/2012 (ECSR, 7 December 2012); *Panhellenic Federation of Public Service Pensioners (POPS)* v. *Greece*, Complaint No.77/2012 (ECSR, 7 December 2012); *Pensioners' Union of the Athens-Piraeus Electric Railways (I.S.A.P.)* v. *Greece*, Complaint No. 78/2012 (ECSR, 7 December 2012); *Panhellenic Federation of pensioners of the Public Electricity Corporation (POSDEI)* v. *Greece*, Complaint No. 79/2012 (ECSR, 7 December 2012); *Pensioners' Union of the Agricultural Bank of Greece (ATE)* v. *Greece*, Complaint No. 80/2012 (ECSR, 7 December 2012).

[201] See e.g. *Federation of employed pensioners of Greece (IKA-ETAM)* v. *Greece*, Complaint No. 76/2012 (ECSR, 7 December 2012), paras. 77–78.

[202] See also HRC, 'IE 2014 Report on first mission to Greece', para. 55.

[203] ILO, 'Social Security (Minimum Standards) Convention, 1952 (No. 102) – Greece', Observation (CEACR) – adopted 2013, published 103rd ILC session (2014).

4.4.2.6 Privatisations

Another key component of the adjustment programmes was the privatisation, restructuring or liquidation of state-owned enterprises (SOEs) and assets in order to contribute to the reduction of the public debt. The target was initially set at €50 billion by the end of 2015, later reduced to €24.2 billion by 2020 as privatisation progressed slowly and produced revenues significantly below expectations. The Hellenic Republic Asset Development Fund (HRADF), which was established by Law 3986/2011, is now responsible for the privatisation programme. As of 2017, only three privatisations of major SOEs were completed (ports, airports and the national lottery).[204] In 2014, the Independent Expert on Foreign Debt and Human Rights expressed its concern that 'several of the enterprises targeted for privatization provide essential public services, such as water and sanitation, transportation and energy, and that there is a likelihood of a significant increase in user fees for the services offered by these entities after privatization'.[205] He also questioned the decision to privatise the Greek national lottery, if the intention was to raise funds to pay down the debt, considering that it was one of the most profitable of the world.[206] It is important to emphasise as well – as the IMF has more recently noted – that, while it is true that privatisations increase revenue and lower deficits (thus, improving the fiscal position of the state in the short term), they nonetheless reduce the government asset holdings, that is, net public wealth over time, creating a 'fiscal illusion' in the short term.[207]

The last part of this chapter discusses the empirical evidence so far reported in light of the existing standards on ESR outlined in Chapter 3, and comments on the bigger picture emerging from the Greek case and more generally from present and past responses to debt crises.

204 OECD, 'Greece Policy Brief – Corporate Governance: Reforming the State-owned Enterprises Sector', March 2016. In April 2016, HRADF sold the 51 per cent of the Piraeus Port Authority to the Chinese state-owned company COSCO Shipping Corporation, which already operates the container terminal in Piraeus under a thirty-five-year concession it acquired in 2009. In August 2016, Athens also approved a deal to hand over the operation of fourteen regional airports under a forty-year contract worth €1.23 billion to a Fraport AG, the German company running Frankfurt's airport, see George Georgiopoulos, 'China's Cosco Acquires 51 pct Stake in Greece's Piraeus Port', Reuters, 10 August 2016; 'Greece's Largest Port Taken Over by Chinese Firm', RT News, 11 August 2011.

205 HRC, 'IE 2014 Report on first mission to Greece', para. 31.

206 *Ibid.*, para. 32. In 2013, Greece sold the government's 33 per cent controlling shareholding to Emma Delta, a Cyprus-based vehicle led by Jiri Smejc, a Czech investor in emerging markets, and Dimitris Melissanidis, a Greek ship-owner and oil trader, Kerin Hope, 'Greece Sells Lottery Stake in Biggest Privatisation', Financial Times, 1 May 2013.

207 IMF, 'Fiscal Monitor: Managing Public Wealth', 5.

4.4.3 *Conditionality under Human Rights Law*

Despite the fact that the adverse impacts of debt and related policies on the enjoyment of human rights, particularly ESR, are now abundantly evidenced[208] and have been conceded, as well, by the IMF itself,[209] initially neither the CESCR nor the Independent Expert on Foreign Debt and Human Rights, as I noted elsewhere,[210] seemed to consider conditionality as particularly problematic from a human rights perspective. On the contrary, they had seemingly accepted (and this might be interpreted as a further proof of the extent to which neoliberal assumptions have become ingrained in our current understanding of the world) that conditionality has conclusively become the rule in the economic governance of financial assistance, also in the EU: all that can be done is to seek out legal solutions compatible with this circumstance. Remarkably, however, in a more recent report, the Independent Expert on Foreign Debt and Human Rights has upheld that there is 'a solid legal basis to make the case for a prima facie inconsistency between the imposition of austerity policies in times of recession and the enjoyment of human rights'.[211]

Nonetheless, it is notable that most reports, including some of the reports of the Independent Expert itself,[212] still use the terms 'violation' or 'breach' to refer to the impact of conditionalities on ESR only in cases where a judicial (e.g.

[208] A vast and long-standing literature exists on the adverse human rights impacts of conditionality, see e.g. the 1978 Report of the Special Rapporteur on the Situation of Human Rights in Chile referenced in Chapter 1. For some recent examples, see inter alia, Juan Pablo Bohoslavsky, 'Complicity of International Financial Institutions in Violation of Human Rights in the Context of Economic Reforms' (2020) 52 *Columbia Human Rights Law Review* 1, 204–250; UN General Assembly, 'Responsibility for complicity of international financial institutions in human rights violations'; Aleksandra Ivanković Tamamović, 'The Impact of the Crisis on Fundamental Rights across Member States of the EU: Comparative Analysis' (2015) *Study for the LIBE Committee of the European Parliament*; Isabel Ortiz, Matthew Cummins, Jeronim Capaldo and Kalaivani Karunanethy, 'The Decade of Adjustment: A Review of Austerity Trends 2010-2020 in 187 Countries', ESS Working Paper No 53 (Geneva: International Labour Office, 2015); Council of Europe, 'The Impact of the Economic Crisis and Austerity Measures on Human Rights in Europe', 2015.

[209] Ostry, Loungani and Furceri, 'Neoliberalism: Oversold?'; Ball et al., 'The Distributional Effects of Fiscal Consolidation'.

[210] Emma Luce Scali, 'The Impact of Conditionality on Economic, Social and Cultural Rights in the Latest Reports of the UN Independent Expert on Foreign Debt and Human Rights’ (2017) 11 *Diritti Umani e Diritto Internazionale* 2, 532–541.

[211] HRC, 'Responsibility for complicity of international financial institutions in human rights violations in the context of retrogressive economic reforms', Report of the Independent Expert on the effects of foreign debt and other related international financial obligations of states on the full enjoyment of all human rights, UN Doc. A/74/178 (16 July 2019).

[212] HRC, 'IE 2016 Report on mission to the EU'; 'Labour rights report'.

a constitutional court) or quasi-judicial body (e.g. the European Committee of Social Rights) has already officially ascertained that a specific measure was in contrast with one or more provision(s) of the relative instrument. In most cases, on the contrary, the impact of conditionality on human rights has been described in generic terms, for example, of 'tension', 'declining respect', 'weakened protection' or 'adverse effects'. This fact suggests that difficulties persisted in effectively qualifying particular conditionality-related actions or omissions as ESR 'violations'. Such difficulties were due, on one side, to genuine methodological challenges. For instance, to assess the empirical dimension of retrogression, that is, the 'empirical backsliding in the effective enjoyment of the rights',[213] requires a comprehensive evaluation of state conduct, including its generation and use of available resources, and the monitoring of the degree of retrogression over time, also through quantitative indicators, whose data are not always readily available.[214] On the other side, difficulties to qualify conditionality in terms of ESR violations are due also to the normative uncertainty that still characterises certain aspects of the ESR framework, for instance the notions of 'maximum available resources' or 'non-retrogression', as discussed in Chapter 3. This normative uncertainty certainly has not been remedied by the reluctance especially of the CESCR, but also of other supranational judicial and non-judicial bodies, to engage thoroughly with responses to the crisis.

The description of conditionalities and their impacts on ESR outlined in the previous section suggests that most of the measures implemented in Greece since 2010 had a deliberately retrogressive nature in terms of ESR realisation, and ignored the requirement, particularly under the ICESCR, to prioritise, in the allocation of the state's maximum available resources, the most vulnerable and the realisation of the minimum core content of each right.

In fact, Greece was required to reduce and in some cases to cap (e.g. health care) the resources allocated to the realisation of ESR, in almost all cases below the average percentage devoted to the realisation of the same rights by EU-28 countries, that is, countries with a similar level of development. As mentioned in Chapter 3, in some of its Concluding Observations, the CESCR has interpreted this as an indication of non-compliance with the obligation to use the maximum available resources. In other cases, for instance, with regard to the right to social security, various monitoring bodies have explicitly

213 Aoife Nolan, Nicholas J. Lusiani and Christian Courtis, 'Two Steps Forwards, No Steps Back? Evolving Criteria on the Prohibition of Retrogression in Economic and Social Rights' in Aoife Nolan (ed.), *Economic and Social Rights after the Global Financial Crisis* (Cambridge University Press, 2014) 121–145.

214 *Ibid.*

remarked, as mentioned earlier, that the post-reform allocation of resources is inadequate to ensure that the right-holders enjoy a decent standard of living. Furthermore, reforms to 'rationalise' the physical and human resources available to the public, healthcare, and educational sectors provoked shortages of personnel and unmet basic needs, for instance, with regard to medicines in public hospitals, or heating in public schools.

Greece was also required, in some cases, to abrogate ESR-favourable legislation without replacing it with equally or more consistent law or compensatory measures, such as in the case of the requested abolition of its only major housing benefits institution, the Workers' Housing Organisation (OEK). In many other cases, conditionalities required 'deregulatory' reforms of legislation, which substantially reduced the level of protection guaranteed to right-holders, both in qualitative and quantitative terms, that is, in terms of the number and range of people who can access their rights. This has occurred prominently in the case of labour rights, but also in respect of all the other rights discussed in the previous section, as evidenced for instance by the appalling rates of people who lost their health insurance cover, could not access necessary medical treatment, or became homeless because of facilitated eviction procedures. Other key social indicators, revealing alarming rates of long-term unemployment, poverty, infant mortality, mental health disorders, suicides, the reappearance of infectious diseases that had been eradicated in the developed world, homelessness and deprivation, especially among children, the elderly, women and migrants, portray a general situation in which the protection of the rights, especially of the most vulnerable, has substantially deteriorated and often fallen below the minimum core.

However, with regard to retrogressive measures in particular, it must be remarked that their prohibition under international human rights law is not absolute, as discussed already in Chapter 3. In times of economic hardship, including due to a financial crisis, states may face constraints in the realisation of ESR and international human rights law does not rule out that they may have to take retrogressive measures contrary to their general obligations.[215] Nonetheless, there are limits on the extent to which states may deviate from their ESR obligations in order to comply with the requirements of conditionality. The adoption of retrogressive measures is, in fact, only justifiable under the criteria reaffirmed by the CESCR, inter alia, in its 2016 Statement on Public Debt.[216] Accordingly, retrogressive measures (i) must be temporary, covering only the period of the crisis, (ii) must be necessary and proportionate

215 'Labour rights report', para. 22.
216 CESCR, '2016 Statement on Public Debt'.

(this meaning that the adoption of any other policy, or failure to act, would be more detrimental to ESR), (iii) must be non-discriminatory and comprising all possible measures, including tax measures, to support social transfers and mitigate inequalities that can grow in times of crisis and to ensure that the rights of the disadvantaged and marginalised individuals and groups are not disproportionately affected and (iv) must identify and ensure protection of the minimum core content of ESR at all times.

As mentioned in Chapter 3, the CESCR first proposed these standards in a 2012 Letter addressed to states parties to the ICESCR,[217] and ever since they have been frequently referenced by various human rights treaty bodies and scholarly work. Nonetheless, their application in practice raises important questions that require careful analysis. When can a retrogressive measure be unequivocally said to be 'necessary', and based on what rationale? The idea of necessity seems to imply that there is a 'natural', perhaps just 'technical' righteousness/wrongness of certain economic decisions, but these are, on the contrary, always highly political in nature. Is an ex ante counterfactual assessment of the harm potentially caused by a retrogressive measure compared to other policy options realistically possible? For instance, with regard to conditionality, the Independent Expert on Foreign Debt and Human Rights has admitted that to prove whether, without financial assistance in this guise, the social impact of the crisis may or may not have been worse is 'an extremely complex counterfactual exercise'.[218] Under what circumstances can retrogressive measures actually 'mitigate inequalities', considering that a positive link between retrogressive measures and inequality has been frequently observed?[219] While the CESCR has recalled these criteria in some of its recent Concluding Observations,[220] it has not further clarified yet how state conduct should be assessed against them in practice.

Furthermore, the 'emergency approach' to economic and social policy-making triggered by the crisis, together with the scarcity of resources caused by the exclusion of Greece from international markets, proved to be a useful

217 CESCR, '2012 Letter on austerity measures'.

218 HRC, 'IE 2016 Report on mission to the EU', para. 14.

219 See e.g. HRC, Report of the Independent Expert on the effects of foreign debt and other related international financial obligations of states on the full enjoyment of all human rights, particularly economic, social and cultural rights on his mission to Greece, UN Doc. A/HRC/31/60/Add.2 (21 April 2016).

220 See i.a. CESCR, Concluding observations on the sixth periodic report of Cyprus, UN Doc. E/C.12/CYP/CO/6 (28 October 2016), para. 12; Concluding observations on the sixth periodic report of the United Kingdom of Great Britain and Northern Ireland, UN Doc. E/C.12/GBR/CO/6 (14 July 2016), para. 19; Concluding observations on the fifth periodic report of Italy, UN Doc. E/C.12/ITA/CO/5 (28 October 2015).

argumentative tool to justify the adoption of (allegedly) temporary measures, regressive or otherwise, incompatible with ESR.[221] As mentioned in the previous section, most monitoring bodies have endorsed such an approach, either justifying the necessity of austerity measures based on the emergency of the crisis and the public interest pursued by the state, as done by the ECtHR, or expressing 'concern' with regard to their ESR impacts, without engaging more thoroughly with the conduct and the justifications put forward by the state. The European Committee of Social Rights has been, so far, the only monitoring body to uphold unambiguously that some of the austerity measures implemented by Greece since 2010 violate welfare rights. It has been, so far, also the only body to attempt to go beyond a 'micro' analysis of the link between conditionality and ESR, to assess, rather, the cumulative effects of the different reforms implemented, on the enjoyment of welfare rights by all those affected. Such attempt must be very positively welcomed.

4.5 CONCLUSIONS

This chapter has attempted to provide a full portrait of the Greek sovereign debt crisis, revealing the intricate interplay of political and economic, national and supranational, country-specific and systemic factors in the build-up of unsustainable debt levels and the formulation of responses to the crisis.

Greece entered the Eurozone in 2001 with a high level of public debt, which was mainly the heir to the country's fiscal behaviour of the 1980s–early 1990s. The architecture of the EMU both facilitated and induced Greek (as other 'peripheral' Euro Area Member States') public and private actors to (over) borrow, and to rely on debt-based economic growth. The global credit crunch that followed the 2007 financial crisis exposed the weakness of this coping mechanism, and the Greek debt crisis, together with the instability of other EU countries, threatened the Eurozone as a whole. In order to provide financial assistance to Greece and the other Euro Area Member States in difficulty, temporary mechanisms and, finally, the ESM were progressively put in place, often circumventing or 'reshaping' as necessary any possible legal obstacle to the interests and the aims of the 'powerful' (i.e. creditors, or the Greek state itself, in some cases); responses to the crisis followed a path riddled with injustices against all those who alternately found themselves in a more vulnerable

221 Catherine Moury and Adam Stranding, 'Going Beyond the Troika: Power discourse in Portuguese austerity politics' (2017) 56 *European Journal of Political Research* 3, 660–679. The authors noted i.a. that 'the crisis exploitation constitutes a tactic of depoliticisation, in which both the material constraints and the discourse used to frame them are employed to construct imperatives around a narrow selection of policy alternatives'.

position, including among the creditors. The existing legal framework not only has not prevented, but has actually worked towards, the prioritisation of economic objectives/interests over any other objectives/interests.

The new financial assistance mechanisms put in place for EU Member States have imported conditionality in the European legal framework, despite it being an opaque and potentially coercive practice, characterised by power asymmetry between debtors and creditors, guided by purely economic objectives, and overtly and extensively criticised for its well-known adverse social impacts. Conditionality has inappropriately become a tool of economic and, indirectly, social governance also in the European context. In Greece, it has enforced a regressive, permanent trend in the realisation of ESR.

5

Conclusions

'*Crisis*. From the Greek word κρίσις, "judgement," "result of a trial," "turning point," "selection," "decision" (according to Thucydides), but also "contention" or "quarrel" (according to Plato), a standard, from which to derive *criterion*, "means for judging," but also "ability to discern," and *critical*, "suitable to judge," "crucial," "decisive" as well as pertaining to the art of judgement."[1] In the original meaning of the word, *crisis* identifies a point of uncertainty and a moment of (inevitable) transition, of change from one condition to another (not necessarily an improved one), which importantly prompts, in the individuals involved, practical moral reasoning and possibly an enhanced understanding of their condition and of themselves. Despite being labelled as such, however, the recent and increasingly recurring global financial, economic, fiscal/debt, climate and health crises seem to elapse, one after the other, without any radical transformation – most notably in the awareness of their witnesses – and to return the various global human and ecosystems involved into a state of permanent malaise: treated enough so not to die (for now) but marked by an unresolved affliction. A state in which further crises are thus to be expected, and may happen very soon indeed.[2]

From the point of view of ESR, the latest Global Financial Crisis and the ensuing Eurozone debt crisis did not represent a critical juncture, as one might have expected, for a rethinking of the nature and aims of the global economic order. To the contrary, they fostered and accelerated global

[1] Zygmunt Bauman and Carlo Bordoni, *State of Crisis* (Cambridge: Polity Press, 2014).

[2] See e.g. Bank for International Settlements, 'BIS Annual Report 2017 – media briefing by Claudio Borio and Hyun Song Shin', 25 June 2017, www.bis.org/publ/arpdf/ar2017e_tcintro .htm; or the warning issued in 2017 by the Bank of England, over the possibility of a rerun of the 2008 financial crisis linked to the spiralling out of control of household debt in the UK, Larry Elliott, 'Bank of England Warns of Complacency Over Big Rise in Personal Debt', The Guardian, 24 July 2017.

regressive tendencies in terms of ESR realisation that were already underway at least since the 1970s, producing a permanent restructuring of most European countries' welfare systems. Ten years later, it is somehow surprising how this seemingly inevitable course of action has been implemented amongst, all things considered, relatively isolated and effectively powerless cries of protest. The crisis silently eroded social and legal achievements that had costed years of unconditional struggle to many in Europe and around the world and, as the Greek case has evidenced, existing legal frameworks proved rather ineffective in protecting ESR and preventing their structural decline.

This book has argued that a possible explanation for this circumstance lies in the affirmation and progressive global diffusion of neoliberalism, not merely as a political economic theory, but more generally as a belief system (however based on a deeper 'psychic' state) characteristic of a certain political philosophy (and characterised by distinctive normative assumptions, especially on the possibilities and role of human knowledge in the construction of the social/political order) that is increasingly reflected in the existing law, and whose core tenets greatly diverge from the fundamental beliefs that inspired the development and affirmation of human rights, including ESR, as international legal rights during the twentieth century. The existing international human rights framework has not been able to effectively prevent this regression also because – as this book's chapters have attempted to describe – the law itself increasingly reflects neoliberalism, and the crisis has actually corroborated and to an extent advanced its neoliberalisation.

This book has reviewed and discussed some of the debt-ESR-related legal developments that seem to evidence such reinforced neoliberalisation.

Firstly, the post-crisis reform of economic governance in the EU (Chapter 2) has increased the convergence of national economic and fiscal policies towards neoliberal standards. It has considerably restricted the fiscal sovereignty of EU Member States and it has made their social policies increasingly contingent upon the realisation of the Union's objectives of financial and monetary stability. Importantly, the reform has also strengthened, in line with neoliberal scepticism against democratic governance, the purported depoliticisation of economic and fiscal decision-making, by promoting, in some cases, the automatic application of EU fiscal rules, to prevent politics, especially national parliaments, from interfering with the ostensibly technical nature of such decisions.

Secondly, the incorporation of the principle of conditionality under EU law (Chapter 4) represents (where conditionality is characterised as above) the legal formalisation of a most probably asymmetrical (power) relationship between debtor states and their creditors, susceptible to intensifying the influence of neoliberal imperative over states' economic and, indirectly, social policymaking. It also signals a possible departure of economic governance in the EU from the principles of sovereign equality, non-intervention, self-determination and international cooperation, rather underlying a different conception of the international order, concerned, at least to a certain extent, with the protection of economically more vulnerable states.

Finally, the CESCR and the European Court of Human Rights in particular (Chapters 3 and 4) seem to have absorbed, in their legal assessment of responses to the crisis, neoliberal assumptions regarding, inter alia, the inevitability of conditionality and austerity, the nature of equality and an understanding of personal responsibility (as in the case of the small private and institutional investors that suffered disproportionally from the 2012 Greek debt restructuring) that overlooks the importance, on the contrary, of structural and contextual variables for individual behaviour. Furthermore, the alterations made by the CESCR, after the crisis, to the doctrine of non-retrogression appear to reconcile ESR and austerity by adjusting the legal requirements of the international ESR regime to the necessities of the latter. The legal protection of ESR risks, thus, being substantially undermined.

The overall trend that emerges from the debt crisis in Europe is thus one characterised by (1) unresolved or even increased legal uncertainty, with regard to both sovereign debt and ESR, since the former remains largely unregulated under international law (also considering that the principles elaborated at the UNCTAD and the UN have so far received only scarce attention by states and monitoring bodies) and the legal protection of ESR is put at risk by the above-mentioned developments in the interpretation of existing international human rights law standards; (2) increased opacity (in terms of the sources, legitimacy and the prospects for accountability of the actors involved) of the economic governance regime of the EMU, due to the espousal of conditionality as a key principle of economic assistance, and to the above-mentioned features of the post-crisis reform of that regime; (3) increased supranational control over the fiscal and social policies of EU Member States, and increased subordination of their social policymaking, and thus potentially of their ability to realise ESR, to the objectives and requirements of debt sustainability, and financial and monetary stability; (4) the consolidation and diffusion of a neoliberalised state model, implying a progressively greater disengagement of the state with its welfare responsibilities; (5) a greater risk of legal opportunism, encouraged and supported by neoliberal morality, and consequently, the danger that the idea of law itself, as a means to achieve and protect any social order, is progressively compromised; and, finally, (6) the thus far completely unchallenged, expanded and expanding impoverishment and indebtedness of many states, including, increasingly, some advanced economies. Some final remarks on the latter seem, thus, worthwhile.

Contrary to rhetorical assertions, in the current neoliberal global economic system, debt seldom represents a genuine opportunity for poorer nations. For these countries, indebtedness often corresponds, more realistically, to a necessity rather than a choice, the only way to survive in the existing economic environment. Hence, *in this context*, sovereign debt more often epitomises the product and perpetuating instrument of economic vulnerability, unfair economic relations and structural injustice. It provides a temporary illusion of redistribution, while de facto transferring resources from those who do not have enough to those who should not need more, and increasing the wealth and influence of the (economically more) 'powerful' over (and against) the 'weak'. Debt has become an expedient to 'counterweight' the increasingly widespread public and private impoverishment and the 'structural deprivation and exclusion' that are, actually, 'systematically produced and maintained by the current [neoliberal] arrangement' of international economic relations.[3] Rather than an enabling tool, debt thus constitutes, more often than not, a tool of oppression and dispossession.[4]

The fact that states generally, and some of them more than others, increasingly 'choose' to rely on borrowing for the resources necessary to implement their functions (Chapter 2), including the realisation of ESR, should raise questions and concerns about not only the *sustainability* but also, most importantly, the *justice* of indebtedness and the current global state of the economy. Moreover, it raises questions about the inevitable repercussions that economic injustice and (asymmetrical) relationships of indebtedness have, more generally, on the structure of the international legal system and the nature of international law. Something can be made 'sustainable', while remaining nonetheless unjust.

Thus, the problem underlying the debt–ESR relationship – one that has not been minimally touched upon by debates about the Eurozone debt crisis, including by a large part of academia and, even more surprisingly, by those responsible for the promotion and the monitoring of ESR, such as the CESCR or the Independent Expert on Foreign Debt and Human Rights – remains primarily a problem of economic justice ('who is to have more and who less, or how much is to have whom, according to which criteria').[5]

[3] Richard Dienst, *The Bonds of Debt: Borrowing against the Common Good* (London: Verso, 2011), pp. 26–32.

[4] Harvey, *A Brief History of Neoliberalism*, pp. 159–165, describing the springing of the 'debt trap' and the use of the credit system as primary means of capitalist 'accumulation by dispossession'.

[5] Carlo Focarelli, *Economia Globale e Diritto Internazionale* (Bologna: Il Mulino, 2016), p. 18.

The relationship between sovereign debt and socio-economic rights is not limited to the regressive impacts of austerity measures on the enjoyment of ESR, in countries threatened by or facing a debt crisis (Chapter 1). It is more intimately founded upon the reality that the resources that are necessary to realise ESR have become increasingly dependent, because of the increasing debt financing of states, on the fate and mood of international credit and of sovereign bond markets. If a state is economically dependent upon its (largely private) international creditors, the realisation of human rights, together with other state functions, risks becoming contingent upon and subordinate to market imperatives. In other words, their realisation is left to the erratic 'benevolence' of the market.

This circumstance represents a *structural* problem for which the existing international, and especially human rights, legal framework provides no solution. As mentioned in Chapters 2 and 4, international law on sovereign debt, on one side, is currently underdeveloped. With regards to the issue of sovereign borrowing and human rights in particular, the only existing standards are represented by the various 'guiding principles' more recently developed under the aegis of the UN. These are soft law instruments with no legal binding force and, apart from some very few exceptions among the UNCTAD Principles, cannot be said to correspond to customary international law.

On the other hand, the international socio-economic rights regime does not offer sufficient safeguards. As noted in Chapter 3, the normative content of the ICESCR in particular remains quite elusive, and the legal protection of ESR under international law de facto relatively weak, as the irrelevance of socio-economic rights considerations in responses to the Eurozone crisis and the deferential approach adopted by monitoring bodies revealed.

More worryingly, there are no signs, at present, that this deficit will be altered or reversed any time soon. In fact, the measures adopted to respond to the Eurozone debt crisis have essentially evidenced and reinforced the neoliberal character of contemporary international law, by buttressing certain transformations in the nature and functions of the law and the state themselves. There is a clear link between the ascent of neoliberalism, current global economic arrangements and, most importantly, international law developments (or lack thereof). Given the absence, at the international level, of a centralised political and legal authority, the content of international law – including human rights law – is necessarily the outcome of the systematic competition between states and groups of states with divergent interests and values. Since the 1980s and still today, despite multiple crises, neoliberal morality has been hegemonic. As long as alternative systems of beliefs will not reach sufficient endorsement, so to overcome neoliberalism's ideological dominion, international law will necessarily reflect the latter.

These closing remarks are not a conclusion to my enquiry, but rather an invitation for further research. The analysis drawn in this book essentially was an attempt at reconstructing a faithful narrative of the facts, taking stock of the existing law, and identifying the underlying problem(s).

A final general observation on law's neoliberalisation is compelling, especially because of its significance for the possibilities of 'neoliberalised' law to constitute a useful means to promote an alternative social order. It has been correctly observed that '[l]aw's embedded and constitutive role in the formulation and dissemination of neoliberal social relations forecloses or severely limits law as a useful terrain for transformative change to those social relations'.[6]

Alternative means to promote such changes have been proposed, including a resurrection of the agonistic element of politics, a tactical use of law in political resistance and, even, alternative regulatory frameworks outside the law. I endorse the need, in particular, for a critical approach to the study of international law, including, in a pervasive neoliberal context, 'a subversive engagement with law that contains an implicit critique of the legal form' itself.[7] In the human rights context, this means, inter alia, the willingness to engage with the possible limitations not only of the normative content of existing legal frameworks but also of the legal form of rights itself.

Nonetheless, I also believe that for the law to move away from its current neoliberal inclination, the existence of a radically different, non-neoliberal 'common sense' will be necessary. And this appears to be foremost a task for culture, education and politics to realise.

6 Brabazon, *Neoliberal Legality*.
7 *Ibid.*

Bibliography

Ali Abbas S. M., Belhocine N., El-Ganainy A. and Horton M., 'Historical Patterns and Dynamics of Public Debt: Evidence from a New Database' (2011) 59 *IMF Economic Review* 717

Ali Abbas S. M., Belhocine N., El-Ganainy A. and Weber A., 'Current Debt Crisis in Historical Perspective', in C. Cottarelli, P. Gerson and A. Senhadji (eds.), *Post-Crisis Fiscal Policy* (MIT Press, 2014) 161–191

Ali Abbas S. M., Blattner L., De Broeck M., El-Ganainy A. and Hu M., 'Sovereign Debt Composition in Advanced Economies: A Historical Perspective' (September 2014) IMF Working Paper WP/14/162

Aliprantis N., 'Social Rights Beyond the National Level – Findings and Challenges', in Nikita Aliprantis and Ioannis Papageorgiou (eds.), *Social Rights at European, Regional and International Level: Challenges for the 21st Century* (Bruylant, 2010)

Alogoskoufis G., 'Greece's Sovereign Debt Crisis: Retrospect and Prospect' (January 2012) GreeSE Paper No 54, Hellenic Observatory Papers on Greece and Southeast Europe

Alston P., *The United Nations and Human Rights: A Critical Appraisal* (Clarendon Press, 1992)

Alston P. and Goodman R., *International Human Rights: Text and Materials* (Oxford University Press, 2013)

Alston P. and Quinn G., 'The Nature and Scope of States Parties' Obligations under the International Covenant on Economic, Social and Cultural Rights' (1987) 9 *Human Rights Quarterly* 173

Alston P. and Simma B., 'Second Session of the UN Committee on Economic, Social and Cultural Rights' (1988) 82 *American Journal of International Law* 3, 603–615

Andrews M., 'Hohfeld's Cube' (1983) 16 *Akron Law Review* 3, 471–485

Antonakakis N. and Collins A., 'The Impact of Fiscal Austerity on Suicide: On the Empirics of a Modern Greek Tragedy' (2014) 112 *Social Science & Medicine* 39–50

'The Impact of Fiscal Austerity on Suicide Mortality: Evidence across the "Eurozone Periphery"' (2015) 145 *Social Science & Medicine* 63–78

Arapoglou V. and Gounis K., 'Caring for the Homeless and the Poor in Greece: Implications for the Future of Social Protection and Social Inclusion', Executive Summary, Hellenic Observatory of the London School of Economics, 2014

'Poverty and Homelessness in Athens: Governance and the Rise of an Emergency Model of Social Crisis Management' (March 2015) GreeSE Paper No 90, Hellenic Observatory Papers on Greece and Southeast Europe

Arnsperger C., *Critical Political Economy: Complexity, Rationality and the Logic of Post-Orthodox Pluralism* (Routledge, 2006)

Attali J., *Tous ruinés dans dix ans? Dette publique: la dernière chance* (Fayard, 2010)

Ball L., Furceri D., Leigh D. and Loungani P., 'The Distributional Effects of Fiscal Consolidation' (June 2013) IMF Working Paper WP/13/151

Bantekas I. and Oette L., *International Human Rights Law and Practice*, 3rd ed. (Cambridge University Press, 2020)

Bates E., 'History', in Daniel Moeckli, Sangeeta Shah and Sandesh Sivakumaran (eds.), *International Human Rights Law*, 3rd ed. (Oxford University Press, 2017)

Bauman Z. and Bordoni C., *State of Crisis* (Polity Press, 2014)

Beddeleem M., 'Fighting for the Mantle of Science: The Epistemological Foundations of Neoliberalism, 1931–1951', unpublished Ph.D thesis, Université de Montréal (2017)

Beveridge W., 'Social Insurance and Allied Services' (American ed. reproduced photographically from the English edition and published by arrangement with His Majesty's Stationery Office, The Macmillan Company, 1942)

Birch K., *A Research Agenda for Neoliberalism* (Edward Elgar, 2017)

Blalock C., 'Neoliberalism and the Crisis of Legal Theory' (2015) 77 *Law and Contemporary Problems* 4, 71–103

Blyberg A. and Hofbauer H., *Article 2 and Governments' Budgets* (International Budget Partnership, 2014), www.internationalbudget.org/wp-content/uploads/Article-2-and-Governments-Budgets.pdf

Blyth M., *Austerity: The History of a Dangerous Idea* (Oxford University Press, 2011)

Bohoslavsky J. P., 'Complicity of International Financial Institutions in Violation of Human Rights in the Context of Economic Reforms' (2020) 52 *Columbia Human Rights Law Review* 1, 204–250

Bohoslavsky J. P. and Černič J. L. (eds.), *Making Sovereign Financing and Human Rights Work* (Hart, 2014)

Bonney R. (ed.), *Economic Systems and State Finance* (Oxford University Press, 1995) 81–100

The Rise of the Fiscal State in Europe, c. 1200–1815 (Oxford University Press, 1999)

Borensztein E., Chamon M., Jeanne O., Mauro P. and Zettelmayer J., 'Sovereign Debt Structure for Crisis Prevention' (2004) IMF Occasional Paper No 237

Brabazon H. (ed.), *Neoliberal Legality: Understanding the Role of Law in the Neoliberal Project* (Routledge, 2017)

Buchheit L. C. and Mitu Gulati G., 'Sovereign Contingent Liabilities', in Rosa M. Lastra and Lee Buchheit (eds.), *Sovereign Debt Management* (Oxford University Press, 2014)

Cahill D., Cooper M., Konings M. and Primrose D. (eds.), *The SAGE Handbook of Neoliberalism* (SAGE, 2018)

Chinkin C., 'Sources', in Daniel Moeckli, Sangeeta Shah and Sandesh Sivakumaran (eds.), *International Human Rights Law*, 3rd ed. (Oxford University Press, 2017) 75–95

Contiades X. (ed.), *Constitutions in the Global Financial Crisis: A Comparative Analysis* (Routledge, 2016)
Corbin A., 'Jural Relations and Their Classification' (1921) Yale Law School Faculty Scholarship Series Paper No 2873
Costamagna F., 'National Social Spaces as Adjustment Variables in the EMU: A Critical Legal Appraisal' (2018) 24 *European Law Journal* 163–190
'Saving Europe "Under Strict Conditionality": A Threat for EU Social Dimension?' (2012) LPF Working Paper No 7
Craven M., *The International Covenant on Economic, Social and Cultural Rights: A Perspective on its Development* (Clarendon Press, 1998)
Crouch C., 'Privatised Keynesianism: An Unacknowledged Policy Regime (2009) 11 *British Journal of Politics and International Relations* 3, 382–399
The Strange Non-Death of Neoliberalism (Polity Press, 2011)
Dardot P. and Laval C., *The New Way of the World: On Neoliberal Society* (Verso, 2013)
Dawes S. and Lenormand M. (eds.), *Neoliberalism in Context* (London: Palgrave Macmillan, 2020)
De Grauwe P. and Ji Y., 'Mispricing of Sovereign Risk and Multiple Equilibria in the Eurozone' (20 January 2012) Centre for European Policy Working Paper No 61
De Schutter O. (ed.), *Economic, Social and Cultural Rights as Human Rights* (Edward Elgar, 2013)
De Schutter O. and Salomon M., 'Economic Policy Conditionality, Socio-economic Rights and International Legal Responsibility: The case of Greece 2010-2015', *Legal Brief for the Special Committee of the Hellenic Parliament on the audit of the Greek debt* (15 June 2015)
de Witte F., 'The Architecture of a "Social Market Economy"', (2015) LSE Law Society and Economy Working Papers 13/2015
Dienst R., *The Bonds of Debt: Borrowing Against the Common Good* (Verso, 2011)
Dornbusch R. and Edwards S. (eds.), *The Macroeconomics of Populism in Latin America* (University of Chicago Press, 1991)
Dowell-Jones M., 'The Sovereign Bond Markets and Socio-Economic Rights: Understanding the Challenge of Austerity' in Eibe Reidel, Gilles Giacca and Christophe Golay (eds.), *Economic, Social and Cultural Rights in International Law: Contemporary Issues and Challenges* (Oxford University Press, 2014)
'International Finance and Human Rights: Scope for a Mutually Beneficial Relationship' (2012) 3 *Global Policy* 467
Contextualising the International Covenant on Economic, Social and Cultural Rights: Assessing the Economic Deficit (Martinus Nijhoff, 2004)
Dowell-Jones M. and Kinley D., 'Minding the Gap: Global Finance and Human Rights' (2011) 25 *Ethics and International Affairs* 183
Dreher A., 'IMF Conditionality: Theory and Evidence' (2009) 141 *Public Choice* 233–267
Drelichman M. and Voth H.-J., *Lending to the Borrower From Hell: Debt, Taxes, and Default in the Age of Philip II* (Princeton University Press, 2014)
Duménil G. and Lévy D., *The Crisis of Neoliberalism* (Harvard University Press, 2011)
Eagleton-Pierce M., *Neoliberalism: Key concepts* (Routledge, 2016)
Eichengreen B. and Hausmann R. (eds.), *Debt Denomination and Financial Instability in Emerging Market Economies* (University of Chicago Press, 2002)

Eichengreen B., Hausmann R. and Panizza U., 'The Pain of Original Sin', in B. Eichengreen and R. Hausmann (eds.), *Other People's Money: Debt Denomination and Financial Instability in Emerging Market Economies* (University of Chicago Press, 2005) 13–37

Espósito C., Li Y. and Bohoslavsky J. P. (eds.), *Sovereign Financing and International Law: The UNCTAD Principles on Responsible Sovereign Lending and Borrowing* (Oxford University Press, 2013)

European University Institute, 'Constitutional Change through Euro Crisis Law: A Multi-Level Legal Analysis of Economic and Monetary Union: Greece – IX. Fiscal Compact – IX.5. Debate Balanced Budget Rule', available at http://eurocrisislaw.eui.eu/country/greece/topic/fiscal-compact/

Ferguson N., *The Cash Nexus: Money and Power in the Modern World, 1700–2000* (Basic Books, 2001)

Finnis J., *Natural Law and Natural Rights*, 2nd ed. (Oxford University Press, 2011)

Flassbeck H. and Lapavitsas C., *Against the Troika: Crisis and Austerity in the Eurozone* (Verso, 2015)

Focarelli C., *Economia Globale e Diritto Internazionale* (Il Mulino, 2016)

'Il pianeta dei balocchi. A proposito della definizione dei diritti umani' (2016) 3 *Diritti umani e diritto internazionale* 659–676

'International Human Rights "in Crisis" and the Neoliberalization of the Human Person' (2020) 19 *Chinese Journal of International Law* 1, 53–100

International Law as Social Construct: The Struggle for Global Justice (Oxford University Press, 2012)

Trattato di Diritto Internazionale (UTET, 2015)

Folz H. E., 'State Debts' in *Encyclopaedia of Public International Law* (North-Holland, 2000), vol. IV

Foucault M., *The Birth of Biopolitics: Lectures at the Collège de France, 1978–1979*, ed. by M. Senellart, General Eds.: F. Ewald and A. Fontana, trans. by G. Burchell (Palgrave Macmillan, 2010)

Fundar-Center for Analysis and Research, International Budget Project and International Human Rights Internship Program, 'Dignity Counts: A Guide to Using Budget Analysis to Advance Human Rights', 2004

Garner B. A. (ed.), *Black's Law Dictionary*, 10th ed. (Thomson Reuters, 2014) 'Debt'

Goldmann M., 'Human Rights and Democracy in Economic Policy Reform: The European COVID-19 Response Under Scrutiny' (2020) 24 *The International Journal of Human Rights* 9, 1290–1310

Goodin R. E., *Reasons for Welfare: The Political Theory of the Welfare State* (Princeton University Press, 1988)

Graeber D., 'On the Moral Grounds of Economic Relations: A Maussian Approach' (2014) 14 *Journal of Classical Sociology* 1, 65–77

Debt: The First 5,000 Years (Melville House, 2011)

Grewal D. S. and Purdy J., 'Introduction: Law and Neoliberalism' (2014) 77 *Law and Contemporary Problems* 4, 1–23

Grant W. and Wilson G. K., 'Introduction' in Wyn Grant and Graham K. Wilson (eds.), *The Consequences of the Global Financial Crisis: The Rhetoric of Reform and Regulation* (Oxford University Press, 2012)

Greek Ministry of Finance, 'Update of the Hellenic Stability and Growth Programme including an Updated Reform Programme' (January 2010), ec.europa.eu/economy_finance/economic_governance/sgp/pdf/20_scps/2009-10/01_programme/el_2010-01-15_sp_en.pdf

Greek National Commission for Human Rights, 'NCHR Recommendation: On the imperative need to reverse the sharp decline in civil liberties and social rights' (8 December 2011), nchr.gr/images/English_Site/CRISIS/nchr_crisis.pdf

Han B.-C., *The Agony of Eros*, trans. by Erik Butler (MIT Press, 2017)

Harvey D., *A Brief History of Neoliberalism* (Oxford University Press, 2005)

Hayek F. A., *Individualism and Economic Order* (University of Chicago Press, 1948)

Law, Legislation and Liberty (University of Chicago Press 1973), vol. I

'Scientism and the Study of Society', in B. Caldwell (ed.), *The Collected Works of F. A. Hayek: Studies on the Abuse and Decline of Reason: Text and Documents* (The University of Chicago Press, 2010), vol. XIII

The Sensory Order: An Inquiry into the Foundations of Theoretical Psychology (Routledge, 1952)

Hermann C., 'Structural Adjustment and Neoliberal Convergence in Labour Markets and Welfare: The Impact of the Crisis and Austerity Measures on European Economic and Social Models' (2014) 18 *Competition and Change* 2, 111–130

Hinarejos A., 'Economic and Monetary Union' in Catherine Barnard and Steve Peers (eds.), *European Union Law* (Oxford University Press, 2014) 567–590

Hocquet J. C., 'City-State and Market Economy' in Richard Bonney (ed.), *Economic Systems and State Finance* (Oxford University Press, 1995) 81–100

Hohfeld W. N., 'Fundamental Legal Conceptions as Applied in Judicial Reasoning' (originally published as two articles in the *Yale Law Journal* for 1913 and 1917) in Walter Wheeler Cook (ed.), *Fundamental Legal Conceptions as Applied in Judicial Reasoning: And Other Legal Essays* (Yale University Press, 1920)

Hull R., 'ICTs, the Knowledge Economy, and Neo-liberalism' (2001) 8 *BRIDGES: An Interdisciplinary Journal of Theology, Philosophy, History & Science* 3/4

'The Great Lie: Markets, Freedom and Knowledge' in D. Plehwe, B. Walpen and G. Neunhöffer, *Neoliberal Hegemony: A Global Critique* (Routledge, 2006)

International Law Association, The Hague Conference (2010), Sovereign Insolvency Study Group, 'State Insolvency: Options For The Way Forward' (August 2010), ila.vettoreweb.com/Storage/Download.aspx?DbStorageId=1451&StorageFileGuid=58bc4db7-4213-440c-93fe-978a0a2896cb

Ioannidis M., 'EU Financial Assistance Conditionality after "Two Pack"' (2014) 74 *Zeitschrift für ausländisches öffentliches Recht und Völkerrecht* 1–44

Ivanković Tamamović A., 'The Impact of the Crisis on Fundamental Rights across Member States of the EU: Comparative Analysis' (2015) *Study for the LIBE Committee of the European Parliament*

Janssen R., *Greece and the IMF: Who Exactly is Being Saved?* (Centre for Economic and Policy Research, July 2010)

Jayasuriya K., 'Globalization, Sovereignty, and the Rule of Law: From Political to Economic Constitutionalism?' (2001) 8 *Constellations* 4, 442–460

Joerges C. and Rödl F., '"Social Market Economy" as Europe's Social Model?' (2004) EUI Working Paper Law 2004/8

Kaltsouni S. and Kosma A., 'The impact of the crisis on fundamental rights across Member States of the EU: Country Report on Greece' (2015) *Study for the LIBE Committee of the European Parliament*

Karagiannis N. and Wagner P., 'The Subject-In-Debt: Notes Towards a Sociology and Philosophy of Indebtedness' (2018), available at www.ub.edu/thedebt/wp-content/uploads/2018/03/Karagiannis-Wagner_The-subject-in-debt.pdf

Katrougalos G., 'A Short Genealogy of Social Rights' in Nikita Aliprantis and Ioannis Papageorgiou (eds.), *Social Rights at European, Regional and International Level: Challenges for the 21st Century* (Bruylant 2010)

Keller L.M., 'The American Rejection of Economic Rights as Human Rights and the Declaration of Independence: Does the Pursuit of Happiness Require Basic Economic Rights?' (2003) 19 *New York Law School Journal of Human Rights* 557

Khan Z. and Burn N. (eds.), *Financing for Gender Equality: Realising Women's Rights through Gender Responsive Budgeting* (Palgrave Macmillan, 2017)

Kilpatrick C., 'On the Rule of Law and Economic Emergency: The Degradation of Basic Legal Values in Europe's Bailouts' (2015) 35 *Oxford Journal of Legal Studies* 2, 325–353

King J., *The Doctrine of Odious Debt in International Law: A Restatement* (Cambridge University Press, 2016)

Klein N., *The Shock Doctrine: The Rise of Disaster Capitalism* (Picador, 2008)

Kocourek A., 'Various Definitions of Jural Relation' (1920) 20 *Columbia Law Review* 4, 394–412

Koskenniemi M., 'Human Rights Mainstreaming as a Strategy for Institutional Power' (2010) 1 *Humanity* 1, 47–58

Koutras A., 'A better translation of Bondholders Act 4050' (5 March 2012), andreaskoutras.blogspot.com.au/2012/03/better-tarnslation-of-bondholders-act.html

Kramer M. H., 'Rights Without Trimmings' in Matthew M. Kramer, N. E. Simmonds and Hillel Steiner, *A Debate Over Rights* (Oxford University Press, 1999)

Lapavitsas C., Kaltenbrunner A., Lindo D., Michell J., Painceira J. P., Pires E., Powell J., Stenfors A. and Teles N., 'Euro-zone Crisis: Beggar Thyself and Thy Neighbour' (2010) 12 *Journal of Balkan and Near Eastern Studies* 4, 321–373

Lastra R. M., *International Financial and Monetary Law* (2nd ed., Oxford University Press, 2015)

Lastra R. M. and Buchheit L., *Sovereign Debt Management* (Oxford University Press, 2014)

Lastra R. M. and Louis J.-V., 'European Economic and Monetary Union: History, Trends and Prospects' (2013) 32 *Yearbook of European Law* 1, 57–206

Lazzarato M., *Governing by Debt* (Semiotext(e), 2015)

The Making of the Indebted Man: An Essay on the Neoliberal Condition (Semiotext (e), 2012)

Lee Mudge S., 'What Is Neo-Liberalism?' (2008) 4 *Socio-Economic Review* 6, 703–731

Levi M., *Of Rule and Revenue* (University of California Press, 1989)

Linarelli J., Salomon M. E. and Sornarajah M., *The Misery of International Law: Confrontations with Injustice in the Global Economy* (Oxford University Press, 2018)

Lowenfeld A. F., *International Economic Law*, 2nd ed. (Oxford University Press, 2008)

Lumina C., 'Sovereign Debt and Human Rights: The UN Approach' in Juan Pablo Bohoslavsky and Jernej Letnar Černič (eds.), *Making Sovereign Financing and Human Rights Work* (Hart Publishing, 2014) 251–268

Matsaganis M., 'The Greek Crisis: Social Impact and Policy Responses' (Friedrich Ebert Stiftung, November 2013)

McCrudden C. , 'Mainstreaming Human Rights', Public Law & Legal Theory Research Papers No. 47, University of Michigan School of Law, 2004

Médecins du Monde, International Network, 'Access to healthcare for people facing multiple vulnerabilities in health in 31 cities in 12 countries' (November 2016) 2016 Observatory Report

Megliani M., 'Private Loans to Sovereign Borrowers', in Ilias Bantekas and Cephas Lumina, (eds.), *Sovereign Debt and Human Rights* (Oxford University Press, 2018) 69–83

Metallinos A., 'The Greek Sovereign Debt Restructuring', in Eugenio Bruno (ed.), *Sovereign Debt and Debt Restructuring: Legal, Financial and Regulatory Aspects* (Globe Business, 2013)

Michalowski S., *Unconstitutional Regimes and the Validity of Sovereign Debt: A Legal Perspective* (Ashgate, 2008)

'Sovereign Debt and Social Rights: Legal Reflections on a Difficult Relationship' (2008) 8 *Human Rights Law Review* 1

Mirowski P., *Machine Dreams: Economics Becomes a Cyborg Science* (Cambridge University Press, 2002)

'Markets as Computer Programs in a Theory of Markets', Lecture, 12 December 2017, available at www.hkw.de/en/app/mediathek/video/62324

'Naturalizing the Market on the Road to Revisionism: Bruce Caldwell's *Hayek's Challenge* and the Challenge of Hayek Interpretation' (2007) 3 *Journal of Institutional Economics* 3, 351–317

Never Let a Serious Crisis Go to Waste: How Neoliberalism Survived the Financial Meltdown (Verso, 2014)

Mirowski P. and Plehwe D. (eds.), *The Road from Mont Pèlerin: The Making of the Neoliberal Thought Collective* (Harvard University Press 2009)

Moury C. and Standring A., 'Going Beyond the Troika: Power Discourse in Portuguese Austerity Politics' (2017) 56 *European Journal of Political Research* 3, 660–679

Müller-Armack A., *Wirtschaftsordnung und Wirtschaftspolitik. Studien und Konzepten zur sozialen Markwirtschaft und zur europäischen Integration* (Rombach Verlag, 1966)

Nolan A., 'Not Fit for Purpose? Human Rights in Times of Financial and Economic Crisis' (2015) 4 *European Human Rights Law Review* 360–371

(ed.), *Economic and Social Rights after the Global Financial Crisis* (Cambridge University Press, 2014)

Nolan A. and Bohoslavsky J.P., 'Human Rights and Economic Policy Reforms' (2020) 24 *The International Journal of Human Rights* 1247–1267

Nolan A. and Dutschke M., 'Article 2 (1)ICESCR and States Parties' Obligations: Whither the Budget?' (2010) 3 *European Human Rights Law Review* 280–289

Nolan A., O'Connell R. and Harvey C. (eds.), *Human Rights and Public Finance: Budgets for the Promotion of Economic and Social Rights* (Hart, 2013)

Norton A. and Elson D., *What's Behind the Budget? Politics, Rights and Accountability in the Budget Process* (Overseas Development Institute, 2002)

Nussbaum M., *Creating Capabilities: The Human Development Approach* (Belknap Press of Harvard University Press, 2011)

'Human Dignity and Political Entitlements', in *Human Dignity and Bioethics: Essays Commissioned by the President's Council on Bioethics* (President's Commission on Bioethics,2008) 351–380, www.google.co.uk/books/edition/Human_Dignity_and_Bioethics/u3AoAQAAIAAJ?hl=en&gbpv=1&printsec=frontcover

O'Connell R., Nolan A., Harvey C., Dutschke M. and Rooney E., *Applying an International Human Rights Framework to State Budget Allocations: Rights and Resources* (Routledge, 2014)

Olivares-Caminal R., *Legal Aspects of Sovereign Debt Restructuring* (Sweet and Maxwell, 2009)

Ortiz I., Matthew Cummins, Jeronim Capaldo and Kalaivani Karunanethy, 'The Decade of Adjustment: A Review of Austerity Trends 2010–2020 in 187 Countries', ESS Working Paper No 53 (ILO, 2015)

Ostry J. D., Prakash Loungani and Davide Furceri, 'Neoliberalism: Oversold?' (2016) 53 *Finance and Development* 2

Paulus C. G., 'Debts', in R. Wolfrum (ed.), *The Max Planck Encyclopedia of Public International Law*, vol. 2 (Oxford University Press, 2012)

Peck J., Brenner N. and Theodore N., 'Actually Existing Neoliberalism', in D. Cahill, M. Cooper, M. Konings and D. Primrose (eds.), *The SAGE Handbook of Neoliberalism* (SAGE, 2018)

Pezzolo L., 'Bonds and Government Debt in Italian City-States, 1250-1650', in William N. Goetzmann and K. Geert Rouwenhorst (eds.), *The Origins of Value: The Financial Innovations that Created Modern Capital Markets* (Oxford University Press, 2005) 145–164

Piketty T., *Capital in the Twenty-First Century* (Belknap Press of Harvard University Press, 2014)

Pinelli C., 'Conditionality' in A. Peters and R. Wolfrum (eds.), *Max Planck Encyclopedia of Public International Law* (November 2013)

Plant R., *The Neo-liberal State* (Oxford University Press, 2010)

Plehwe D., Slobodian Q. and Mirowski P. (eds.), *Nine Lives of Neoliberalism* (Verso, 2020)

Plehwe D, Walpen B. and Neunhöffer G., *Neoliberal Hegemony: A Global Critique* (Routledge, 2006)

Polackova H., 'Contingent Government Liabilities: A Hidden Fiscal Risk' (1999) 36 *Finance and Development* 1, 46–49

Porzecanski A. C., 'Behind the 2012 Greek Default and Restructuring', in Eugenio Bruno (ed.), *Sovereign Debt and Debt Restructuring: Legal, Financial and Regulatory Aspects* (Globe Business, 2013)

QUB Budget Analysis Project, *Budget Analysis and Economic and Social Rights: A Review of Selected Case Studies and Guidance* (Queen's University Belfast, 2010)

Rasmussen R. K., 'Sovereign Debt Restructuring, Odious Debt and the Politics of Debt Relief' (2007) 70 *Law and Contemporary Problems* 4, 249–261

Reinhart C. M. and Rogoff K. S., 'From Financial Crash to Debt Crisis American Economic Review' (2011) 101 *American Economic Review* 5, 1676–1706

Reinhart C. M., Reinhart V. R. and Rogoff K. S., 'Public Debt Overhangs: Advanced-Economy Episodes Since 1800' (2012) 26 *Journal of Economic Perspectives* 69

Reinisch A., *State Responsibility for Debts: International Law Aspects of External Debt and Debt Restructuring* (Böhlau, 1995)

Riedel E., Giacca G. and Golay C. (eds.), *Economic, Social and Cultural Rights in International Law: Contemporary Issues and Challenges* (Oxford University Press, 2014)

Roberts A., *The Logic of Discipline: Global Capitalism and the Architecture of Government* (Oxford University Press, 2011)

Robertson R. E., 'Measuring State Compliance with the Obligation to Devote the "Maximum Available Resources" to Realizing Economic, Social, and Cultural Rights' (1994) 156 *Human Rights Quarterly* 702

Rocholl J. and Stahmer A., 'Where did the Greek bailout money go?' (2016) ESMT White Paper No WP–16–02

Rodgers G., Lee E., Swepston L. and van Daele J., *The International Labour Organization and the Quest for Social Justice* (ILO, 2009)

Roosevelt F. D., *Annual Message to Congress on the State of the Union* (11 January 1944), fdrlibrary.marist.edu/archives/address_text.html

Ruiz Almendral V., 'The European Fiscal Consolidation Legal Framework: Its Impact on National Fiscal Constitutions and Parliamentary Democracy', in Thomas Beukers, Bruno de Witte and Claire Kilpatrick (eds.), *Constitutional Change through Euro-Crisis Law* (Cambridge University Press, 2017)

Ruggie J., 'International Regimes, Transactions and Change: Embedded Liberalism in the Postwar Economic Order' (1982) 36 *International Organization* 2, 379–399

Salomon M. E., 'Europe's Debt to Greece', *EJIL: Talk!* (25 August 2015)

'Of Austerity, Human Rights and International Institutions' (2015) 21 *European Law Journal* 4

'Poverty, Privilege and International Law: The Millennium Development Goals and the Guise of Humanitarianism' (2008–2009) 51 *German Yearbook of International Law* 39–73

'Winners and Others: Accounting for International Law's Favourites', in C. Gearty and C. Douzinas (eds.), *The Cambridge Companion to Human Rights Law* (Cambridge University Press, 2012) 271–292

Sapir A., Wolff G. B., de Sousa C. and Terzi A., 'The Troika and Financial Assistance in the Euro Area: Successes and Failures' (European Union, 2014) *Study on the Request of the Economic and Monetary Affairs Committee of the European Parliament*

Scali E. L., 'Sovereign Financing During the COVID-19 Pandemic: The Debt Implications of Italy's Socio-Economic Measures for 2020 and the Response of the European Union', in Pia Acconci and Elisa Baroncini (eds.), *Gli effetti della pandemia Covid-19 su commercio, investimenti e strumenti finanziari* (Editoriale Scientifica, 2020) 369–387

'Sovereign (over)borrowing during the COVID-19 pandemic: Do creditors have a responsibility to prevent unsustainable debt situations?', *EJIL: Talk!* (17 July 2020)

'The Impact of Conditionality on Economic, Social and Cultural Rights in the Latest Reports of the UN Independent Expert on Foreign Debt and Human Rights' (2017) 11 *Diritti Umani e Diritto Internazionale* 2, 532–541

Schmidt V. A., 'Ideas and the Rise of Neoliberalism in Europe', in D. Cahill, M. Cooper, M. Konings and D. Primrose (eds.), *The SAGE Handbook of Neoliberalism* (SAGE, 2018)

Schumpeter J. A., 'The Crisis of the Tax State' (originally published in 1918 as 'Die Krise der Steuerstaates'), trans. by Stolper W. F. and Musgrave R. A. in (1954) 4 *International Economic Papers* 5–38

Sepúlveda M., *The Nature of the Obligations under the International Covenant on Economic, Social and Cultural Rights* (Intersentia, 2003)

Sheppard S. M. (ed.), *The Wolters Kluwer Bouvier Law Dictionary*, vol. 1 (Wolters Kluwer, 2012), 'Debt'

Shue H., *Basic Rights: Subsistence, Affluence and US Foreign Policy* (2nd ed., Princeton University Press, 1996)

Simitis C., *The European Debt Crisis: The Greek Case* (Manchester University Press, 2014)

Simma B. and Alston P., 'The Sources of International Human Rights Law: Custom, *Jus Cogens*, and General Principles' (1992) 12 *Australian Yearbook of International Law* 1, 82–108

Skogly S., 'The Requirement of Using the 'Maximum of Available Resources' for Human Rights Realisation: A Question of Quality as Well as Quantity?' (2012) 12 *Human Rights Law Review* 3

Slobodian Q., *Globalists: The End of Empire and the Birth of Neoliberalism* (Harvard University Press, 2018)

'Social Market' in 'Economics A-Z', *The Economist*, www.economist.com/economics-a-to-z/s#node-21529660

Soederberg S., *Debtfare States and the Poverty Industry: Money, Discipline and the Surplus Population* (Routledge, 2014)

Spector H., 'Value Pluralism and the Two Concepts of Rights' in Brian H. Bix and Horacio Spector (eds.), *Rights: Concepts and Contexts* (Routledge, 2012) 115–134

Springer S., Birch K. and MacLeavy J. (eds.), *The Handbook of Neoliberalism* (Routledge, 2016)

Streeck W., *Buying Time: The Delayed Crisis of Democratic Capitalism* (Verso, 2014)

'The Politics of Public Debt: Neoliberalism, Capitalist Development and the Restructuring of the State' (2013) 15 *German Economic Review* 1

'The Rise of the European Consolidation State' (2015) MPIfG Discussion Paper No 15/1

Stuckler D. and Basu S., *The Body Economic: Why Austerity Kills* (Basic Books, 2013)

Tan C., 'Life, Debt and Human Rights: Contextualising the International Regime for Sovereign Debt Relief', in K. Nadakavukaren Schefer (ed.), *Poverty and the International Economic Law System: Duties to the Poor* (Cambridge University Press, 2013) 307–324

Theodorikakou O., Alamanou A. and Katsadoros K. , '"Neo-homelessness" and the Greek Crisis' (2013) 7 *European Journal of Homelessness* 2, 203–210

Thomadakis S. B., 'Growth, Debt and Sovereignty Prolegomena to the Greek Crisis' (May 2015) GreeSE Paper No 91, LSE Hellenic Observatory Papers on Greece and Southeast Europe

'The Greek Economy: Performance, Expectations and Paradoxes', in Graham Allison and Kalïpso Nicolaidis (eds.), *The Greek Paradox* (MIT Press 1997) 39–60

Tilly C., *Coercion, Capital, and European States: AD 990–1992* (Blackwell, 1990)

Trubek D. and Santos A., 'Introduction: The Third Moment in Law and Development Theory and the Emergence of a New Critical Practice', in David Trubek and Alvaro Santos (eds.), *The New Law and Economic Development: A Critical Appraisal* (Cambridge University Press, 2006) 1–18

Truth Committee on Public Debt, 'Illegitimacy, Illegality, Odiousness and Unsustainability of the August 2015 MoU and Loan Agreement' (August 2015), cadtm.org/Illegitimacy-Illegality-Odiousness

'Preliminary Report' (18 June 2015), cadtm.org/Preliminary-Report-of-the-Truth

Tuori K. and Tuori K., *The Eurozone Crisis: A Constitutional Analysis* (Cambridge University Press, 2014)

Varoufakis Y., *Adults In The Room: My Battle With Europe's Deep Establishment* (Vintage Digital 2017)

'Minister No More!' (6 July 2015), yanisvaroufakis.eu/2015/07/06/minister-no-more/

'As It Happened – Yanis Varoufakis Intervention During the 27th June Eurogroup Meeting' (28 June 2015), yanisvaroufakis.eu/2015/06/28/as-it-happened-yanis-varoufakis-intervention-during-the-27th-june-2015-eurogroup-meeting/

Viterbo A., 'La ristrutturazione del debito sovrano greco allo scrutinio della Corte europea dei diritti umani: nessuna tutela per i piccoli investitori' (2017) 11 *Diritti Umani e Diritto Internazionale* 1, 294–300

Viterbo A. and Costamagna F., 'L'impatto sociale della politica di condizionalità nel contesto della crisi nell'area euro: profili giuridici', in Nicola Napoletano and Andrea Saccucci (eds.), *Gestione internazionale delle emergenze globali. Regole e valori* (Editoriale Scientifica, 2013) 167–194

Waibel M., *Sovereign Defaults Before International Courts and Tribunals* (Cambridge University Press, 2011)

Warwick B., 'Socio-Economic Rights During Economic Crises: A Changed Approach to Retrogression' (2016) 65 *International and Comparative Law Quarterly* 1

Wellman C., *The Moral Dimensions of Human Rights* (Oxford University Press, 2011)

Williamson J., 'What Washington Means by Policy Reform', in John Williamson (ed.), *Latin American Readjustment: How Much Has Happened?* (Institute for International Economics, 1990) 7–20

Winkler M., *Foreign Bonds: An Autopsy. A Study of Default and Repudiations of Government Obligations* (Roland Swain, 1933)

Wrobel M., *Fiscal Rules for the Control of Government* (Research Branch, Library of Parliament, Ottawa, 1993)

Yianni A. and Aggarwal N., 'Eurozone Financial Rescue and Stabilization Measures, and their Legal Foundations', in Rosa M. Lastra and Lee Buchheit (eds.), *Sovereign Debt Management* (Oxford University Press, 2014)

Zacher H. F., 'Social Market Economy, Social Policy, and the Law' (1982) 138 *Zeitschrift für die gesamte Staatswissenschaft/Journal of Institutional and Theoretical Economics* 367–388

Zettelmeyer J., Trebesh C. and Gulati M., 'The Greek Debt Restructuring: An Autopsy' (2013) 28 *Economic Policy* 75, 513–563

NEWSPAPER ARTICLES

Allen K., 'Greece crisis timeline: the rocky road to another bailout (2015)', *The Guardian* (20 August 2015)

Alloush A., 'George Soros Donates Funds to Help Heat Schools in Greece', *Greek Reporter* (15 December 2013)

Alloway T., 'Goldman's Trojan currency swap', *Financial Times* (9 February 2010)

Armitage J. and Chu B., 'Greek Debt Crisis: Goldman Sachs could be sued for helping hide debts when it joined the euro', *The Independent* (10 July 2015)

Arnold M., 'Soaring Eurozone government debt reignites call for cancellation', *Financial Times* (8 December 2020)

Balzli B., 'Greek debt crisis: How Goldman Sachs helped Greece to mask its true debt', *Spiegel Online International* (8 February 2010)

Barber T., 'Greece vows action to cut budget deficit', *Financial Times* (20 October 2009)

Brunsden J. and Jenkins P., 'Bank rescues: putting bondholders on the hook', *Financial Times* (4 January 2016)

Christoforou A., 'EU austerity killing Greece. Report shows suicide, infant death, and mental illness on the rise', *Global Research* (18 June 2016)

Clark A., Stewart H. and Moya E., 'Goldman Sachs faces FED inquiry over Greek crisis', *The Guardian* (26 February 2010)

Cohan W. D., 'Plenty deserve blame for Greece's woes, but maybe not Goldman Sachs', *The New York Times* (13 July 2015)

Cooper C., 'Tough austerity measures in Greece leave nearly a million people with no access to healthcare, leading to soaring infant mortality, HIV Infection and Suicide', *The Independent* (21 February 2014)

Darvas Z. and Hüttl P., 'How to reduce the Greek debt burden?', *Bruegel* (9 January 2015)

Dunbar N., 'Revealed: Goldman Sachs' mega deal for Greece', *Risk.net* (July 2003)

ECB Watch, 'EU ignores falsification of Greek public finance data' (18 December 2011)

ECB Watch, 'Falsification of Greek public finance data: EU regulatory bodies' (absence of) response' (12 December 2011)

Elliott L., 'Bank of England warns of complacency over big rise in personal debt', The Guardian, 24 July 2017

Georgiopoulos G., 'China's Cosco acquires 51 pct stake in Greece's Piraeus Port', *Reuters* (10 August 2016)

Gopinath G., 'The Great Lockdown: Worst economic downturn since the Great Depression', in *IMFBlog* (14 April 2020)

Hope K., 'Greece sells lottery stake in biggest privatisation', *Financial Times* (1 May 2013)

Inman P., 'Greek debt crisis: timeline (2009–2012)', *The Guardian*

Inman P. and Treanor J., 'Britain's debt timebomb: FCA urges action over £200bn crisis', *The Guardian* (19 September 2017)

Jones C., Hope K. and Foy H., 'Greek banks given one-day reprieve as depositors pull out €1.6bn', *Financial Times* (22 June 2015)

Krugman P., 'Ending Greece's bleeding', *The New York Times* (6 July 2015)
Moore E., 'What is the message from Greece's bond market?', *Financial Times* (21 February 2017)
Nardelli A. and Merler S., 'The Greek debt: What creditors may stand to lose', *The Guardian* (19 June 2015)
Phillips M., 'The complete history of the Greek debt drama in charts', *Quartz* (30 June 2015)
Ranasinghe D., Ramnarayan A. and Papadimas L., 'Pariah no more? Greece needs big bond investors to seal its comeback', *Reuters* (30 April 2019)
Reiermann C. and Reuter W., 'The State's silent takeover: Germany's big banking bailout', *Spiegel Online* (2 February 2009)
Saragosa M., 'Greece warned on false euro data', *BBC News* (1 December 2004)
Shokar P., 'Will COVID-19 usher on another decade of austerity within the United Kingdom? What does this mean for the protection of economic, social and cultural rights (ESCR)?', *EJIL: Talk!* (13 May 2020)
Smith H., 'Greek crisis: episodes of despair and drama as moment of truth nears', *The Guardian* (21 June 2015)
Smith H., 'Papandreou unveils radical reforms to salvage Greece's public finances', *The Guardian* (14 December 2009)
Smith H. and Seager A., 'Financial markets tumble after Fitch downgrades Greece's credit rating followed by Moody's downgrading from A1 to A2', *The Guardian* (8 December 2009)
Syal R. (and agencies), 'Government finances at "significant risk" from debt-laden councils due to Covid', *The Guardian* (22 January 2021)
Vihriälä V., 'Make room for fiscal action through debt conversion', *VoxEU.org* (15 April 2020)
Wachman R. and Fletcher N., 'Standard & Poor's downgrade Greek credit rating to junk status', *The Guardian* (27 April 2010)
Wearden G., 'Greece debt crisis: timeline (2001–2010)', *The Guardian* (5 May 2010)
Wroughton L., Schneider H. and Dina Kyriakidou, 'How the IMF's Greek misadventure is changing the fund', *Ekathimerini.com* (28 August 2015)
'Greek economy sinks back into recession', *BBC News* (16 May 2017)
'Can Tsipras' new proposals revive a deal?', *The Guardian* (24 June 2015)
'Juncker says EU must "respect Greek dignity"', *Reuters* (16 March 2015)
'Greek debt tracker', *Financial Times* (2015)
'Greek debt haircut led 15 bondholders to kill themselves', *The National Herald* (4 December 2014)
'Greece's largest port taken over by Chinese firm', *RT News* (11 August 2011)
'Greek bonds rated "junk" by Standard & Poor's', *BBC News* (27 April 2010)
'Exposure to Greece weighs on French, German banks', *The Wall Street Journal* (17 February 2010)
'EU accepts Greek debt plan, but begins infringement proceedings', *Leadership* (3 February 2010)
'Greece debt rating downgraded by third agency', *BBC News* (22 December 2009)
'Greece is downgraded by a second credit rating agency', *BBC News* (16 December 2009)

OTHER DOCUMENTS

United Nations

Commission on Human Rights

Sub-Commission on Prevention of Discrimination and Protection of Minorities, 'The realization of economic, social and cultural rights', Second progress report prepared by Mr Danilo Türk, Special Rapporteur (18 July 1991) E/CN.4/Sub.2/1991/17

Sub Commission on Prevention of Discrimination and Protection of Minorities, 'The Right to Adequate Food as a Human Right', Report prepared by Mr. Asbjørn Eide, Special Rapporteur (7 July 1987) E/CN.4/Sub.2/1987/23

Special Rapporteur on the Situation of Human Rights in Chile, 'Study of the impact of foreign economic aid and assistance on respect for human rights in Chile', Report prepared by Antonio Cassese (1978) E/CN.4/Sub.2/412 (Vol. IV)

Commission on Human Rights, Drafting Committee, 'International Bill Of Rights: Documented Outline Part I – Texts', 11 June 1947, UN Doc. E/CN.4/AC.1/3/Add.1, available at www.un.org/en/ga/search/view_doc.asp?symbol=E/CN.4/AC.1/3/Add.1

General Assembly

'Addressing, from a human rights perspective, the debt-related problems of developing countries caused by the coronavirus disease (COVID-19) pandemic', Report of the Independent Expert on the effects of foreign debt and other related international financial obligations of states on the full enjoyment of all human rights, particularly economic, social and cultural rights, Yuefen Li, UN Doc. A/75/164, 31 July 2020

Report of the Independent Expert on the effects of foreign debt and other related international financial obligations of states on the full enjoyment of all human rights, particularly economic, social and cultural rights (5 August 2016) A/71/305

Report of the independent expert on the effects of foreign debt and other related international financial obligations of states on the full enjoyment of all human rights, particularly economic, social and cultural rights (14 August 2008) A/63/289

Human Rights Council (HRC)

'Private debt and human rights', Report of the Independent Expert on the effects of foreign debt and other related international financial obligations of states on the full enjoyment of human rights, particularly economic, social and cultural rights (3 January 2020) A/HRC/43/45

Guiding Principles for Human Rights Impact Assessments for Economic Reform Policies' (19 December 2018) A/HRC/40/57

Report of the Independent Expert on the effects and foreign debt and other related international financial obligations of states on the full enjoyment of all human rights, particularly economic, social and cultural rights on his mission to institutions of the European Union (28 December 2016) A/HRC/34/57/Add.1

Report of the Independent Expert on the effects of foreign debt and other related international financial obligations of states on the full enjoyment of all human rights, particularly economic, social and cultural rights (27 December 2016) A/HRC/34/57

Report of the Independent Expert on the effects of foreign debt and other related international financial obligations of states on the full enjoyment of all human rights, particularly economic, social and cultural rights on his mission to Greece (21 April 2016) A/HRC/31/60/Add.2

Working Group on the Universal Periodic Review, 'Summary prepared by the Office of the United Nations High Commissioner for Human Rights in accordance with paragraph 15 (c) of the annex to Human Rights Council resolution 5/1 and paragraph 5 of the annex to Council resolution 16/21 – Greece' (22 February 2016) A/HRC/WG.6/25/GRC/3

Report of the Independent Expert on the effects of foreign debt and other related international financial obligations of states on the full enjoyment of human rights, particularly economic, social and cultural rights (12 January 2016) A/HRC/31/60

End-of-Mission Statement. Visit to the European Union institutions' (8 December 2015)

End-of-mission statement by Mr. Juan Pablo Bohoslavsky, United Nations Independent Expert on the effects of foreign debt and other related international financial obligations of states on the full enjoyment of all human rights, particularly economic, social and cultural rights. Mission to Iceland, 8–15 December 2014' (15 December 2014)

Report of the Independent Expert on the effects of foreign debt and other related international financial obligations of states on the full enjoyment of all human rights, particularly economic, social and cultural rights, Cephas Lumina, 'Draft Commentary to the Guiding Principles on foreign debt and human rights' (10 March 2014) A/HRC/25/51

Report of the Independent Expert on the effects of foreign debt and other related international financial obligations of states on the full enjoyment of all human rights, particularly economic, social and cultural rights, Cephas Lumina, Addendum: Mission to Greece (22–27 April 2013) (7 March 2014) A/HRC/25/50/Add.1

Report of the Independent Expert on the effects of foreign debt and other related international financial obligations of states on the full enjoyment of all human rights, particularly economic, social and cultural rights, Cephas Lumina (7 March 2014) A/HRC/25/50

Mandate of the Special Rapporteur on adequate housing as a component of the right to an adequate standard of living, and on the right to non-discrimination in this context, 'Communication to Greece', (19 February 2013) GRC 1/2013 in Communications report of Special Procedures, 'Communications sent, 1 December 2012 to 28 February 2013; Replies received, 1 February to 30 April 2013' (22 May 2013) A/HRC/23/51

Report of the Independent Expert on the effects of foreign debt and other related international financial obligations of states on the full enjoyment of all human rights, particularly economic, social and cultural rights, Cephas Lumina: Guiding principles on foreign debt and human rights (10 April 2011) A/HRC/20/23

Report of the independent expert on the effects of foreign debt and other related international financial obligations of states on the full enjoyment of all human rights, particularly economic, social and cultural rights, Cephas Lumina (3 April 2009) A/HRC/11/10

Office of the High Commissioner for Human Rights (OHCHR)

'Realizing Human Rights Through Government Budgets', 2017 (co-authored with International Budget Partnership)

'Promoting a Rights-Based Approach to Economic Stabilization, Recovery and Growth', Background paper, April 2013

'Report on austerity measures and economic and social rights', 2013

'Fact Sheet No. 33: Frequently Asked Questions on Economic, Social and Rights', 2008

'Economic, Social and Cultural Rights: Handbook for National Human Rights Institutions', 2005

'Fact Sheet No 16 (Rev 1): The Committee on Economic, Social and Cultural Rights', 1991

Secretariat

United Nations Secretariat's Division on Human Rights, headed at the time by Professor John Humphrey, see 'Draft Outline of International Bill of Rights (prepared by the Division of Human Rights)', UN Doc. E/CN.4/AC.1/3, 4 June 1947, available at www.un.org/en/ga/search/view_doc.asp?symbol=E/CN.4/AC.1/3

United Nations Conference on Trade and Development (UNCTAD)

The Concept of Odious Debt in Public International Law (July 2017) Discussion paper No 185

Sovereign debt workouts: going forward. Roadmap and guide (April 2015) http://unctad.org/en/PublicationsLibrary/gdsddf2015misc1_en.pdf

Council of Europe (CoE) Commissioner for Human Rights

'The Impact of the Economic Crisis and Austerity Measures on Human Rights in Europe', 2015

'Safeguarding human rights in times of economic crisis', November 2013

International Labour Organization (ILO)

Social Security (Minimum Standards) Convention, 1952 (No 102) – Greece, Observation (CEACR) – adopted 2013, published 103rd ILC session (2014) www.ilo.org/dyn/normlex/en/f?p=NORMLEXPUB:13100:0::NO::P13100_COMMENT_ID,P11110_COUNTRY_ID,P11110_COUNTRY_NAME,P11110_COMMENT_YEAR:3150771,102658,Greece,2013

Conclusions of the Report on the High Level Mission to Greece (Athens, 19–23 September 2011)

International Monetary Fund (IMF)

Fiscal Monitor: Policies for the Recovery (October 2020)

World Economic Outlook, October 2020: A Long and Difficult Ascent (October 2020)

World Economic Outlook Update, June 2020: A Crisis Like No Other, An Uncertain Recovery (June 2020)

World Economic Outlook, April 2020: The Great Lockdown (April 2020)

Fiscal Monitor: Managing Public Wealth (October 2018)

Greece, Preliminary debt sustainability analysis – Updated estimates and further considerations (May 2016) IMF Country Report 13/130

Fiscal Monitor: Now is the time: Fiscal Policies for Sustainable Growth (April 2015)

International Monetary Fund and World Bank, 'Revised Guidelines for Public Debt Management' (2014)

Greece: Ex Post Evaluation of Exceptional Access under the 2010 Stand-By Arrangement (June 2013) IMF Country Report No 13/156

Greece: 2013 Article IV Consultation (5 June 2013) IMF Country Report No 13/154

Sovereign Debt Restructuring—Recent Developments and Implications for the Fund's Legal and Policy Framework (26 April 2013)

Greece: Request for Stand-By Arrangement (10 May 2010) Country Report No 10/111

World Economic Outlook: Coping with High Debt and Sluggish Growth (October 2012)

Annual Report of the Executive Board for the Financial Year Ended April 30, 1990 (1990)

Organisation for Economic Co-operation and Development (OECD)

Greece (March 2016) Economic Surveys www.keepeek.com/Digital-Asset-Management/oecd/economics/oecd-economic-surveys-greece-2016_eco_surveys-grc-2016-en#WUFHkTN2q8U#page1

Greece Policy brief – Corporate governance: Reforming the state-owned enterprises sector (March 2016) www.oecd.org/policy-briefs/greece-reforming-the-state-owned-enterprises-sector.pdf

In It Together: Why Less Inequality Benefits All (2015)

Government at a Glance 2015: General government structural balance (6 July 2015) www.oecd-ilibrary.org/governance/government-at-a-glance-2015/general-government-structural-balance_gov_glance-2015-9-en

Economic Surveys: 'Greece', November 2013 www.oecd.org/eco/surveys/GRC_Overview_Eng_2013.pdf

Divided We Stand: Why Inequality Keeps Rising (2011)

OECD Public Debt Markets: Trends and Structural Changes (2002)

Public Debt Management and Government Securities Markets in the 21st Century (2002)

Aggregate National Accounts, SNA 2008 (or SNA 1993): Gross Domestic Product www.oecd-ilibrary.org/economics/data/aggregate-national-accounts/gross-domestic-product_data-00001-en

World Bank

'Impacts of COVID-19 on poverty' www.worldbank.org/en/topic/poverty/coronavirus

World Health Organization (WHO)

Barriers and facilitating factors in access to health care services in Greece (2015) www.euro.who.int/en/countries/greece/publications/barriers-and-facilitating-factors-in-access-to-health-services-in-greece-2015

Bank for International Settlements (BIS)

Bank for International Settlements, 'BIS Annual Report 2017 – media briefing by Claudio Borio and Hyun Song Shin', 25 June 2017, available at www.bis.org/publ/arpdf/ar2017e_tcintro.htm

Consolidated positions on counterparties resident in Greece, Q4 2009 http://stats.bis.org/statx/srs/table/B4?c=GR&p=20094

Bank of Greece

'Monetary Policy Report 2015-2016', 2016 (in Greek only)

'Governor's Report for the Year 2010', 2011

European Union

European Parliament

At a Glance: Broad Economic Policy Guidelines and Employment Guidelines (2015) www.europarl.europa.eu/RegData/etudes/ATAG/2015/542652/IPOL_ATA(2015)542652_EN.pdf

Report on the enquiry on the role and operations of the Troika (ECB, Commission and IMF) with regard to the Euro Area programme countries (2013/2277(INI)) (28 February 2014)

European Commission

The Second Economic Adjustment Programme for Greece – March 2012 (March 2012), European Economy Occasional Papers No 94 http://ec.europa.eu/economy_finance/publications/occasional_paper/2012/pdf/ocp94_en.pdf

The Fiscal Compact – Taking Stock (22 February 2017) https://ec.europa.eu/info/publications/fiscal-compact-taking-stock_en

Macroeconomic imbalance procedure https://ec.europa.eu/info/business-economy-euro/economic-and-fiscal-policy-coordination/eu-economic-governance-monitoring-prevention-correction/macroeconomic-imbalance-procedure_en

Financial assistance to Greece https://ec.europa.eu/info/business-economy-euro/economic-and-fiscal-policy-coordination/eu-financial-assistance/which-eu-countries-have-received-assistance/financial-assistance-greece_en#economicadjustmentprogrammes

Europe 2020: Integrated guidelines for the economic and employment policies of the Member States (27 April 2010) http://ec.europa.eu/eu2020/pdf/Brochure%20Integrated%20Guidelines.pdf

Report on Greek Government Deficit and Debt Statistics (COM(2010)) 1 Final, 8 January 2010

European Financial Stabilisation Mechanism (EFSM) https://ec.europa.eu/info/business-economy-euro/economic-and-fiscal-policy-coordination/eu-financial-assistance/loan-programmes/european-financial-stabilisation-mechanism-efsm_en

The Euro Plus Pact: How Integration into the EU Framework can Give New Momentum for Structural Reforms in the Euro Area (8 May 2015) https://ec.europa.eu/epsc/publications/strategic-notes/euro-plus-pact_en.

The European Semester https://ec.europa.eu/info/strategy/european-semester_en

Europe 2020 strategy https://ec.europa.eu/info/strategy/european-semester/framework/europe-2020-strategy_en

Medium-term Budgetary Objectives (MTOs) https://ec.europa.eu/info/business-economy-euro/economic-and-fiscal-policy-coordination/eu-economic-governance-monitoring-prevention-correction/stability-and-growth-pact/preventive-arm/medium-term-budgetary-objectives-mtos_en

Balance of Payments (BoP) Assistance https://ec.europa.eu/info/business-economy-euro/economic-and-fiscal-policy-coordination/eu-financial-assistance/loan-programmes/balance-payments-bop-assistance_en

Eurogroup

Ministerial Statement of 27th June 2015, No 534/15 (27 June 2015) www.consilium.europa.eu/press-releases-pdf/2015/6/40802199989_en.pdf

European Central Bank

ELA to Greek banks maintained at its current level (28 June 2015) Press Release www.ecb.europa.eu/press/pr/date/2015/html/pr150628.en.html

Eurostat

Report by Eurostat on the revision of the Greek government deficit and debt figures (22 November 2004) http://ec.europa.eu/eurostat/documents/4187653/5765001/GREECE-EN.PDF/2da4e4f6-f9f2-4848-b1a9-cb229fcabae3?version=1.0

Structure of government debt http://epp.eurostat.ec.europa.eu/statistics_explained/index.php/Structure_of_government_debt

Government Finance Statistics (GFS) http://ec.europa.eu/eurostat/web/government-finance-statistics/overview

GDP and main components, volumes: GDP at market prices, percentage change on previous period http://ec.europa.eu/eurostat/data/database

Index

For EU product safety concerns, contact us at Calle de José Abascal, 56–1°, 28003 Madrid, Spain or eugpsr@cambridge.org.

www.ingramcontent.com/pod-product-compliance
Lightning Source LLC
LaVergne TN
LVHW011813200926
848484LV00005B/1184